BUS

D0773056

Strategies
FOR THERAPY
WITH THE ELDERLY

— 2ND EDITION —

Claire M. Brody, PhD, is in private practice in West Orange, New Jersey. She is currently an adjunct in the psychology department at Fairleigh Dickinson University (Madison Campus), teaching courses primarily in gerontology. Formerly, she taught in the Psychology and Women's Studies departments at William Paterson College in Wayne, New Jersey. Previous to that she was an adjunct associate professor in the Department of Psychology, Sociology, and Anthropology at the College of Staten Island, City University of New York (CUNY), in addition to teaching and counseling at several other branches of CUNY for more than 20 years. Dr. Brody is a Diplomate of the American Board of Professional Psychology and a Fellow of the American Psychological Association. In addition to articles and papers on psychotherapy with women and women in nursing homes, she has written on college counseling and teaching. She received a master's degree in Human Development from the University of Chicago, and a PhD in psychology from New York University. Dr. Brody edited two prior books and co-authored another in the Springer Focus on Women Series, *Women Therapists Working With Women*, *Woman's Therapy Groups*, and *Psychotherapy and Counseling With Older Women* (with Frances K. Trotman). She also was the co-author, with Vicki G. Semel, of an earlier edition of this book.

Vicki G. Semel, PsyD, is in private practice in West Orange, New Jersey, and New York City. She is currently the executive director, a training analyst, and supervisor at the Academy of Clinical and Applied Psychoanalysis (ACAP) in West Orange and an adjunct professor at Centenary College in their Master's Degree in Psychoanalysis program at ACAP. She is also on the faculty, a supervisor, and director of admissions at the Center for Modern Psychoanalytic Studies in New York City. Dr. Semel is the Chair of the Board of Accreditation of the Society of Modern Psychoanalysts and a member of the New Jersey State Certified Psychoanalysts Advisory Committee. She was formerly an adjunct assistant professor at the University of Medicine and Dentistry of New Jersey and a consulting psychologist at Daughters of Israel Geriatric Center, a nursing home in West Orange. Dr. Semel has doctorates in both political science and clinical psychology from Rutgers University. She is a certified psychoanalyst, trained at the Center for Modern Psychoanalytic Studies. She has written articles and a book chapter on working with the aging patient, as well as on teaching psychoanalytic treatment of the narcissistic disorders.

CLAIRE M. BRODY, VICKI G. SEMEL
WITH CONTRIBUTORS

Strategies
FOR THERAPY
WITH THE ELDERLY

— 2ND EDITION —

LIVING WITH HOPE AND MEANING

SPRINGER PUBLISHING COMPANY

Springer Publishing Company, Inc.
11 West 42nd Street
New York, NY 10036

Acquisitions Editor: Sheri Sussman
Production Editor: Betsy Day
Cover design by Mimi Flow
Typeset by International Graphic Services, Inc., Newtown, PA

05 06 07 08 09 / 5 4 3 2 1

Library of Congress Cataloging-in-Publication Data

Brody, Claire M.
    Strategies for therapy with the elderly: living with hope and meaning / Claire M. Brody, Vicki G. Semel—2nd ed.
        p. cm.
    Includes bibliographical references and index.
    ISBN 0-8261-8011-6 (hardcover)
1. Psychotherapy for older people. 2. Older people—Mental health services. 3. Older people—Mental health services—Planning. I. Semel, Vicki Granet. II. Title.
RC480.54.B76 2006
618.97'68914—dc22
                                    2005016898

Printed in the United States of America by Maple-Vail Book Manufacturing Group.

Contents

Contributors

Marilyn S. Denninger received her PhD in psychology from the Pennsylvania State University. Currently she serves as specialist professor in the department of Psychological Counseling at Monmouth University, and is a psychotherapist in private practice. She has prior teaching experience at the Pennsylvania State University and in college and community counseling centers, and has done extensive consulting and training in the areas of stress and lifespan issues with depression and anxiety. She also has conducted workshops for post-polio syndrome support groups, helping group members deal with adjustment issues.

Michael Duffy, PhD, is Professor and past Director of Training of the Doctoral Program in Counseling Psychology at Texas A&M University, in College Station, and also directs a proficiency program in clinical gerontology. He is past president (1995) of the Texas Psychological Association, Fellow of the American Psychological Association, and Chair of Division 17 Section of Independent Practice. He holds graduate degrees in theology (Angelicum University, Rome, Italy) and in psychology (University College, Dublin, Ireland and the University of Texas at Austin). Dr. Duffy teaches psychotherapy with adolescents, couples, and families, and older adults. He is a licensed psychologist and has been in independent practice since 1978. He is a Diplomate of the American Board of Professional Psychology and practices with children, adults, couples, and families, with a specialty in working with older adults. He is the author of many articles and chapters and editor of the *Handbook of Counseling and Psychotherapy With Older Adults* (John Wiley & Sons, 1999).

x STRATEGIES FOR THERAPY WITH THE ELDERLY

Miriam E. Lemerman, MA, NCPsyA, is in private practice in West Orange, New Jersey. For more than 30 years she was a guidance counselor at West Essex Senior High School in North Caldwell, New Jersey. Ms. Lemerman has a master's degree in personnel and guidance from Montclair State University. She is a certified psychoanalyst, trained at the Psychoanalytic Center of Northern New Jersey, recently renamed The Academy of Clinical and Applied Psychoanalysis. She is the author of a handbook for high school students and their families entitled *Taking the Right Steps: A Guide Through the College Process.*

Benjamin W. Pearce is the president and chief executive officer of Potomac Homes, in Ramsey, New Jersey, a residential alternative to institutional care for Alzheimer's disease and related dementias. He was formerly the senior vice president at Senior Housing of Genesis Health Ventures, senior vice president for operations for A.D.S Senior Housing, and Vice President of Operations for Classic Residence by Hyatt. Mr. Pearce is a former director of the National Association of Senior Living Industries (NASLI) and the Assisted Living Federation of America (ALFA). He is the author of *Accounting Systems and Risk Management for Assisted Living* (Assisted Living University Press, 1998) and *Senior Living Communities: Operations Management and Marketing for Assisted Living, Congregate, and Continuing Care Retirement Communities* (Johns Hopkins University Press, 1999).

Jennifer L. Rutberg, MSW, LSW, received a master's degree in social work with a specialization in gerontology from the University of Pennsylvania, in Philadelphia. Her experiences as a social worker include both the Adult Day Health Care Center and the Geriatric Assessment Center at Newark Beth Israel Medical Center in New Jersey, as director of social services at Isaiah House in East Orange, New Jersey, and as director of Herr Adult Medical Day Services at Daughters of Israel in West Orange. She has served on the patient and family services committee for the Alzheimer's Association in New Jersey and is currently on the board of the New Jersey Adult Day Services Association. Ms. Rutberg has extensive experience as an educational speaker for caregivers, paraprofessionals, and professionals, including two years at the statewide conference for the New Jersey Activity Professionals Association.

Foreword

Sheldon S. Tobin, PhD
Professor Emeritus, State University of New York, Albany

When I began my studies of adult development and aging, almost fifty years ago, scant attention was given to therapeutic strategies for the elderly, which is quite understandable given the newness of the field and before the burgeoning of the aging population. With burgeoning, clinical practice escalated and so too the literature, as is readily evident in this significant collation. Reviews of literature include managing of stress, therapy for persons with dementing disorders, using the life review, caregiving issues, care in long-term care facilities, and psychoanalysis. The several reviews attest to knowledge gained in recent times. Still, what is likely to be of special interest to readers are the personal clinical reports.

Denninger reduces stress by meditative techniques that encompass relaxation, guided imagery and mindfulness. Duffy approaches elderly with dementing disorders by pushing for psychological contact that includes persistent verbal and visual interaction. Brody observes how participants in a reminiscence group in a nursing home were able to shift from support by the leader to support for each other. Lemerman, in her clinical examples of caregiving, illustrates for her not only the inherent strain but also deriving "pleasure from the reciprocal act of caring." Rutberg notes how living in an environment that is not safe and secure diminishes working effectively in therapy. Pearce comments that an important component of activity programs in assisted living facilities is the encouragement and fostering of relationships. Then there are Semel's rich reports of her psychoanalysis of elderly persons. It is certainly rare to be provided with case reports that show so clearly the psychoanalytic process.

In a series of case reports, Semel illustrates her "Modern Psychoanalysis" approach to therapy. For her, the process of psychoanalytic therapy is not changed by the age of the patient. The first case is of a woman with "serious lifelong pathology" who uses rage as a defense against abandonment and loneliness. Next is a man with "work inhibition" who welcomes retirement. Two couples are then presented who sought treatment because of unsatisfactory relationships in their marriages. Whereas treatment may not vary by age, age-associated issues, such as retirement and illness of spouse, can induce elderly persons to seek treatment. Countertransference, too, may be different because elderly persons readily evoke feelings of vulnerability and dependency. In her sparkling chapter on countertransference, she details reports by psychoanalysts on their age biases followed by illustrations of how countertransference has "intertwined" with ageism in her practice. In her final example, she uses "the idea of age" as a way to consider excusing herself from continuing treatment of a difficult patient.

An optimism is shared by the several writers regarding what can be accomplished by therapeutic strategies. Apparently when less-impaired clients or patients are discussed, more positive outcomes can be expected, as suggested by the subtitle "Living With Hope and Meaning" and in the Introduction by "empowered to develop more mature coping styles." Semel talks of "ego strength" as basic to Modern Psychoanalysis. When working with the more impaired elderly, however, less ambitious outcomes are anticipated. Duffy hopes that successful treatment of persons with dementing illness will lead to less cognitive disorganization, fewer difficult behaviors, and less depression. Brody's goal for demented elderly in her life review groups in nursing homes is to recapture meaningfulness of the self. This outcome is similar to the therapeutic goal I propose (Tobin, 1999); that is, the preservation of the essential self, a task that is normative for the oldest old. So I share the optimism of therapeutic strategies evidenced for elderly persons with varying degrees of deficits and in a diversity of settings. The strength of this book is in the detailing of these therapeutic strategies.

REFERENCE

Tobin, S. S. (1999). *Preservation of the self in the oldest years with implications for practice.* New York: Springer.

Preface

Claire M. Brody and Vicki G. Semel

This book encompasses three major areas of work with elderly clients (aged 60 and older) functioning on a continuum of autonomy: living in nursing homes; living in assisted living housing, while participating in community-oriented activities for the aged; living independently and being seen in private practice. It also explores issues of the new political reality—reimbursement of non-medical mental health providers under Medicare—and deals with some caregiving issues at home.

Part I has two new chapters: treatment of stress and mental disorders in the elderly, and treatment of Alzheimer's disease, a fairly new area of expertise. The overall theme of this book continues to be that meaningful therapy can be accomplished with an aging/elderly population wherever they are found. Furthermore, we contend that what can truly be unique with the aging client are the feelings, thoughts, and assumptions of the therapist. If the therapist initially experiences negative reactions to a client because of stereotypes about aging, acknowledging the possibility of maturation and hope through psychotherapy can shape his or her perspective.

A sub-theme of this book is the contention that persons with serious mental disorders—such as dementia—no matter what their ages or condition, can be empowered to develop more mature coping styles. Therapy for elderly male and female clients is described throughout the book, using case history material and group vignettes to illustrate the process.

The work is composed of a variety of approaches, ranging from eclectic small group formats for nursing home residents, to group and individual counseling for the elderly in assisted living houses, to home care for the elderly, to psychoanalytic therapy techniques in private practice. What emerges from the work we have done with clients in different settings are basic themes of dependence and independence, failure and success, friendship and loneliness, trust and suspicion, involvement and separation, as well as many of the hopes and aspirations of a younger population. In each of the settings in which we work, we have noted small but significant changes in client adjustment. The changes are just as apparent in clients in long-term care (residents in nursing homes) as they are for those who live independently and seek help in private practice or day care settings for their depression or frustrating marriages. The zest for living and the increase in hopefulness are as significant for one group as for the other. This is a major thesis of this book.

Therapeutic endeavors with elderly women and men are framed within a feminist system of thinking by one author (Claire M. Brody) and a modern psychoanalytic therapy orientation by the other author (Vicki G. Semel). (The reader will find that the terms "client" and "patient" are used to reflect these different approaches.) In the cohort of today's elderly persons, there are far more women than men and the premise is that the *process* of aging may be different for men and women. Women have most often been victims of both ageism and sexism (Trotman & Brody, 2002).

Some of the problems that have been particularly exacerbated in recent times for women, as compared with men, are those connected with inadequate preparation for role changes: the end of parenting, but assuming the care of an elderly parent; retirement with major changes in income level; or crime and violence in neighborhoods where the women have lived peacefully in the past (E. M. Brody, 2004). Society's dual standards for older men and older women reinforce women's problems with the aging process.

Day (1991) researched a variety of variables for women in their seventies and eighties that characterized whether they were "successful" or not at aging. Her object was to carefully define the markers for a positive outcome. Among significant findings were that "challenges associated with aging are most readily discernible and have the greatest potential for causing distress at times of acute change in status" (pp. 156–157). These changes still include going from married woman to widow, from strong and hardy to frail, and from independent homemaker to dependence on others. One stereotype about old age is that it is a time for fruition, release from responsibilities, and postponed creative activity. In fact, it may rock the foundation of self and security; whether a woman survives a major life transition may depend on the *extent of her own role in making the decisions.* This may be especially important when considering caregiving options, discussed in chapter 7.

Women in mid-life and older are more likely than younger women to experience burnout in their jobs, as explained by Richter (1990). They experience less control over their environment, tend to deny their personal needs, and use less effective strategies for coping with stress. With age, this author says, the level of self-confidence of women increases; with men, it decreases. Especially when caring for an aging parent, a daughter who has become independent has an especially difficult time.

We need to look at some of the reasons for inadequacies in providing mental health services for elderly men and women as compared with other age cohorts. Until recently, these would include the paucity of prevention and outpatient care available through either psychological or medical aegis, or an elderly person might have been reluctant to admit to psychological problems. This was especially true prior to 1988 when changes occurred in the Medicare system that made more psychological help available (see chapter 14). Evidence of emotional problems was more likely to result in confinement to a custodial nursing home. This is not as true anymore; many nursing homes routinely provide mental health services. In the past, perception of psychopathology in the aged was more likely to be seen as part of a permanent decline due to aging; this attitude of ageism when considering psychopathology also is no longer as true.

PART I: INTRODUCTION

The first chapter of this book, under the heading "Introduction," discusses the kinds of disorders that are characteristic of elderly people, with an emphasis on those that cause stress and their implications for other disorders. The second chapter is on the treatment of Alzheimer's disease, often in nursing homes, but also with many such elderly now residing in assisted living residences. There is much new literature and thinking about this common disorder and many myths to dispel.

PART II: NURSING HOMES

The first chapter in Part II (chapter 3) examines the literature on staff, family, and residents of nursing homes. It also offers a new view of residents, with effective models of individual and group therapy for them. Management techniques that have evolved for nursing homes are also dealt with and new areas for research are suggested. One recent article (Corder & Hernandez, 2004) distinguishes between *consumers* and *recipients* of long-term care services, with the residents able to *choose* the kind of care they want. This new model of nursing home care has much to say about "elderspeak," defined as patronizing talk that characterizes much of the communication by staff with the residents of nursing homes and its potentially negative effects on the elders.

Chapter 4 describes a series of reminiscence groups with elderly women in a private nursing home. Participants in these groups varied widely in their cognitive ability and capacity for sustained communication. The therapist functioned as a leader/participant and used a form of life review and directed memory-jogging to elicit responses. While different eras of their lives were being reviewed, there was an opportunity for brief discourses on such topics as feminism, comparative child-rearing practices, and changing roles of women. Excerpts from group sessions are included to illustrate the process of life review with impaired residents.

In chapter 5, three myths of motherhood are outlined, along with the realities aging women face today. Women living in nursing homes are seen in their roles as mothers of caregiving daughters, and the daughters' conflicts are examined. The subject of mothers and daughters has been a focus of several books (see, especially, the revision of Elaine Brody's book, *Women in the Middle*, 2004), and many articles (notably Peters-Davis, Moss, & Pruchno, 1999). The latter authors talk of daughters-in-law as not being that different than daughters: "When care is needed within an extended family unit it appears that the in-law status is not an impediment in many cases" (p. 73). It should be of special interest here to explore feelings about this significant relationship in a woman's life.

Alzheimer's disease clients are becoming a major group in nursing homes and assisted living residences, and so the final chapter of this section (chapter 6) describes a pilot project with a small group of these elderly in a nursing home. Other innovative programs for these residents are also described and compared, with an emphasis on programs within the last few years. Until recently there were very few programs for this diagnostic cohort.

PART III: ISSUES OF THE ELDERLY IN THE COMMUNITY

There are many communities in this country with a sizeable number of independent and semi-independent elderly people in need of varied services. There are those elderly who no longer have families—widows, widowers, older divorced individuals, and singles. Those with families frequently find their middle-aged children involved with their own families. The elderly are often sandwiched between their older, frail parents and their children (a newer trend with our increasingly aging population).

In response to these issues, many innovative programs utilizing different services and modalities have been developed. Our experience over the last decades has shown that when institutions provide supportive living and socialization, along with medical care, client functioning is enhanced and the deteriorations of old age are significantly delayed. Several of these programs are discussed in this book.

The first chapter in this section (chapter 7) discusses caregiving. The emphasis is on seniors who live alone or with family members and either do or do not take part in community activities. In addition to giving a historical and statistical view of those we are talking about, this chapter discusses the needs of the *caregiver* as well as of the elderly person who is cared for, and the variety of needs of the older person. For example, one of the key roles of the caregiver is communicating with the elder's physician and other health care professionals, and being sure that medications and procedures are understood by all. For the caregiver who does not live close to the elder, or who just needs to call in an advisor, a list of resources is included at the end of the chapter.

The second chapter in this section (chapter 8) describes a day treatment program in a community center. This arrangement addresses the social, psychological, emotional, and physical needs of this group. There is a description of many varieties of residences for seniors, with varying therapies and other options. Therapists often help residents assess their own needs, and the case illustrations deal with this situation effectively. Ms. Rutberg describes a particular senior center, and one can easily extrapolate to other communities.

The last chapter in this section (chapter 9) deals with a variety of therapy programs for people in assisted living facilities. It deals with different staff people's roles, including volunteers. It also describes how to recruit volunteers and how an activity department works. The author of this chapter indicates that there are no industry guidelines for staffing ratios across all levels of care, but he compares activity staffing under different types of living arrangements and provides a sample of activity programming for an assisted living facility (ALF). Mr. Pearce also defines "Validation Therapy" and gives examples of different kinds that are in use.

PART IV: PRIVATE PRACTICE

In this section of the book, psychoanalytic therapy in private practice with the aging person is explored. Modern Psychoanalytic treatment of the more disturbed aging person is described in case study format. Chapter 10 examines the treatment of a borderline paranoid woman as she deals with the aging process and issues particular to her age group (mid-sixties): retirement of a spouse, the last child leaving home, the husband's illness, and the couple's decision to move to a retirement village. The focus is on how her extraordinary rage was dealt with in the sessions.

Chapter 11 explores the work with another aging and disturbed client who was never able to achieve occupational success. The meaning of his retirement as it related to unresolved preoedipal issues was addressed in the therapy. Chapter 12 describes two aging couples trying to deal with long-term frustration in their marriages. One couple, in their late seventies, started treatment after a serious illness and the husband's symptomatology affected the marriage.

The second couple, in their late sixties, was treated in a more unorthodox fashion, as only the dissatisfied wife would come to the office. Her husband participated through letters he would write to the therapist. The wife presented physical symptoms, which her internist suggested were related to stress. She, in turn, associated these problems with long-term frustrations with her husband and sought help for the marriage.

Chapter 13 deals with the issues of ageism and countertransference, as such processes influence therapists who treat older and frequently more disturbed clients. Two cases of patients in their sixties illustrate countertransference problems. One describes the person previously discussed in chapter 11 whose difficulties were centered around working; in chapter 13, countertransference issues are the focus. The second case involves a client's hostile and sarcastic style, which became an issue of ageism for the therapist.

For these cases, the thesis is that an experience of hopelessness in an aging person's psychotherapy may reside more in the therapist than in the client. If the therapist believes that the person is not treatable, the idea may not be a comment on the client but on the reactions of the therapist (Semel, 1990). The theoretical perspective of Modern Psychoanalysis (Spotnitz, 1987, 2004; Spotnitz & Meadow, 1976) is described and made relevant for private practice work with aging women, men, and couples.

In the final section of the book, on Medicare, we define some of the wide-ranging and unique problems engendered by the law passed in July 1990, which makes it possible for psychologists, social workers, and other mental health professionals to work independently with aging clients under Medicare. It can be expected that, as a result of this legislation, many more non-medical professionals will become involved with diverse treatment strategies for the elderly.

PART V: RELEVANT ISSUES AND APPROACHES FOR THERAPY

The literature in therapy with aging women and men was especially sparse until about 20 years ago. Most of the research and descriptive material available appeared in professional journals.

The Modern Psychoanalytic approach to working with elderly clients in private practice, as described by Semel (1990), is a revision of the classical psychoanalytic stance. This permits work with elderly clients by means of ego-strengthening approaches. The person's contact with the therapist, that is, the client's "contact functioning," is studied and respected (Spotnitz, 2004). It is within this theoretical framework that a format is provided for working individually with an elderly population of clients.

Back in 1984, Lurie and Rich wrote of a developing continuum of comprehensive therapy services for the high-risk elderly population as an outreach from a community medical center. They provided evidence that individual and group therapy are viable forms of psychological help for older persons. (Knight, 1983, and Zarit, 1980, also wrote about this issue at that time.)

Betty Friedan (1985) said that one way to view aging is as the second stage of the women's movement. However, just as we cannot understand personhood by using a male model, we also cannot understand this second stage only in terms of women; it must include men (p. 42). Friedan also said that similar to a feminine mystique there is also an age mystique that frustrates and depresses elderly people by diminishing their self-esteem and expectations. A popular view of the aging process too often denies them the very real vitality of men and women in their sixties, seventies, eighties, and sometimes even in their nineties. Too often age is associated with disease, and often not at all with the growth that can accompany aging.

When Claire Brody began to work with people in a nursing home she focused first on the women there because they made up the larger cohort of residents; this is still the case. *Counseling and Therapy With Older Women: Cross-Cultural, Family, and End-of-Life Issues* by Fran Trotman and Claire Brody (2002), was one of the first books that focused on working with older *women*. Steuer (1982) searched the literature up to that year and found little data on therapy with older women. What there was, up to then, was on therapy with the elderly using a medical model, with little on gender-focused issues.

One possible reason for this lack is that therapists reflect society's basic discriminatory attitudes toward this cohort, which continues to have less social status. In all fairness, however, the number of books on women's therapy and outlook is certainly increasing.

For a variety of reasons, such as reluctance or inability of the aged to ask for attention and the unavailability and perceived insurmountable obstacle (recent changes in the Medicare law might remedy this) of the high cost of professional help in nursing homes, mental health care has been a sorely neglected arena of attention. A special issue of *Clinical Gerontologist* (9, 3/4, 1990), titled "Mental Health in the Nursing Home," addressed many aspects of residential treatment for residents and their families. Some of that material is dealt with in this book.

Golant said recently (2004) that the nursing home "is the most institutionalized, long term care setting in the United States with the highest prevalence of older persons who are chronically ill and who have difficulty functioning because of their cognitive and physical difficulties" (p. S68). Actually, more care is provided outside the nursing home, in assisted living facilities (ALFs) and in less institutional settings (see chapter 9). And Elaine M. Brody (2004) reminds us, in her reissue of an older book, that "the chances of being in a nursing home increase with advancing age" (p. 289), especially in view of our population's aging and the expectation that the number of people over age 85 will also increase.

The literature for therapy, both individual and group, with elderly clients in community centers, assisted living residences, and in private practice, as well as new uses of institutional projects, is reported and expanded upon in the individual chapters of this book. The present authors anticipate that by collecting their own and others' experiences, this book can become a valuable source of information for a population that will undoubtedly need creative designs to help them in the decades to come.

REFERENCES

Brink, T. L. (Ed.). (1990). Mental health in the nursing home [Special issue]. *Clinical Gerontologist, 9*, 3/4.

Brody, E. M. (2004). *Women in the middle: Their parent-care years* (2nd ed.). New York: Springer.

Corder, P. C., & Hernandez, M. (2004). Consumer discourse in assisted living. *Journals of Gerontology, 59B*, S58–S67.

Day, A. T. (1991). *Remarkable survivors: Insights into successful aging.* Washington, DC: The Urban Institute.

Friedan, B. (1985). The mystique of age. In R. N. Butler & H. P. Gleason (Eds.). *Productive aging: Enhancing vitality in later life* (pp. 37–45). New York: Springer.

Golant, S. M. (2004). Impaired older persons with health care needs occupy US assisted living facilities: An analysis of six studies. *Journals of Gerontology, 57B*(2), S68–S79.

Knight, B. G. (1983). Assessing a mobile outreach team. In M. A. Smyer & M. Gatz (Eds.). *Mental health and aging: Programs and evaluations* (pp. 23–40). Beverly Hills, CA: Sage.

Lurie, A., & Rich, J. C. (1984). The medical center's impact on the network to sustain the elderly in the community. *Journal of Gerontological Social Work, 7*(3), 65–73.

Peters-Davis, N. D., Moss, M. S., & Pruchno, R. A. (1999). Children-in-law in caregiving families. *Gerontologist, 39*(1), 66–75.

Richter, J. (1990). Crossing boundaries between professional and private life. In H. Y. Grossman & N. L. Chester (Eds.). *The experience of work in women's lives* (pp. 143–161). Hillsdale, NJ: Erlbaum.

Semel, V. G. (1990, August). *Confrontations with hopelessness: Private practice treatment of the older woman.* Paper presented at the APA Annual Meeting, Boston, MA.

Spotnitz, H. (1987). *Psychotherapy of preoedipal conditions: Schizophrenia and severe character disorders.* Northvale, NJ: Jason Aronson.

Spotnitz, H. (2004). *Modern psychoanalysis of the schizophrenic patient* (2nd ed.). New York: YBK.

Spotnitz, H., & Meadow, P. W. (1976). *Treatment of the narcissistic neuroses.* New York: Manhattan Center for Advanced Psychoanalytic Studies.

Steuer, J. L. (1982). Psychotherapy with older women: Ageism and sexism in traditional practice. *Psychotherapy, 19*(4), 429–436.

Trotman, F. K., & Brody, C. M. (2002). *Psychotherapy and counseling with older women: Cross-cultural, family, and end-of-life issues.* New York: Springer.

Zarit, S. H. (1980). *Aging and mental disorders.* New York: Free Press.

Acknowledgments

We would like to thank the following people:

Sheldon S. Tobin, who generously contributed our Preface. Dr. Tobin's life work has been the psychology of the "oldest old"—elders of 85 years and beyond. He has explored the unique adaptive coping mechanisms, from religion to reminiscence to aggression in these elders, and brought new knowledge into gerontological practice for psychologists, psychiatrists, medical clinicians, social workers, gerontological nurses, and students of aging.

Ilene Manahan, whose invaluable editing assistance made this book finally come together.

Paterson Smith, for his inimitable help with computer problems, and Tom Kelly, for his, with the index.

And a special thank you to Sheri W. Sussman and Betsy Day, our editors, whose support and gentle encouragement helped bring this second edition to fruition.

We would also like to thank the rest of Vicki Semel's family: her mothers Lois Granet and Gertrude Semel; her daughters Debra Semel Goldenring and Robin Semel, who are maturing wonderfully; and her "guys": her son-in-law, Stephen Goldenring, and grandchildren Jacob and Samuel Goldenring, all of whose affection and energy have been central in the evolution of this book.

We also acknowledge Claire's daughters Jessica, Laurie, and Naomi, for their support and kindnesses, and Claire's newest granddaughters, Katie and Eva, along with the others, Anna, Lily, Leah, Sophie, and Emily, who, someday, will benefit from our premise about aging: a time of hope and meaning.

I love sitting on a bench by some old person, for now I no
longer fear the old, but wait for when they trust me enough
to tell me their tales, so full of history. I ask, tell me, what did
you wear on your wedding day? And for some reason
there's always a laugh, a smile . . . And I sit and listen, listen.

The Diaries of Jane Somers
Doris Lessing

Part I

Introduction

Chapter 1

Stress and Mental Health in the Elderly

Marilyn S. Denninger

Stress, which presumes the need to adapt, is ubiquitous. It pervades life in that living requires constant adaptation. We routinely adjust to positive and negative shifts and events in our lives, to hassles and demands, as well as to our own physical and psychological progressive and regressive patterns of change.

Because stress is omnipresent, explicit and implicit assumptions abound among mental health practitioners that we automatically deal with stress issues in treatment and therefore need not make specific reference to them. However, this line of thought is fast becoming outdated as stress has gained ascendance as a topic in itself and in relation to various mental disorders and physical problems (Aldwin & Gilmer, 2004; Lovallo, 2005; Zautra, 2003). Further, if stress presumes the need for adaptation, and if the adult years are a time of rapid and multiple changes at the same time as they are years of altered stress reactivity and increased vulnerability (Sapolsky, 1998), then stress becomes a critical topic in treatment considerations with the older population.

WHAT AND WHY STRESS?

Stress is a partner in life. Whether facing major transitions, daily hassles, or even significant positive changes, the individual must adapt. Selye (1956) has referred to the body's response patterns to stress as the general adaptation syndrome (GAS). This syndrome consists of three discrete stages referred to as alarm reaction, resistance, and exhaustion, in which the body first enters a general arousal state, then a more organ/system-specific state of activation, followed by depletion of adaptation energy if the stress continues. Specifically, exposure to stress activates the mind–body arousal system. The requirement to adapt is accompanied by a physical and psychological homeostatic imbalance, also referred to currently as the allostatic load or allostasis. The higher the level of demand on the individual for adaptation, the greater the chance that effects will be experienced and that adverse outcomes will be manifest. To the extent that the demands for adapting and coping strain or exceed the individual's resources, to the extent that the perceived or actual threat to the individual's stability of current functioning is high, to the extent that the outcome or network of outcomes of the situation is significant to the individual, a state of physical, emotional, and cognitive arousal ensues. Though there is disagreement in the literature regarding whether older adults are more or less reactive to stress, more discriminative findings indicate that although in general the older respond to fewer daily stressors, when they do respond it is with greater reactivity (Mroczek & Almeida, 2004). Kindling, or changes in sensitivity of neural pathways associated with stressors, is one possible explanation offered by these researchers. Aging-related alterations in neuroendocrine, organ, and metabolic functioning inherent to the stress reaction also appear to be responsible (Sapolsky, 1998). The elderly, then, are at risk for experiencing the negative effects of "overwhelm," which can include problems with memory and attention, irritability, sleep disruption, a sense of helplessness, and loss of control. More serious outcomes include precipitation of or exacerbation of already existing mental health problems such as depression, anxiety disorders, and schizophrenia, as well as heightened susceptibility to disease and pathogens.

Stress has also been implicated in aging and mortality (Smith, 2003). Stress hormones create decrements in immune function and increments in inflammation, both of which are associated with mortality and almost all of the major health issues experienced by aging individuals. Some of the most serious include Alzheimer's disease, and diabetic, cardiovascular, gastrointestinal, malignant, disability-

and frailty-related conditions (Kiecolt-Glaser, McGuire, Robles, & Glaser, 2002; Lovallo, 2005; Sapolsky, 1998). These mental health and physical problems themselves increase stress, thereby creating a reciprocal stress-pathology interaction.

With this host of implications, addressing stress when treating the population of older adults, both in terms of preventive and postventive interventions, is a salient concern for practitioners.

STRESS POTENTIATORS

There are numerous risk factors or potentiators for the stress reaction in vulnerable individuals. Categories of potentiators include acute and chronic or ongoing stressors. The former is characterized by suddenness, the latter by a sense of relentlessness. Hassles, or low-level annoyances, can also stress the individual, especially if they occur in conjunction with other more severe acute or chronic life events.

Further distinction needs to be made between "normative" stress, considered life-stage appropriate, and "non-normative" stress, those events that are not expected for a given age group. These latter life events are more challenging because they create a greater sense of novelty-related overwhelm. Luckily, normative events are in the majority in younger years. As the individual ages, however, the ratio between what are defined as normative and non-normative events changes such that events considered catastrophic and less likely to occur during the younger years are more the norm with advancing age, posing an additional overwhelm threat for the elderly.

Another useful conceptual distinction bearing impact on working with the elderly is that between sequential and simultaneous stressors (Petersen, Kennedy, & Sullivan, 1991). Sequential stressors occur over time, allowing for coping, adaptation, and restoration of balance within the individual's mental and/or physical coping repertoire. Because of temporal proximity and repetition of stress, when stressors are simultaneous, such rebalancing is either extremely difficult or impossible, leaving the individual depleted and at greater risk for negative outcomes. Here, too, a shift in the ratio of these kinds of patterns is seen with advancing age. The occurrence of stressful events among the elderly becomes more frequent and repetitive so that the distinction blurs and stress is experienced as more simultaneous. Again the threat of overwhelm is increased.

STRESSFUL EVENTS

Numerous life events commonly observed among the elderly have been identified as stress-inducing. Although some disagreement exists in the literature regarding individual, cohort, and contextual differences in the potential that each poses in terms of intensity of reactivity, there is general consensus that they do constitute risk factors among the elderly.

Widowhood and bereavement can be stressful in that loss of a spouse creates pain and changes in life circumstances. Not only is there loss of the person but loss of intimacy and all of the emotional attachment patterns associated with the beloved. If over time this emotional sense of loss cannot be mitigated through the salience of positive memories (Bonanno, Wortman, & Nesse, 2004), protracted negative sequelae are more likely. In addition, the loss of a helpmate often creates numerous financial and instrumental lifestyle changes—changes that may be experienced for some time following the loss, if not for the rest of the individual's life. In addition, the loss of one's role or roles in the marriage (spouse, friend, co-parent, co-grandparent, being half of a couple) creates pain and strain (Foos & Clark, 2003). To the extent that these roles were valued, their loss exerts differential stressful effects: the more valued the role, the more disruption its loss causes (Krause, 2004).

Although parallel and adequate data are sorely lacking with regard to gay and lesbian couples, practitioners working with bereaved partners can combine awareness of the stress caused by multiple marginalization and living in a cultural context that fosters both ageist and homophobic thinking with the research discussed above (Greene, 2002). Regarding intimate relationships, loss of friendships is also noted as a significant stressor for the elderly (Hardy, Concato, & Gill, 2002). Within my practice it has not been uncommon for individuals, especially those living alone, to cite loss of a companion pet as a major challenging life event.

Physical changes and health-related life events are a diverse set of stressors. Changes in physical appearance involving skin, hair, height, and weight (Foos & Clark, 2003) mark the older years. Though these changes are not well researched as a major source of stress, in my clinical work with older adults I have frequently heard reference made to them with worry, resentment, and unhappiness. Regarding cumulative stress and/or how valued youth and physical attractiveness have been to the individual's sense of self, these changes do represent an area of potential stress reactivity. Declines in physical capacity and in muscular strength and endurance, and new or incremental aches and pains are met with concern and voiced complaints. Frailty in the advanced years is the most severe of the physical decline syndromes. Severe pain, especially if associated with some form of disability, is a psychological stressor and has been shown to evoke a biological stress reaction whose potential outcome is lowered immune and mental functioning (Kiecolt-Glaser, McGuire, Robles, & Glaser, 2002). Physical disability and health-related changes are other acknowledged sources of stress. One study (Reich, Zautra, & Garnaccia, 1989) found the recently disabled to suffer more stress-related distress and decrements in well-being than the recently bereaved.

Illness both causes and can worsen stress. Chronic illness involves loss. The patient has lost his or her identity as a well person. Assuming the sick-person identity or patient role (Knight, 2004) means numerous psychological and social adjustments. Those for whom independence has been an integral aspect of their healthy sense of self may suffer additional stress in coming to terms with being more dependent and compliant than is comfortable. Additional strain arises when individuals suffer from multiple chronic conditions, which is often the case among the elderly (Wrosch, Schultz, & Heckhausen, 2002). Other stressors arising from increased illnesses are higher rates of hospitalization among those 65 and older (Merluzzi & Nairn, 1999). Post-hospital admissions to rehabilitation sites also increase with age, thus adding further demands for adaptation and potential for stress reactions, which can impair mental functioning. Relocation has long been known to create high levels of stress and to be linked to increased death rates (Jessen, Cardiello, & Baun, 1996).

Related to the increase of illnesses in the elderly is the need for caregiving by a healthy other, which can be a potent source of stress. The stress that results from caregiving is referred to as the *caregiver burden* and leads to higher rates of illness and mental health difficulties (Whitbourne, 2005). The person in the primary caregiver role also must be a focus of consideration for stress-modifying interventions, especially where there is little or no help from the larger family network (Knight, 2004).

In addition to these more typical stressors among the elderly, it is important to assess what our elderly patients themselves consider to be stressful. To assume that we as practitioners and researchers know better than our patients what events are causing them stress-related distress reflects ageist and patronizing attitudes. The elderly deserve the same status and dignity we accord younger clients in helping us to identify what they consider salient to their levels of stress. Given the relationship of stress to negative mental health and physical illness outcomes, there is a press to do a thorough assessment. In my work I have used an ecological model derived from Bronfenbrenner's idea that the individual is nested in environmental levels, or ecologies, which create multiple reciprocal interactions with the person (Bronfenbrenner, 1995).

I include this line of thinking as part of the intake process by asking for a description of all important intimate, social, and economic aspects of the individual's life as well as for salient cultural beliefs and how that person evaluates them. Also of importance are any interactions among these aspects as they impact my patient. In this collaborative way, I gain a panoramic overview of potential stressors unique to that individual. Importantly, the therapeutic relationship is quickly strengthened by the patient's feeling important and cared about. For the elderly, who are often treated perfunctorily, this approach overcomes many initial hesitations about seeking therapy and helps build a stronger therapeutic alliance. For later stages of the therapy process, such detailed knowledge of the person's positive and negative perceptions of self in context leads to greater idiosyncratic specificity of intervention techniques. Not a small focus in this process is the reflecting on cultural beliefs. This includes pertinent racial, ethnic, religious/spiritual, and immigration information, all of which have been shown to have impact on the way stress and emotionality are experienced (Helman, 2002; Kitayama & Markus, 1994; Lewis, 2002).

STRESS AS A UNIFYING PRINCIPLE IN PSYCHOTHERAPY CONCERNS

Most recently, the area of positive psychology, with its focus on the role of maximizing individuals' strengths and positive subjective experiences as buffers in the etiology and maintenance of pathology, has subsumed much of this thinking.

Research has defined numerous factors related to helping counter the deleterious effects of stress in vulnerable older adults. Some researchers have referred to these factors as resilience (Garmezy, Mastern, & Tellegen, 1984); others refer to them as emotional intelligence (Goleman, 1995; Salovey, Mayer, & Caruso, 2002). Most recently, the area of positive psychology has subsumed much of this thinking (Seligman, 2002). Meditative techniques also help rebalance the person's mental and physical reactivity in response to stress (Kabat-Zinn, 1990). In my work, I have found certain of these techniques beneficial in dealing with stress and both mental and physical disorders.

MEDITATIVE TECHNIQUES

Relaxation as a technique to manage stress and to achieve homeostatic balance enjoys a long tradition. Both positive psychological and physical effects have been observed (Kabat-Zinn, 1990). Progressive relaxation (PR), by its specific focus on muscle groups, is useful where increased awareness of tension patterns is desirable. I have also found that anxious patients feel more comfortable with PR than with other, less focused relaxation exercises. These are people who often experience relaxation-induced anxiety, especially in response to the lack of structure and the potential flood of affect that can occur with simply enjoying a sense of timelessness. With patients who can tolerate more ambiguity and affect, guided imagery fostering an enjoyment of letting go of mundane awareness is quite effective. Creating an image based in the person's positive perceptions of self in relation to his or her respective ecologies has more significance than a generic image and therefore more power to heal.

Mindfulness, a term associated with Kabat-Zinn's work (1990), refers to teaching the individual to stay focused in the present moment and to appreciate it as if observing it for the first time. One benefit of this technique is that it engenders an appreciation for how much uniqueness can be observed even in the very familiar, freeing up the ability to see new meaning even in the most stressful of situations. I refer to this as *transformative reframing* and find it most useful for depressed, stressed individuals. Attention on the present moment also helps combat ruminative tendencies, both past-focused and anticipatory. This is quite helpful with depressed and anxious patients. Where ruminative anger and an associated sense of victimization and impotent rage are part of the problematic pattern, mindfulness can help the individual create options for viewing the perceived stressor differently. This type of anger has also been related to hostility, a known stress-related risk factor for adverse mental and physical health (Ewart & Jorgensen, 2004).

EMOTION-RELATED INTERVENTIONS

The importance of the expression of emotion has been shown to relate to the interface of healthy emotional and physical functioning (Kennedy-Moore & Watson, 1999; Ketrie, Booth, & Davison, 1996). Writing about severe stressors accompanied by disclosure of emotion has been shown to enhance immune function (Pennebaker, 1997). The positive effects of expressive writing on numerous aspects of psychological health, stress reduction, and physical health have been demonstrated (Lepore & Smyth, 2002). For the older adult who is physically able to write, these techniques offer unique opportunities for creative accomplishment as well. I have found this to enhance a sense of competence and pride.

The therapist can also be helpful by aiding in expanding the patient's emotional lexicon in terms of categories and intensities. Emotion differentiation allows for a more balanced use of different emotion categories by which to describe troublesome experiences, as well as for enhancing comprehension and use of intensity nuances within each category. Realizing that one can feel more than one emotion and/or intensity at the same time is particularly helpful for combating the negative set in the stressed, depressed, and anxious. The therapist can also encourage use of active voice as opposed to overgeneralized passive voice when describing emotional experience. For example, I have found (Denninger, 1995) that older women frequently have difficulty giving voice to their anger in well-differentiated active voice statements. Health status benefits when anger is expressed in ways that give options to feel less victimized. I have also found that anxious individuals, regardless of gender, can overcome stress-generated anxiety by being aware of their overuse of passive-voice constructions in their relationship to stressors.

In my clinical work, I have found that emotion differentiation can also be a useful technique in helping alexithymics become more expressive. Alexithymia, the inability to clearly experience and verbalize emotion, has been found to relate to higher incidences of somatic complaints and mood disturbance (Paez, Velasco, & Gonzalez, 1999). For such individuals, a first step is having them replace inappropriate descriptions of emotional states with appropriate emotion words. Simple homework involves practice in replacing an emotion word for the behavioral or other non-emotion descriptor of an emotional state. Patience is needed, as much repetition is required before the use of the emotion word becomes reflexive. Following this, I refine and modify the emotion word—"angry," for example—with intensity differentiations representing high and low, such that "very angry" might become "furious" and "a little angry" might become "annoyed." Again, this is followed by a lengthy period of practice before becoming part of the person's emotion lexicon. Alexithymic mood–disordered individuals with whom I have worked have indicated pleasure at being able to "after all these years, talk to others in ways I am understood."

Positive states also have been found to be related to better health. In addition, Salovey, Rothman, Detweiler, and Steward (2000) found that positive affect motivates health-promoting behaviors. More recent findings have shown that positive affect lowers the risk of frailty in older adults (Ostir, Ottenbacher, & Markides, 2004). It would thus seem that helping the elderly to deal more effectively with negative emotionality, especially where related to stress overwhelm, depression, and physical problems, should be prominently included in therapeutic interventions.

Findings indicate that with advancing age, levels of positive affect increase, suggesting that older adults naturally tend to regulate their emotionality in the direction of maximizing positive emotions (Mroczek & Kolarz, 1998). Other research has shown that those elderly with the ability to savor positive affect states, in contrast to muting or dampening them, experience higher self-esteem (Wood, Heimpel, & Michela, 2003). Significantly, self-esteem problems are common to many areas of pathology. Taken together, these findings imply that the elderly may have a natural propensity for being responsive to interventions designed to increase feeling good, enabling therapy to address issues of self-esteem and comorbid conditions via this mediating modality. Teaching distressed older individuals other skills designed to foster a positive focus would also seem age-relevant. Here the use of "uplifts," or reflections on positive life domains as a means of countering negative life events is relevant (Larsen & Asmussen, 1991). The inability to manage stress and negative emotionality can instill a sense of helplessness and hopelessness. In the depressive, this poses an increased risk of suicide, lending additional import to therapeutic intervention, which fosters a positive bias.

To conclude, explicit focus on stress as a unifying principle in psychotherapy allows for an integrative mind–body approach to working with a population who need, and perhaps more importantly deserve, such holistic care.

REFERENCES

Aldwin, C., & Gilmer, D. (2004). *Health, illness and optimal aging: Biological and psychosocial perspective*. Thousand Oaks, CA: Sage.

Bonanno, G. A., Wortman, C. B., & Nesse, R. M. (2004). Prospective patterns of resilience and maladjustment during widowhood. *Psychology and Aging, 19*(2), 260–271.

Bronfenbrenner, U. (1995). The bioecological model from a lifespan perspective: Reflections of a participant observer. In P. Moen, G. H. Elder, Jr., & K. Luscher (Eds.). *Examining lives in context* (pp. 599–618). Washington, DC: American Psychological Association.

Denninger, M. S. (1995). *Therapeutic implications of a gender-based theory of self—women's anger and affiliative needs revisited*. Presented at the Gender and Diversity Conference, Monmouth University, Long Branch, NJ.

Ewart, C. K., & Jorgensen, R. S. (2004). Agonistic interpersonal striving: Social-cognitive mechanism of cardiovascular risk in youth. *Health Psychology, 23*(1), 75–85.

Foos, P. W., & Clark, M. C. (2003). *Human aging*. Boston: Allyn and Bacon.

Garmezy, N., Mastern, A. S., & Tellegen, A. (1984). The study of stress and competence in children: A building block for developmental psychopathology. *Child Development, 55*, 97–111.

Goleman, D. (1995). *Emotional intelligence: Why it can matter more than IQ*. New York: Bantam.

Greene, B. (2002). Older lesbians' concerns and psychotherapy: Beyond a footnote to the footnote. In F. K. Trotman & C. M. Brody (Eds.). *Psychotherapy and counseling with older women: Cross-cultural, family, and end-of-life issues* (pp. 161–174). New York: Springer.

Hardy, S. E., Concato, J., & Gill, T. M. (2002). Stressful life events among community-living older persons. *Journal of General Internal Medicine, 17*, 841–844.

Helman, C. (2002). *Culture, health and illness* (4th ed.). London: Arnold.

Jessen, J., Cardiello, F., & Baun, M. (1996). Avian companionship in alleviation of depression, loneliness and low morale of older adults in skilled rehabilitation units. *Psychological Reports, 78*, 339–348.

Kabat-Zinn, J. (1990). *Full catastrophe living: Using the wisdom of your body and mind to face stress and illness*. New York: Delta.

Kennedy-Moore, E., & Watson, J. (1999). *Expressing emotion, myths: Realities and therapeutic strategies*. New York: Guilford.

Ketrie, K. J., Booth, R. J., & Davison, K. P. (1996). Repression, disclosure and immune function: Recent findings and methodological issues. In J. W. Pennebaker (Ed.). *Emotion, disclosure and health* (pp. 223–240). Washington, DC: American Psychological Association.

Kiecolt-Glaser, J., McGuire, L., Robles, T. F., & Glaser, R. (2002). Emotions, morbidity, and mortality: New perspectives from psychoneuroimmunology. *Annual Review of Psychology, 53*, 83–107.

Kitayama, S., & Markus, H. (Eds.). (1994). *Emotion and culture: Empirical studies of mutual influence*. Washington, DC: American Psychological Association.

Knight, B. (2004). *Psychotherapy with older adults* (3rd ed.). Thousand Oaks, CA: Sage.

Krause, N. (2004). Stresses arising in highly valued roles: Meaning in life and health status of older adults. *Journals of Gerontology, 59B*(5), S287–S297.

Larsen, R., & Asmussen, L. (1991). Anger, worry and hurt in early adolescence: An enlarging world of negative emotions. In M. Colten & S. Gore (Eds.). *Adolescent stress: Causes and consequences* (pp. 21–42). New York: Aldine deGruyter.

Lepore, S. J., & Smyth, J. (Eds.). (2002). *The writing cure: How expressive writing promotes health and emotional well being*. Washington, DC: American Psychological Association.

Lewis, M. (2002). *Multicultural health psychology: Special topics acknowledging diversity*. Boston: Allyn and Bacon.

Lovallo, W. (2005). *Stress and health: Biological and psychological interactions* (2nd ed.). Thousand Oaks, CA: Sage.

Merluzzi, T., & Nairn, R. (1999). Adulthood and aging; Transitions in health and health cognition. In T. Whitman, T. Merluzzi, & R. White (Eds.). *Lifespan perspectives on health and illness* (pp. 189–206). Hillsdale, NJ: Erlbaum.

Mroczek, D., & Almeida, D. (2004). The effect of daily stress, personality and age on daily negative affect. *Journal of Personality, 72*(2), 355–378.

Mroczek, D., & Kolarz, C. (1998). The effect of age on positive and negative affect: A developmental perspective on happiness. *Journal of Personality and Social Psychology, 75*(5), 1333–1349.

Ostir, G. V., Ottenbacher, K. J., & Markides, K. (2004). Onset of frailty in older adults and the protective role of positive affect. *Psychology and Aging, 19*(3), 402–408.

Paez, D., Velasco, C., & Gonzalez, J. L. (1999). Expressive writing and the role of alexithymia as a dispositional deficit in self disclosure and psychological health. *Journal of Personality and Social Psychology, 77*(3), 630–641.

Pennebaker, J. W. (1997). *Opening up: The healing power of expressing emotions* (Rev. ed.). New York: Guilford.

Petersen, A. C., Kennedy, R. E., & Sullivan, P. (1991). Coping with adolescence. In M. Colten & S. Gore (Eds.). *Adolescent stress: Causes and consequences* (pp. 93–110). New York: Aldine deGruyter.

Reich, J. W., Zautra, A., & Garnaccia, C. (1989). Effects of disability and bereavement on the mental health and recovery of older adults. *Psychology and Aging, 4*(1), 57–65.

Salovey, P., Mayer, J. D., & Caruso, D. (2002). The positive psychology of emotional intelligence. In C. R. Snyder & S. Lopez (Eds.). *Handbook of positive psychology* (pp. 159–171). Oxford, UK: Oxford University Press.

Salovey, P., Rothman, A. J., Detweiler, J. B., & Steward, W. T. (2000). Emotional states and physical health. *American Psychologist, 55*, 110–121.

Sapolsky, R. M. (1998). *Why zebras don't get ulcers: An updated guide to stress, stress-related diseases and coping.* New York: W. H. Freeman.

Seligman, M. E. P. (2002). Positive psychology, positive prevention, positive therapy. In C. R. Snyder & S. Lopez (Eds.). *Handbook of positive psychology* (pp. 3–13). Oxford, UK: Oxford University Press.

Selye, H. (1956). *The stress of life.* New York: McGraw Hill.

Smith, J. (2003). Stress and aging: Theoretical and empirical challenges for interdisciplinary research. *Neurobiology of Aging, 24*(1), 77–80.

Whitbourne, S. K. (2005). *Adult development and aging: Biopsychosocial perspectives* (2nd ed.). New York: Wiley.

Wood, J. V., Heimpel, S. A., & Michela, J. L. (2003). Savoring versus dampening: Self esteem differences in regulating positive affect. *Journal of Personality and Social Psychology, 85*(3), 566–580.

Wrosch, C., Schultz, R., & Heckhausen, J. (2002). Health stresses and depressive symptomology in the elderly: The importance of health control engagement strategies. *Health Psychology, 21*(4), 310–348.

Zautra, A. (2003). *Emotions, stress and health.* Oxford, UK: Oxford University Press.

Chapter 2

Psychotherapeutic Interventions for Older Persons With Dementing Disorders

Michael Duffy

INTRODUCTION

Recently, as I was entering a local nursing home, I met a lady who was serving as an in-home caregiver for a previous older client of mine. I asked after my previous client and she indicated that the client was doing well and made a point of saying that "I just keep on talking to her and she seems to appreciate that." I recognized the simple power of what she was saying and encouraged her, saying that she was doing exactly the right thing for her older demented client.

In thinking about this chapter, this example came to mind. I asked myself: "If I were allowed to give only one prescription for a therapeutic intervention with older persons with dementia, what would it be?" I believe the answer I would give is exactly what the caregiver gave to me: "Just keep on talking to her." I believe that this simple naturalistic prescription is perhaps the most critical ingredient in working with older adults who suffer from a dementing disorder. The process of talking, conversing, sharing feelings, and imparting information, even asking questions that may not receive clear answers, is surely a powerful method of maintaining a healthy and therapeutic psychological connection with the older patient, despite the many and increasing cognitive impairments that accompany dementia. This advice is in many ways counterintuitive; our natural reaction to someone who is no longer capable of logical discourse is to reduce conversation as a means of relating and, frequently, to withdraw from the older person. This reaction is completely understandable and represents an intuitive-level assumption that there is little point in continuing conversation when the capacity for clear comprehension is no longer present. In fact, this reaction, however intuitively reasonable, is perhaps the single most lethal threat to the well-being of older persons with dementia and is alarmingly common both among family members and professional caregivers. In the nursing home it is relatively rare to find a caregiver, even the most well-intentioned, spending time conversing with an older adult who is afflicted with dementia. However counterintuitive it may seem, continuing conversation is the most important single prescription for psychological and even cognitive well-being of the older person with dementia. Although there are many other effective specific interventions that we will discuss in this chapter, this simple prescription is, in my experience, the most fundamental.

The continuing conversation between an adult caregiver and an older person with dementia is highly reminiscent of the unquestionable power of the "nonsensical" conversations that exist in parent/new infant interactions. Much of this early conversation is prerational and is not characterized by logical sequencing of language, and yet it is the primary vehicle both for emotional intimacy and, as we now know, of intellectual stimulation and the actual physical growth of the neonatal brain. This example is not intended to show equivalence of development of older clients and neonatal children. Rather, it illustrates the power of natural human conversation with its many complex levels of impact, meaning, and purpose, in addition to the logical transmission of ideas. We also now know well that the outcome of psychological withdrawal from an older person with dementia is very frequently the onset of comorbid affective disorders (Olin et al., 2002).

This chapter reviews a series of approaches to providing psychotherapeutic interventions for older adults with dementia. We first review a range of interactive dynamics in psychotherapy with demented clients. We also examine the logistical structure of therapy sessions with older adults who have a diagnosis of dementia. This material is then applied to a discussion of training and utilizing psychotherapeutic "surrogates" to extend and enhance this psychotherapeutic influence. Finally, the chapter reviews a series of specific treatments for the management of symptoms that are comorbid with cognitive impairment, including behavior therapy, memory enhancement, and treatment of depression.

INTERACTIVE DYNAMICS OF DOING PSYCHOTHERAPY WITH DEMENTED CLIENTS

This section explores detailed interactions that can occur in working with older adults with dementia. These provide therapeutic opportunities for psychotherapeutic change, which may be missed when the focus is exclusively on specific interventions directed toward symptom management. I hope the reader will forgive me for conveying my experiences in this area as a series of prescriptions, which I believe have enhanced the intensity and effectiveness of my own work with older adults.

Push for Psychological Contact

As mentioned earlier, our intuitive reaction with a client who is both cognitively and emotionally out of touch or disordered is to lessen our urge to continue to communicate. This is the not-uncommon pattern among family members and even professional caregivers. Indeed a similar pattern of professional detachment can often be detected in adult psychiatric treatment in which the thought-disordered patient is often sidelined with very little communication with mental health staff. When interaction does occur it often expresses the implicit and demeaning assumption that no meaningful interaction or conversation is possible. This message can be detected in impoverished eye contact, in trivial topics of conversation, and in a covert but palpable lack of confidence on the part of the caregiver that the patient can be reached. This pattern of emotional and cognitive neglect is also very common in our nursing facilities, especially with residents with dementing disorders, but also including patients who have suffered strokes and have impaired cognitive or language function. The therapeutic prescription here is to vigorously reverse this natural pattern and strive with each client for meaningful psychological contact. How often have we, for example, in visiting a nursing home client, failed to make contact with a silent and withdrawn (apparently demented) roommate of our client? Colluding in the implicit "diagnosis" and subsequent neglect, our client will frequently signal the roommate's cognitive impairment by a meaningful raising of the eyebrows or silent circular movement of the finger at the temple (Duffy, 1988). Our tendency to leave well enough alone in such circumstances does not serve us well in psychotherapeutic work with older adults. In an astonishing number of cases the roommate is not cognitively impaired at all, but of introverted temperament or depressed. Recently, while on therapy rounds with doctoral psychology trainees in a specialized dementia unit, we met a group of unit residents sitting around the day room table. We encountered the fascinating diversity that one finds among demented patients, ranging from what appeared to be the natural group leader with a bubbling and effervescent personality, to the resident at an advanced vegetative level of impairment. One of the apparent vegetative-level residents was an interesting case in point. She sat silently at the head of the table with a slumped posture, eyes tightly closed, with seeming inattention and lack of interest in the fairly vibrant conversation stimulated by our student therapists. When we focused on this silent client we were initially met with no reaction whatsoever. However, as we patiently stayed with the continuing invitation to talk with us, the client opened her eyes and began to converse with us. Our understanding of the group dynamics became reversed. The lady with the talkative and leadership-oriented personality was perhaps one of the most impaired residents and our "vegetative" resident turned out to have the clearest cognitive functioning in the group. Such experiences are amazingly common in working with older adults who have cognitive impairments. It would have been understandable and intuitively reasonable to have assumed that the noninteraction and nonparticipation of this silent resident represented the highest level of cognitive impairment when in fact, this was not so. I have found that pushing for psychological contact is the most rewarding experience for the therapist and is almost always a means of either maintaining or enhancing the current level of cognitive functioning.

Parenthetically, in conducting psychological assessment, appearances can also be misleading. How often do we discover that the interpersonally competent older adult with the vibrant personality manifests significant cognitive impairment in the course of a careful assessment? This provides a useful segue to the next section.

Explore Personality Dynamics

As was also illustrated in the above examples, the personality style of the older person with dementia becomes an important vehicle for understanding and for psychotherapeutic intervention. There is growing evidence of the continuity of personality in late life (Neugarten, Havighurst, & Tobin, 1968) and also in dementia, including the continuity of attachment style (Magai & Cohen, 1988) in later life. As was evident in the roundtable discussion of older persons with dementing disorders mentioned earlier, the personality and temperament of the participants had a critical influence on the caregiving and therapeutic process. Many therapists have recognized that the natural interpersonal skills of nursing home residents are critical in engaging caregiving staff and will frequently enhance the quality not only of interactions but also of caregiving tasks. In my own work I have intervened in problems of caregiver indifference and neglect, not only by training and consultation with staff, but also by working with and enhancing interpersonal skills in residents. Residents who reach out to nursing home staff very frequently can create a more positive interpersonal environment that is mutually satisfying to themselves and the caregiver. As a part of this empathy, training can help residents understand the unenviable role of the typical nurse's aide: underpaid, underappreciated, and frequently a worried parent and sole wage earner. This empathic capacity in the resident illustrates the power of personality in the caregiving process and is also true in the case of those residents who suffer from a dementia.

Coming to understand the older person's personality style, or personality disorder, is a critical ingredient in guiding therapeutic strategy. For example, a temperamental variable that influences therapeutic effectiveness is the natural disposition of a person to prefer and find intimacy and closeness with either the same or opposite gender. In assigning clients to my doctoral students, I take this into account, assigning a therapist in a gender-sensitive manner. This will usually mean that the psychotherapeutic relationship will be more intimate and intensive and will avoid the risk of a somewhat shallow and polite relationship. Note that this is not an issue of sexual orientation or age but of natural personality disposition. In another example, recognizing an older client's lifelong pattern of manipulative behavior will help the caregiver understand the therapeutic interactions more precisely and enhance the success of interventions. In the case of a resident with a long history of emotional deprivation and even victimization, understanding the client's attachment style and related psychological injuries is helpful in formulating therapeutic strategy, especially the most effective psychological "posture" with the client. In this case the therapeutic relationship itself becomes the primary vehicle for change. Carol Magai (Magai & Cohen, 1988), in her study of attachment style in persons with dementia, found a remarkable continuity of early attachment style throughout the life-cycle and continuing even within the period of cognitive impairment. Another example is identifying a pervasive passive/dependent personality style that becomes an impediment to caregiving. Caregivers initially feel drawn into an overly helping relationship, but eventually begin to resent the lack of independence in an older person, even when that person is cognitively impaired. In all these cases, understanding the prevailing and pervasive personality structure and style, whether at the level of a trait or a disorder, is imperative in formulating therapeutic strategy and also guiding the interpersonal process of therapy. This is also true when the therapist is using specific techniques designed to alleviate symptoms such as anxiety, depression, or behavior problems. Understanding the prevailing personality dynamics of the patient will help enhance the success of the technique and avoid undercutting by the patient.

Discriminate Among Cognitive Deficits

Most practitioners recognize that the cognitive symptoms of dementia can be the result of many unrelated disorders, ranging from delusional reactions to major surgery to constipation. Although we know that Alzheimer's disease and vascular dementia represent the largest portion of dementing disorders in older adults, we also recognize now that the variety of cognitive deficits in dementia may have many different meanings. Memory problems, for example, clearly have implications that do not necessarily signal the beginning of a degenerative process. We recognize that memory problems can be caused by affective disorders such as anxiety or depression, and by attentional deficits, and can also be short term and situational. Likewise, cognitive orientation to person, place, and time can have variable meanings, especially in long-term care facilities. It cannot be assumed that orientation difficulties are an unambiguous sign of a dementing process. In a clearly institutional phenomenon, many older persons find it difficult to distinguish the passage of time, the complexity of a confusing multi-corridor nursing home, personal address and phone number (often they do not have a phone), and current political events. Similarly, aphasia and communication problems are frequently reversible and do not give a clear indication of internal cognitive difficulties. This is especially pertinent in the case of post-stroke expressive aphasia. I can recall situations where family members of the stroke victim essentially abandoned their spouse or relative, physically and emotionally, when the patient was unable to converse after a stroke. There can be a natural but erroneous assumption that expressive aphasia implies the loss of logical intellectual process. It is as if the stroke victim is living in a glass coffin where family members and staff persons are physically present but completely cut off and isolated (Duffy, 1999). In fact, most stroke victims are completely capable of logical and coherent thought and are devastated by the abandonment. There are some cognitive processing effects of stroke—for example, memory problems—and this is an area that needs further clinical study and research (McDowd, Filion, Pohl, Richards, & Stiers, 2003).

In the converse situation, it is important to recognize those likely signs of severe a dementing process. Primary among these clues, in my experience, is the loss of logical language that occurs in mid-stage dementia, including Alzheimer's disease. This is the phase of logical non sequiturs, of "nonsense talk," which is often a sign of an advanced stage of dementia. This should be distinguished, however, from delusions and visual and auditory hallucinations that may be a function of Alzheimer's or multi-infarct dementia, but are also frequently the result of transitory cognitive impairments such as brief postoperative psychosis or delirium. Such is the randomness of pathophysiology of dementia that even in middle or advanced stages of the disorder there are frequently windows of cognitive clarity. These moments of clear consciousness appear as a break in the clouds, and are quite striking. A personal example occurred when I was conducting a psychological assessment with a woman with middle–stage Alzheimer's disorder, whom I had met briefly only once, two weeks before. I was amazed to find that in the middle of a completely incoherent and confused language exchange she suddenly called me by my correct name, presumably pulled out of a remaining memory trace. In another recent example, while doing rounds with doctoral students in a local assisted living facility, we also encountered a surprising window of consciousness in a woman who had already (and accurately) been diagnosed with Alzheimer's disease. She had consistently reported that her deceased husband was simply "out of town working and was expected back in a short time," but on this occasion (only) she suddenly recalled that he had in fact passed away. This case was also notable in that she had also blocked memory of the recent death of her 55-year-old son caused by a heart attack. These types of experiences also point to the influence of psychological and emotional processes that remain involved in cognitive impairments. It seemed striking that she had "forgotten" not only the death of her husband but also the premature death of a son—losses that are frequently the precipitant of a complicated bereavement. It is important to entertain the possibility that her cognitive behavior also represented the presence of a grieving process that still needed resolution. Again, this is a helpful segue into our next consideration.

Search for Feelings and Affective Themes

It is now well understood by researchers and clinicians that the presence of cognitive impairments, even in the dementing disorders, does not eliminate an active affective life in the older person (Duffy, 1999; Feil, 1999). Therapists increasingly recognize the presence of intact feelings in the internal world of the cognitively impaired older person. Those who have engaged older adults in psychological assessment will recognize the sense of embarrassment that mid-stage Alzheimer's patients often experience as they struggle with cognitive tasks and clearly demonstrate self-awareness of the impairment.

Obviously, embarrassment *is* affect and is only one example of the range and depth of the feelings that still exist even into quite late-stage impairment in older adults with dementia. The therapist's task is to listen carefully for affective themes or clues within the often confused logic of the conversation, within the delusions or even hallucinations. In a recent situation involving a brief reactive psychosis, probably due to a medical condition, we were struck by the meaningful affective qualities of "Bob," who figured in high relief in the delusional system. Bob had known our older female client in her pre-delusional stage, so it seemed reasonable for her to associate him with the comforting authoritative figure of John, who was her recently deceased spouse. It was then possible, even in her delusional state, for us to listen for important affective themes that, oddly enough, were not as vividly available in the pre-psychotic state. These affective themes clearly are not simple and sole evidence, but can be factored into the understanding of the dynamics and needs of the older person and guide the content of therapeutic discourse. In an earlier example, the episodic recall of the death of a husband and an adult son was clearly, in the midst of severe cognitive impairment, a window into understanding the existence of profound and unfinished relationships, and an indication of the patient's position in the grief trajectory. And although this patient was not considered to have agnosia (non-recognition of self or other familiar persons), she did fail to recognize her son in a family portrait, while clearly recognizing herself and her spouse and daughter. These phenomena lend an intriguing possibility to understanding affective and emotional characteristics of advanced dementia. We are indebted to the pioneering work of social worker Naomi Feil in her description of Validation Therapy (1999). Although the precise procedures of validation therapy are complex and have limited support in conventional research methods, many practicing clinicians recognize the pertinence of Feil's ideas and approach to working with patients suffering from dementia. Feil's Validation Therapy films clearly illustrate the gains to be made in demented patients by tuning in to the affective domain and by affirming rather than disputing the meaningfulness of the inner world of the older person.

Work With Emotional Memories

Related to the above considerations are the considerable therapeutic gains that can be made when we attend to the emotional memory traces in our older clients. One of the most devastating effects of agnosia is for the adult child who suddenly realizes that the parent no longer remembers the child's name or position in the family. However, some consolation can be offered. In fact, in such cases, although there is a failure to *identify* the person involved, there is usually clear evidence of *emotional recognition.* In other words, though the cognitive *identification* of name and relationship is lost, there is a clear *recognition* of the affective significance of the family member. There can be a parallel experience for therapists who feel ineffective when they realize that their clients do not remember them or their sessions from week to week. In our intuitive manner we may assume that such therapeutic contacts are without value and we may be tempted to discontinue therapy. However, there is a counterintuitive reality often operating; the therapeutic presence and work of a trusted therapist do not diminish with the failure to identify the therapist or recall the events of the sessions. The truth of this assertion can often be noticed in the natural behavior of older clients with dementia. Even though the older person cannot identify the family member or therapist, there is clearly an affective recognition of the person's presence, which is, we hope, comforting and soothing. Contrariwise, this emotional memory trace will also reveal the reaction of the demented person to a visitor who is experienced as antagonistic, impatient, or critical. In these cases we will notice an upsurge in agitation and anxiety or outright anger. The presence of emotional memory, now often identified as a midbrain function (van der Kolk & McFarlane, 1996), is also an asset in the therapeutic agenda. These emotional clues very frequently help set the therapeutic agenda. This was the case in the earlier example, in which emotional clues suggested the presence of unfinished grieving, especially for the premature death of the adult son.

STRUCTURE AND LOGISTICS OF PSYCHOTHERAPEUTIC INTERACTIONS

Flexible Time

Even for experienced therapists, learning to continue conversation with persons with middle or advanced-age dementia is a learned skill.

Learning to continue conversation, often in a "nonsensical manner," goes against the intuitive grain for most of us. Speaking with a middle-stage demented patient is somewhat reminiscent of a dreamlike state with regard to the dissociative and dreamlike cognitive sequence and content. Learning to tolerate and even welcome such apparently disjointed conversations requires a tolerance that is not easy to acquire. Therefore it is important to be patient with ourselves as we learn this counterintuitive approach. Even when we have chosen to engage in such challenging therapeutic conversation, and although it may be helpful to occasionally push these limits and extend our capacity for such conversations, it is important not to overextend and try to go beyond our comfort zone. When we are beginning to have relatively short interactions of this type with older persons with dementia we will often be surprised by the cognitive and affective impact of our early attempts. Our conversations are always a source of pleasure to our clients, and even though our presence and conversation may not be clearly recalled, we often have a sense of renewed welcome in subsequent visits. It is quite common to notice a significant improvement in mood over successive visits. We may be somewhat skeptical of such rapid change in our older charge. However, if we recognize that our session may be the *only occasion* in the week where there is any kind of *intensive interpersonal contact* with the client, such mood change may be more understandable.

Use Therapeutic Monologue

Because we cannot expect to have a logical discursive and reciprocal conversation with our older clients with dementia, it can be helpful to be willing to engage in a monologue with a client. *Therapeutic monologue* is a technique used in a series of dyadic interactions where the client is unwilling or unable to engage in reciprocal conversation. In therapeutic monologue the therapist performs *both* sides of the conversation, using nonverbal and subverbal clues as well as collateral information about the client. This can occur, for example, in working with a five-year-old child whose parents are recently deceased or are going through a divorce, and where the child has only limited capacity to understand or converse. It can also be used in cases of acting-out adolescents who typically will be ostentatiously silent during the clinical interview or psychotherapy. Therapeutic monologue is particularly pertinent in working with stroke patients who have expressive aphasia; they are almost always cognitively intact but unable to engage in reciprocal conversation. And, finally, therapeutic monologue can help considerably in working with older adults with dementing disorders. Again, in therapeutic monologue, the therapist basically plays both sides of the conversation. Although there is no verbal exchange, there are many nonverbal and subverbal signals that the therapist monitors in the client and that essentially constitute the other side of the conversation. The therapist attempts to tune in and "speak to" the salient psychological and affective issues of the client even though they cannot be directly or clearly expressed. When the therapist is willing to engage in therapeutic monologue with a stroke or dementia patient it helps considerably to seek collateral information prior to and during the course of therapy. To understand from family or relatives the premorbid personality style and difficulties that the person has encountered will help the therapist to be on-target. Also helpful are the details and experiences of a person's life, and the nature and quality of contacts with parents and adult children, which bear on the therapeutic conversation in important ways.

Engaging in therapeutic monologue is a learned skill requiring patience with self, willingness to tolerate uncomfortable silences, ambiguity in identifying salient emotional issues, and so forth. However, in many cases it is the only manner in which our conversation can be pursued.

Use a Slow and Relaxed Pace

Younger therapists frequently operate at a much more frenetic pace than their older clients. As we approach an interaction with an older person, and especially an older person with dementia, it helps to deliberately slow down, both physically and psychologically. Most of us have iconic images that represent newly learned experiences. In my case, it was the experience of taking my 87-year-old mother to a shopping mall many years ago. Fitting this expedition into my busy activities of academic and clinical life meant that my internal and external pace was considerably faster than that of my aging parent. I recall the initial impatience I felt with her cumbersome pace as we set off on our visit to the mall. After a few minutes of my encouraging her to move just a little faster, I became aware of a pertinent question: Whose pace is better? At that moment (surely an example of "one-shot learning"), I recognized the unreasonableness of the assumption that she should speed up to my pace. This iconic memory has had an influence on my practice with older adults. Today, as I approach the entrance of a nursing home, it signals me to slow down my own internal and external pace in a way that comports with the life and pace of the nursing home and its residents. This personal and professional experience has become an important part of the orientation I provide to graduate students learning to work with older adults. I suggest that we systematically use informal relaxation techniques, such as breathing and slowed walking, as we approach the therapy with an older person. This is especially helpful in working with a person with a dementing process. This approach helps enter a reflective and contemplative mindset that allows us to join the internal world of our clients in a manner that considerably enhances therapeutic process.

Use Flexible Session Structure

Working in nursing homes, and especially with demented elderly, does not comport well with the typical structure of outpatient psychotherapy with its quiet 10' × 10' room furnished with chairs, table, and lamp, with a receptionist and a 50-minute hour. To work in nursing homes is often to survive a booming buzzing confusion, where there is little privacy, private space, or opportunity to work with fixed time limits. All too often our sessions are interrupted and joined by interested other older persons who have little sense of therapeutic propriety and, for example, will delightedly join in and provide answers to our designated client's psychological assessment questions! Or the "intruder" will be happy to engage in a therapy session along with our client! Another feature of working in nursing homes is the occasional presence of family members who can be either intrusive or constructive in the therapeutic session. In all these contexts, it is helpful to adopt a flexible approach that rolls with the many interruptions and intrusions. More positively, these interruptions can be understood and used as valuable collateral information about the interpersonal functioning of our older clients, their connections with other important relationships, and the family dynamics that affect the therapeutic process. Rather than reactively attempting to exclude such interruptions, it is much more helpful, at least initially, to engage these other persons in the process. There will be times, of course, when a completely private session is required, either by the confidentiality of the topic or the need for unambiguous test results. However, this usually can be better achieved by first welcoming the inevitable interruptions and then moving on to a request for privacy.

Another aspect of flexible structure is the location for conducting therapy or assessment. All too often in Medicaid-reimbursed nursing homes, our clients have roommates who cannot be moved or are bedridden. In these circumstances it is sometimes impossible to go elsewhere as our client also may be bedridden, and we have to choose either to not provide the service or to use whatever aids for privacy that are available, including tone of voice and environmental aids such as curtains. When our clients are movable we may be able to take them outside to an open area or to an unused room. There are occasions, however, especially with our demented patients, when even this is not possible. Recently I was asked to do an initial interview/psychological assessment of a demented patient in a local rural nursing home. I found this patient wandering and pacing up and down the nursing home corridors. When I gently asked her to accompany me to an office that was at my disposal, she was clearly agitated and unwilling to comply. She seemed to feel threatened, and this is the type of situation when a demented older patient is likely to be aggressive. At this point, typically, we have a choice: we can either not perform the professional service, or we can make the best of an imperfect situation in order to provide the service. In this case, I was able to guide the patient (using an inviting rather than a constraining gesture) to a reasonably quiet corner of the day room, where she was willing to engage in an interaction with me. Such experiences are typical in working with older adults who have dementing disorders.

TRAINING AND USING PSYCHOTHERAPEUTIC SURROGATES

As mentioned earlier in this chapter, one or two weekly therapeutic interactions with a professional therapist can have powerful effects on both mood and cognitive status. Precisely because of this, it can be effective to *involve others* in providing equivalent experiences for the older person, thus increasing the intensity and frequency of such experiences throughout the week. Recently, having worked intensively with a stroke patient who was experiencing a typical post-stroke depression as well as memory impairment, I saw the effects of enhanced mood and gradual improvement in orientation and attention and thought it was likely that more of the same would be helpful. I was able to work with the activity director to provide a volunteer who would continue this work during the week. Also, I had discovered that this particular patient seemed to thrive when taken outside the nursing home in order to enjoy our sessions in the Texas sunshine. The volunteer was able to repeat the therapeutic experience in this manner throughout the week.

Involve Family Members

Family members are typically at a loss as to how to interact with their relatives who are beset with dementing disorders or stroke. It can be helpful to orient family members to the nature of the cognitive impairment, explain predictable limitations and teach available opportunities along the lines discussed earlier. Family members simply do not know how to talk to their older relative and can be included, often serendipitously, in therapy sessions where therapeutic monologue can be modeled for them. In this manner they can be helped to avoid intrusive behavior and to avoid reacting negatively to dependent and symbiotic behavior that is sometimes the result of cognitive impairment.

Family members sometimes react to dementia in a hyperattentive and symbiotic fashion. The therapist can help them avoid this behavior as well as help nursing home staff appreciate how this reactive behavior makes sense in terms of threatened relationship loss. Thus, involvement of family members as psychotherapy surrogates can have a double effect by helping them interact more helpfully and therapeutically with the older parent and simultaneously helping them cope with their inevitable painful struggle at the apparent "loss" of their parent.

Formal and Informal Consultation With Professional Caregivers

Our work with older clients provides opportunities to help professional, but not psychologically trained, caregiving staff to understand the dimensions of dementia in older residents. In "messages" in our clinical case notes, in informal corridor consultations, and in formal training sessions we have the opportunity to induct staff into sensitive interactive behavior. The point is not to turn nurses into formal counselors or psychotherapists, but to help them appreciate how powerful it can be if they turn their routine tasks of medical caregiving into opportunities to interact therapeutically in a life-giving way with their residents. Parenthetically, it has been demonstrated that this more intensive involvement with residents is not only beneficial to their clients, but also tends to offset the potential burnout that can easily occur in caregivers, especially in long-term care. When we engage intensively in a therapeutic relationship there is a paradoxical effect. Whereas it may seem that more intensive relationships with residents place greater emotional stress on the caregiver, in fact the opposite is the case. Burnout actually exists in situations where there is a high incidence of contact with minimal intimacy. This makes sense; in a more emotionally meaningful and intimate relationship, the caregiver receives as well as gives in a much more reciprocal manner.

Training Volunteers and Paraprofessionals

Another avenue for extending our psychotherapeutic reach is to involve and train volunteers or paraprofessionals. In a demonstration project, my colleagues and I developed a training program for volunteers to enable them to provide paraprofessional psychotherapy to older adults in nursing homes. Project Oasis (Crose, Duffy, Warren, & Franklin, 1987) trained volunteers to a paraprofessional level of skill in a series of typical clinical scenarios with older adults, including working with depression, cognitive confusion, and difficult clients. This type of volunteer work is relatively demanding and should involve only those persons who have the relevant natural skill and interpersonal temperament that will sustain them through training and service. Training emphasizes practice and clinical supervision, and is capable of bringing a volunteer to a surprisingly high level of therapeutic sophistication.

Using Program-Level Interventions

Recently developed, special-purpose dementia care units (Davis, Sloane, Mitchell, et al., 2000) have incorporated many important intervention approaches for older adults suffering from dementing disorders. With the increased survival rates for older persons, combined with the high prevalence of dementia progressively increasing in the 85+ age range, it has become imperative for nursing homes and assisted living facilities to develop a programmatic approach to working with older residents with dementing disorders. This is partly a positive strategic change on the part of nursing homes and partly a matter of survival.

Practitioners familiar with nursing home work will be well aware of the often intrusive and disruptive effect of dementia and demented older adults on the daily life of nursing homes. This pressure has led to the development of innovative and effective strategies in working with older residents. The literature on special–purpose dementia care units is extensive and will not be cited or discussed here. Many of the prescriptions in the earlier part of this chapter have become at least informally enshrined in caregiving practices in dementia care–settings. For example, it is understood that in general, high activity levels and high social participation levels help reduce agitation in older adults with dementia, especially as a result of sustained and systematic attempts to maintain as many family connections as possible. There is also some evidence (Davis et al., 2000) that "homeliness" and small program size have been associated with less disorientation, anxiety, and agitation in residents. Small homes/units may be an especially therapeutic care model for dementia. Because of this concern for environmental design there has been an increased involvement of architectural designers in the field of dementia care. The environmental design of homes for older persons has been studied by psychologists and architects alike. Lawton (1999) has proposed the concept of "person–environment fit" as a model for psychological and architectural design of optimal facilities. Duffy, Bailey, Beck, and Barker (1986) have investigated a multidimensional perspective on preferences in facility design. Residents, administrators, and architects were surveyed as to their preferences for social aspects of the nursing home design. It was interesting that both nursing home administrators and architects chose institutional designs that were "sociopetal" in nature—that is, designs that encourage social interaction. Residents, on the other hand, chose "sociofugal" designs—designs that promote greater privacy. This was not surprising, in retrospect, because in many institutional settings privacy is in short supply. In fact, designs of facilities with associated programs need to provide both for social interaction and for privacy.

DEMENTIA SYMPTOM
MANAGEMENT INTERVENTIONS

We turn now to a summary of a rich array of specific techniques designed to help with various symptoms encountered in dementia. These methods are not intended to replace, but rather to add to the interactive techniques mentioned earlier—techniques that undergird and enhance the effectiveness of the specific interventions to follow. In the hands of a competent and sensitive clinician, both domains are always present, at least implicitly. Interpersonal/interactive approaches will need to use specific techniques for the aggressive treatment of symptoms, especially distressing ones such as depression and anxiety. Specific symptom management techniques will be more powerful if accompanied by relational and interactive sensitivity and sophistication. Thus, manualized treatments in the hands of experienced therapists will likely outperform the use of these same methods by novice or inflexible therapists.

It is generally acknowledged that the cognitive techniques available and effective with younger and non-cognitively impaired elderly are frequently less effective with older adults with dementing disorders (Teri et al., 2003). The greater the impairment, the less we are able to tap and utilize cognitive capacity. It is not surprising that as a patient loses higher cortical and intellectual functioning through degenerative or vascular impairment, cognitively based interventions are increasingly limited. Thus, interventions such as cognitive restructuring and reminiscence, which rely on reasoning with or "disputing" negative thoughts, will decline in effectiveness. In fact, as neurological control in the older person becomes more "primitive," more traditional behaviorist principles, based on classical and operant conditioning, become highly relevant. Also, in current theory and practice, cognitive and behavioral approaches have been almost uniformly linked under the rubric of "cognitive-behavioral." They quickly become unlinked in working with demented older persons. In the profoundly limiting later stages of dementia, where vegetative functions predominate and are themselves eventually depleted, it is the behavior intervention techniques that appear to be most appropriate (Hussian & Lawrence, 1987). Even with less impaired and younger groups it has been suggested that behavioral techniques are of equal efficacy to cognitive methods (Jacobson & Dobson, 1996; Lewinsohn, Antonuccio, & Steinmetz, 1984). The Gatz (Gatz et al., 1998) review of empirically validated treatments for older adults gives special consideration to treatments of elderly with dementia in which the efficacious techniques are predominantly behavioral.

We now review briefly the available techniques for a series of problems associated with dementia. These include memory problems and associated memory training programs, behavior management of difficult comorbid behaviors, and treatment approaches for depression in dementia.

Memory Training

Cameron Camp (1998) has pointed out that memory interventions with demonstrated positive effects on older adults often have little effect on persons with dementia. Thus, enhancing memory function in older adults with dementing process is challenging and difficult. Camp takes a cognitive rehabilitation perspective in which the older adult works with a cognitive psychologist to optimize the level of functioning by alleviating cognitive deficits. The cognitive rehabilitation approach focuses less on simply measuring impairment in such structures as frontal lobe lesions and more on ways that impairments manifest themselves in everyday problems, such as difficulty completing a task; forgetting names; or problems with work, living, or recreation. These are the associated social and environmental effects of memory loss, and the attempt is to create practical rehabilitation-oriented interventions for memory problems associated with dementia. These practical applications might include maintaining a routine schedule for daily activities, keeping frequently used items in the same place, writing down notes using a calendar, using printed labels with objects, using name cards, giving retrieval props, using a large clock face, using a large wristwatch, using a bulletin board to list the day's activities and menus, and so forth. This approach is clearly proactive and it appears to fit very well with the interactive, interpersonal principles discussed early in this chapter. Using more technical interventions, Camp suggests the use of spaced retrieval, which involves giving a person practice at recalling information over successively longer time intervals. Using these everyday principles in memory enhancement, Camp also developed a memory game called memory bingo. Clients are presented with a set of cards with typed words belonging to a particular category. The bingo caller holds up a card and has a client read it out loud and then check to see if he or she has such a card. If the card is there, the client has won a round of bingo. These naturalistic methods of memory enhancement are clearly very compatible with everyday life and the often unstimulating world of long-term care.

The traditional technique of reminiscence may also provide a useful platform for memory enhancement. Kasl-Godley and Gatz (2000) reviewed evidence for reminiscence and life review for older adults and found that several investigations have offered evidence on the effectiveness of this approach. The nature of reminiscence and description of programs are well documented elsewhere (Molinari, 1999). These authors also suggest a series of other methods, including support groups, reality orientation, memory training, and behavior approaches.

Behavior Management

In many cases, dementia is accompanied by changes in behavior that include agitation, acting out, and aggression. Although such behavior is not present in all cases of dementia, it is extremely taxing on caregivers and on nursing home resources. As mentioned earlier, behavioral and even strictly behaviorist approaches to management of difficult behaviors have been found to be more pertinent than rational approaches. This field is greatly indebted to Richard Hussian, who unfortunately died prematurely, for his early and insightful work on adapting behaviorist strategies to manage difficult behavior of demented patients. In a seminal article, Hussian and Lawrence (1987) described the use of a classical conditioning approach of stimulus manipulation in helping to shape the difficult behavior of the demented elderly. He describes in detail plans for stimulus manipulation to allow control over such things as wandering, entering another's room, inappropriate urination, and aggressive behavior. These and other similar approaches have become invaluable in helping nursing home staff and family members care for older adults with dementia, especially those in advanced stages.

Depression in Dementia

We know that traditional methods of treating depression, such as cognitive, interpersonal, or brief dynamics are of limited utility in working with older adults who experience depression within a dementing syndrome. There are very few controlled studies showing the efficacy of the non-cognitive interventions that have been primarily used. We are indebted to the work of Linda Teri and colleagues for more than a decade of clinical research into this area. She has conducted a series of studies that use creative behavioral and family therapy techniques to minimize depression in older persons with dementia. In their 2003 (Teri, Gibbons, McCurry, et al., 2003) study, Teri examined the efficacy of exercise plus behavior management on depression in demented older adults. Parenthetically, it appears that this use of exercise in treating depression is a promising new treatment for depression in all age groups.

In other studies, researchers have used such techniques as training caregivers in problem-solving strategies, emphasizing communication skills training, structured programs aimed at increasing social engagement, and programs designed to modify sensory and environmental stimulation. In this latter technique, it is assumed that depression in the older demented client can be minimized by reducing sensory overload.

CONCLUSION

Using psychotherapeutic techniques with older adults with dementia is challenging and difficult, but rewarding. It is rewarded by a recognition of potential in the older person that could otherwise be unknown, ignored, and lost. The surprising latent resources that can still exist despite the dementing process are striking and gratifying to the therapist. Such work requires a flexibility and willingness to shift customary paradigms in order to be responsive to the very different conditions that face the therapist working with dementia. These attitudes also translate well into utilizing the growing number of specific treatment techniques designed to work with comorbid behavioral problems in older adults with dementia. This is truly an area of incredible growth, matched only by the incredible need of these older persons.

REFERENCES

Camp, C. J. (1998). Memory interventions for normal and pathological older adults. *Annual Review of Gerontology, 18*, 155–189.

Crose, R., Duffy, M., Warren, J. L., & Franklin, B. (1987). Project OASIS: Volunteer mental health paraprofessionals serving nursing home residents. *Gerontologist, 27*, 359–362.

Davis, K. J., Sloane, P. D., Mitchell, C. M., Preisser, J., Grant, L., Hawes, M. C., Lindeman, D., Montgomery, R., Long, K., Philips, C., & Koch, G. (2000). Specialized dementia care programs in residential care settings. *Gerontologist, 40*(1), 32–42.

Duffy, M. (1988). Avoiding clinical detachment in working with the elderly in nursing homes. *Clinical Gerontologist, 7*(3/4), 58–60.

Duffy, M. (1999). Reaching the person behind the dementia. In M. Duffy (Ed.). *Handbook of counseling and psychotherapy with older adults* (pp. 577–589). New York: Wiley.

Duffy, M., Bailey, S., Beck, B., & Barker, D. G. (1986). Preferences in nursing home design: A comparison of residents, administrators and designers. *Environment and Behavior, 18*(2), 246–257.

Feil, N. (1999). Current concepts and techniques in validation therapy. In M. Duffy (Ed.). *Handbook of counseling and psychotherapy in older adults* (pp. 590–615). New York: Wiley.

Gatz, M., Fiske, A., Fox, L. S., Kaskie, B., Kasl-Godley, J. E., McCallum, T. J., & Wetherell, J. L. (1998). Empirically validated psychological treatments for older adults. *Journal of Mental Health and Aging, 4*(1), 9–46.

Hussian, R. A., & Lawrence, P. S. (1987). Use of two-dimensional grid patterns to limit hazardous ambulation in demented patients. *Journal of Gerontology, 42*, 558–560.

Jacobson, N. S., & Dobson, K. S. (1996). A component analysis of cognitive-behavioral treatment for depression. *Journal of Consulting and Clinical Psychology, 64*(2), 295–304.

Kasl-Godley, J., & Gatz, M. (2000). Psychosocial interventions for individuals with dementia: An integration of theory, therapy and a clinical understanding of dementia. *Clinical Psychology Review, 20*(6), 755–782.

Lawton, M. P. (1999). Environmental design features and the well-being of older persons. In M. Duffy (Ed.). *Handbook of counseling and psychotherapy in older adults* (pp. 350–363). New York: Wiley.

Lewinsohn, P., Antonuccio, D., & Steinmetz, J. (1984). *The coping with depression course.* Eugene, OR: Castalia.

Magai, R., & Cohen, C. I. (1988). Attachment style and emotional regulation in dementia. *Journals of Gerontology: Psychological Sciences, 5*(3), 147–154.

McDowd, J. M., Filion, D. L., Pohl, P. S., Richards, L. G., & Stiers, W. (2003). Attentional abilities and functional outcomes following stroke. *Journals of Gerontology: Psychological Sciences, 58B*(1), 45–53.

Molinari, V. (1999). Using reminiscence and life review as natural therapeutic strategies in group therapy. In M. Duffy (Ed.). *Handbook of counseling and psychotherapy in older adults*, (pp. 154–165). New York: Wiley.

Neugarten, B., Havighurst, R., & Tobin, S. (1968). *Personality patterns of aging: In middle age and aging.* New York: McGraw-Hill.

Olin, J. T., Schneider, L. S., Katz, B. S., Meyers, B. S., Alexopoulos, G. S., Breitner, J. C., Bruce, M. L., Caine, R. D., Cummings, J. L., Devenand, D. P., Jeste, D. V., Krishnan, K. R. R., Lyketsos, C. G., Lyness, J. M., Rabins, P. G., Reynolds, C. F. III, Rovner, B. W., Steffans, D. C., Unützer, J., & Liebowitz, B. D. (2002). Provisional diagnostic criteria for depression of Alzheimer's disease: Rationale and background. *American Journal of Geriatric Psychiatry, 10*, 129–141.

Teri, L., Gibbons, L. E., McCurry, S. M., Logsdon, R. G., Boehner, D., Barlow, W., Kukoll, W., LaCroix, A., McCormick, W., & Larson, E. (2003). Exercise plus behavioral management in patients with Alzheimer's disease. *Journal of the American Medical Association, 290*(15), 2015–2022.

Teri, L., Logsdon, R. G., Uomoto, J., & McCurry, S. M. (1997). Behavioral treatment in dementia patients: A controlled clinical trial. *Journal of Gerontology: Psychological Sciences, 52B*(4), 159–166.

van der Kolk, A. C., & McFarlane, A. C. (1996). The black hole of trauma. In B. A. van der Kolk, A. C. McFarlane, & L. Weisaeth (Eds.). *Traumatic stress: The effects of overwhelming experience on mind, body and society* (pp. 3–23). New York: Guilford.

Part II
Nursing Homes

Chapter 3

Working With Staff, Families, and Residents in an Institution: Review of the Literature

Claire M. Brody

It was said recently (Golant, 2004) that the nursing home "is the most institutionalized, long term care (LTC) setting in the United States with the highest prevalence of older persons who are chronically ill and who have difficulty functioning because of their cognitive and physical difficulties" (p. S68). However, more care is actually provided outside the nursing home in group residential care in assisted living facilities (ALF), a more residential-like and less institutionalized setting. The ALF can also provide personal care and supportive services and, sometimes, skilled nursing services to meet the needs of the frail elder person. Golant's was the first analysis that reported a national study of ALFs that assessed the extent to which assisted living facilities are occupied by older persons with cognitive and physical impairments and health care needs (see chapter 9).

In a study by Corder and Hernandez (2004) about consumer discourse in assisted living facilities, they stated that people living in ALFs are *consumers* rather than *recipients* of LTC services; that is, the residents *choose* to consume ALF services and the social model values are attributed to the setting. They make the choice in a marketplace of informed shoppers. They also take on the managed risks that the consumers choose. In considering the competing consumer priorities of services, they come to recognize that their loss of control results in a reduction of consumer choice and the range of options available. It is questioned in the study what, in fact, this cohort of seniors would demand if they were not "educated" to choose independence over other variables, so there are both benefits and pitfalls in practices based on "consumer discourse." There is also the pitfall to be considered that the residents may not be "educated" to the role expected of them, or they may be too cognitively impaired to negotiate the consumer role. It is also not always clear who the "client" is; the resident may not be the primary consumer. It is to be noted that the Assisted Living Federation of America and the Assisted Living Quality Coalition advocate practices such as resident assessment, negotiated services, and managed risk agreements, but the actual use of these in terms of prevalence is unknown.

Elaine M. Brody (2004) reminds us that with advancing age, the chances increase of being in a nursing home. According to the 2000 report of the U.S. Department of Health and Human Services, Administration on Aging, at age 85 or older, over 21 percent of older people reside in nursing homes. The effect on families and on the residents are interlocked no matter where they reside. The notion, Brody says, "that older people are dumped into nursing homes by uncaring families is the most virulent expression of the myth that children nowadays do not care for their elderly parents as was done 'in the good old days' " (p. 290). She adds that besides being a myth that families "dump" elderly parents in nursing homes, once such placement is made by these families, they are then relieved of the responsibility and stress they have endured. Adult children continue to be vitally interested in their parents and behave accordingly, and may experience a whole new set of strains. The fact is that the most rapid increase in the number of beds available in nursing homes is for the very old who will increase in numbers and who are the most vulnerable for disabling ailments, even though the percentage of individuals in nursing homes has remained essentially the same (U.S. Department of Health and Human Services, National Center for Health Statistics, 1999).

In this new model of the nursing home, a recent article (Williams, Kemper, & Hummert, 2003) talks about improving communication, generally, among residents. They talk about unintentionally communicating dependency through "elderspeak," defined as "patronizing talk" (p. 242). It reinforces dependency and induces isolation and depression in residents. By educating health care providers about "elderspeak" and its potential negative effects on older adults, staff use of this type of interaction can be reduced, thereby improving residents' cognitive functional levels and increasing satisfaction in the nursing home. Because institutional living is different from living alone or with one's family, investigating what these differences might mean to the elderly in a nursing home environment is a question more researchers need to address.

Tappen, Williams, Barry, and DiSesa (2001) also did a study using conversation intervention with Alzheimer patients in a nursing home. They found that the effectiveness of conversation might improve the relevance of communication in this particular group of patients. They found that the significance of this intervention was *not* increased by the stimulation of walking at the same time as they initiated the conversation, which was originally hypothesized.

Many residents have lost life partners and might, given stereotypical assumptions, be expected to have prolonged and untreatable depression. However, this is not always the case. A recent statement (D'Andrea & Cassidy, 2000) suggests that "although wide variability has been observed, depressive symptoms associated with bereavement usually remit within six months" (p. 15). In some instances, a major depression occurs, with persistent symptoms. And for caregivers, grieving can begin even before the loved one's death; with dementia it is related to the gradual loss of identity. It can resolve itself with the death of the patient, and the caregivers often express some relief.

One exception to the treatment of depression in nursing home residents was reported by one of the authors of this book (Vicki Semel). She describes two women in a nursing home who were successfully treated for depression using a modified psychoanalytic approach (Semel, 1986). In the women's groups that are described in chapter 4, a feminist therapy value system is echoed wherein women are considered competent adults who can develop self-definition and autonomy as they learn to care for and about themselves (C. M. Brody, 1987).

GROUPS IN NURSING HOMES

In nursing homes, a resident's concept of self as competent is continuously eroded by decreasing physical and mental skills and loss of meaningful relationships. With fewer significant others available, and less opportunity for talking to interested listeners, the aged person in an institution needs another chance to share memories and connect with others. A group program whose objective is to explore feelings is essential for emotional survival. In a chapter in a recent book, Ruckdeschel (2000) talks of group psychotherapy in the nursing home. She says that it can provide "the opportunity for the resident to be viewed as and responded to as a whole person, taking into account the full range of lifetime experiences that have made the person who he or she is" (p. 115).

One of the techniques that addresses this need is the use of reminiscing groups (see chapter 4). Ruckdeschel says that by reminiscencing, it allows the individual to make a connection with meaningful past experiences to identify strengths and successes and to rework unresolved conflicts. Very often, elderly who feel devalued have little desire to socialize with their own age group; in a reminiscing group they can once again identify as well as share problems. However, confused or memory-impaired residents are often the ones denied such group experiences that would challenge them cognitively and provide an opportunity for emotional catharsis. This is a population to whom reminiscing groups can be offered. There are many challenges in running such groups. Ruckdeschel says that the therapist must be respectful of the habits and needs of the residents and attempt to schedule the groups at a time that is least interruptive of the usual nursing home activities and routines.

Primary goals of groups in nursing homes are social integration, a decrease in isolation, and change in affect for the residents. Of great importance is the initial commitment of the administrative person in the institution to incorporating psychotherapeutic goals into the overall program scheme. Of equal importance is the commitment to make the changes in the system that are required to start an individual or group therapy service for the residents, and possibly their families (Abramson & Mendis, 1990).

Brown-Watson (1999) states that some people are admitted to nursing facilities unnecessarily or prematurely. They can be helped to maintain their well-being and independence through participation in groups that provide them with both exercise and socialization opportunities (restorative groups). People with a variety of chronic conditions (stroke, hypertension, arthritis, sensory losses, cancers, among others) may respond and receive comfort in knowing they are not alone in their physical decline. The social support they receive in the group helps to protect them against further stress and illness.

"PATIENTS" OR "BOARDERS"

Mary Schmidt (1990), in her lively and revealing book about elderly people in residential settings, chooses to distinguish between those who live in skilled nursing homes and those who live in residences where they have a degree of autonomy: "patients" in the one case, and "boarders" in the other. She says, "Most elderly patients entering a home for the aged view this move as their last one. But whatever sense of loss they may feel, they are concerned also with the life they can make there" (p. 1). The two different statuses also affect elderly patients' success in negotiating a degree of control over their last years, and is evidence of their "defense of self." As Schmidt says, "the designation as patient in and of itself discounts the individual's capacity for decision-making" (pp. 2–3).

As "patients," behavioral prescriptions imply passivity; as "boarders," the same prescriptions imply prudent activity, according to Schmidt. She also reports that many nursing home administrators think that activity programs for elderly residents exist chiefly to salve the feelings of families and staff, as the very old themselves wish mainly to be left alone. The stereotype is that a climate of sufficient warmth and a standard of cleanliness and care are all that are required for residents' relatives. There are also many reasons why clients may not attend a group regularly, such as conflicting medical appointments, physical therapy sessions, or just a "bad day" resulting from exacerbated symptoms of a chronic illness. With the cooperation of the administration of the nursing home to offer a popular activity at a different time as the group meeting, clients can be encouraged to attend the reminiscence group as a distraction from somatic concerns. Entering a nursing home from the community or hospital implies to older persons that they are not expected to get better, and this sense of finality explains the reluctance of family and doctor to discuss placement with them. The official criteria for transfer to a nursing home—a failure of self-care and the need for supervision—are not always used.

A study (Rantz et al., 2004) evaluating nursing home quality of care was recently reported in relation to one state (Missouri). Similar data should also be examined in other parts of the country for comparison. In this state, the care was determined to range from "good" to "poor." The findings suggested that delivering good quality of care might not necessarily result in higher costs. This was consistent with findings from other research cited. The staff mix and staffing levels were virtually the same in good and poor nursing homes. It would appear that the additional costs were not related to significantly higher wages or hours of care, but it is possible that *turnover* is a significant problem in nursing homes. Lower costs in good-outcome homes may also be explained by their more effective care *processes* that were revealed by qualitative analysis. This was focused on basics of care, such as walking with residents, helping them to eat and drink, taking them to the bathroom regularly, bathing them, and managing pain. For example, toileting them when they request it may positively affect cost of incontinence supplies; helping a resident regain walking ability may reduce the demand for multiple staff to assist individual residents. The authors note that consistency by care staff is key to implementing systems of toileting, bathing, and helping residents to eat and drink. The size of the facility may also promote use of team processes to accomplish work. Nursing home owners may want to consider smaller "nursing homes" within the facility, decentralizing to these smaller areas. In this way, different work groups can be created.

WORKING WITH FAMILIES

Qualls (2000) discusses many aspects of working with families in LTC settings. She describes a complex set of "political, legal, economic, regulatory, professional, and cultural systems" that impinge. In addition, psychologists may be called upon to address problems that not only involve conflicts among these overlapping systems, but also to deal with interfamilial problems: "Psychologists need an intimate understanding of the inner workings of the particular facilities in which they work, but they also need to know the larger regulatory, legislative, and funding contexts in which care is provided" (p. 94). She says, the word "home" is itself an oxymoron, as the medical model it implies is anything but a home. For example, the staff is told to be "personal" but they wear latex gloves! Further, staff is told to be involved with family, but are offered little in the way of mechanisms to participate with them.

Although families are responsible for maintaining the resident's hope, dignity, and family connectedness, at the same time they often get the message that they are in the way. Families' expectations about nutrition, dress, and general care conditions are not always met. Family therapy sessions can be a significant variable in the early adjustment of a nursing home resident. It can be crucial to the success of a placement for a therapist to provide (verbal) support for the families in the decision. This can be done by utilizing a support group composed of other caregivers, or providing a family "confidante" for the caregiver. Coming to accept the particular institution as a good one is essential; comparing it to other homes, and weighing proximity versus acceptability, are very important as well.

In a study (Tornatore & Grant, 2004) examining satisfaction among family caregivers of nursing home residents with dementia, the researchers found that more advanced stages of dementia may undermine family satisfaction because most nursing homes have very little to offer in the way of specialized programs and activities for residents with Alzheimer's disease (see also chapter 6). The longer family members were caregivers before institutionalization, the more satisfied they were after placement. These results contradicted previous findings that caregiving over extended periods of time negatively impacted caregiver outcomes. "Family members who became caregivers shortly before placement or at placement may experience a higher degree of stress and therefore be less satisfied" (p. S84). One explanation for this is that caregivers with more experience better understand what it means to care for a person with Alzheimer's disease; they have more realistic expectations of the nursing home after placement. Another finding was that the more often caregivers visit, the more satisfied they are; they get to know the nursing staff better so they can communicate their preferences for care.

Coping capacities vary, but the residents depend on the responses of significant adults in their lives, the amount of energy they have available and, perhaps most important, the response of the nursing home staff to their needs. It is in this realm that a trained professional can have the most input, by being supportive and educational in his or her efforts, and by dealing with the whole social system. The environmental setting becomes an increasingly important determinant of behavior and well-being. If caregivers expected the care to be adequate after placement in the nursing home, they are more likely to be satisfied after placement. One reason is that family members who have high expectations are more likely to choose nursing homes that meet those expectations.

In a study (Kramer, 2000) of families where the husbands were debating whether to institutionalize their wives with dementia, the author found that gerontological social workers who work with these husbands have to help them sort out the potential benefits for the caregivers of institutionalization. If a husband does place his wife in a nursing home, he needs help with the transition, possibly for the depression related to the move. The author also suggests that with the anticipated increase in individuals requiring such placement in the near future, energy needs to be devoted to devising creative alternatives to nursing home placement, and recommends that work be done to replicate the findings of this study.

SURVIVAL ISSUES FOR CAREGIVERS AND CARE RECEIVERS

A recent study (Burton, Zdaniuk, Schulz, Jackson, & Hirsch, 2003) dealt with the transition from caregiving at home to an institution. The authors found that those who made the transition from heavy caregiving at home had many more symptoms of depression and poorer health. This implies that caregivers whose status changes within the caregiving role should be monitored for adverse health effects. Another study that dealt with caregiving (Amirchanyan & Wolf, 2003) found "strong support for the hypothesis that parental care need is associated with depressive symptoms among non-caregivers" (p. 825). Thus, having a caregiving relative can become a separate pathway of stress for non-caregivers. Schmidt (1990), mentioned earlier, discusses the significant power differential between nursing home resident and staff. For example, in a nursing home, even the family paying a staggering bill for the care of its elderly member often does not feel entitled to complain forthrightly. The family believes it needs the nursing home more than the nursing home needs the family. To a degree this is reality; the person may be dependent on an aide for an item as mundane as a timely bedpan, but a complaint about this can be experienced as risky.

In discussing survival in an institution, Schmidt distinguishes "negotiation" for getting what one wants from other means of getting things done such as threatening, persuading, or appealing to authority. More often there is an interplay among these behaviors. Negotiation is defined as "the interpersonal work that determines status and action, and requires everything the patient can bring to bear on an obdurate social structure" (p. 71). In some institutions, the ability to tap into the social resources, the system that will respond to the resident's needs, is dependent on a complex interplay of forces, including a form of "social outreach" and "particularization" (p. 73). "Outreach" is defined as the individual's willingness or ability to become engaged with the social world around him; "particularization" involves relating to persons as distinct individuals. Thus, the resident who calls out, "Help me, help me . . . " all day long, is appealing for a personal rescuer but is addressing a vaguely generalized other; she neither particularizes nor really reaches out. In addition, the health and physical mobility of the person, the ownership of resources that could be bestowed or withheld, the individual's cognitive and self-care skills, all contribute to a sense of having or lacking power to get what one wants in a nursing home setting.

Because nursing home residents depend on their caregivers for essential services, it is customary to think of residents as passive victims of the staff, says Schmidt. The error is in the assumption that "*Mental incapacity invariably accompanies physical deficits*" (author's italics) (Schmidt, p. 114). If complaining is seen as a method that residents use to maintain a sense of personal control (to be sure that needs, likes, and dislikes are known), as well as control over staff, then it may be easier to deal with. For the resident it is an important aspect of expressing individuality; it is a case of whether the person is active and pursues a solution to a problem versus being a non-complainer, with the attendant need to be noticed by the staff, but with a different style.

Social adjustment is another measure of nursing home engagement by residents (Washburn, Sands, & Walton, 2003). Frail seniors who are residents of nursing homes often exhibit changes in levels of social participation and engagement. The definition used here of "social engagement" refers to a "collection of cognitive abilities that enable us to make sense of our social world and to interact effectively with others . . . recognizing emotions in facial expressions or gestures, forming impressions of others, explaining or predicting others' behavior and solving interpersonal problems" (pp. 203–204). The Washburn (2003) study showed that measures of social cognition and assessed domains of competency could not be directly tested by measures of memory, attention, and other cognitive abilities. In the nursing home, the measures of social cognition and so forth were especially related to a variety of cognition ratings of social functioning. The conclusion was that in future studies the effects of ethnicity and culture also need to be dealt with in relation to social cognition and the effect of various dementing illnesses.

Another way residents may exhibit emotional stress is through psychosomatic symptoms. Staff should be trained to be sensitive to this. D'Andrea and Cassidy (2000) state that depression in LTC residents often needs to be assessed and diagnosed as unrelated to physical causes. For example, poor appetite could be a reaction to placement in the nursing home away from familiar surroundings; cancer; a swallowing disorder; or a side effect of medications.

STAFF: WORKING IN NURSING HOMES

An article about how staff is trained (Lee & Carr, 1993) focused on what nursing home staff needed to learn and be reminded of, and what they recognized as barriers to women residents' empowerment. The authors cited "institutional constraints and burnout as the major problems, and lack of recognition on the part of society, as well as lack of support, as immediate occupational problems and issues of concern" (p. 197).

Evers, Tomic, and Brouwers (2002) found that in caring for the elderly in a nursing home, staff may experience "burnout," defined as becoming exhausted by their work—a syndrome of emotional exhaustion, depersonalization, and reduced sense of personal accomplishment. This is exhibited as early as one year after starting to work. A clear relationship then often exists between the well-being of staff and the behavior of residents. In the present study (Evers, Tomic, & Brouwers, 2002), aggressive behavior (physical and psychological) of the elderly is examined in relation to the dimension of burnout of staff. The burnout was seen as a *process*, an increasing growth of stress and symptoms. In order for preventive strategies to be developed, and to anticipate aggression in homes for the elderly, it must be acknowledged that such aggression can occur.

A study done in the UK (MacPherson, Eastley, Richards, & Mian, 1994) found that staff who worked in a variety of LTC settings, were *not* more likely to perceive a lack of support at work and to report "shouting back" at aggressive residents; they did *not* have significantly high levels of psychological disturbance. At the same time, "a strongly significant relationship was demonstrated between staff psychological disturbance and reports of aggression by residents" (p. 385). In another study in the UK (Proctor, Stratton-Powell, Tarrier, & Burns, 1998), the researchers found that developing skills in individual care planning, or coping with the conflicts and ambiguities of caring for the increasingly dependent clients in residential care, could be helpful. This training for staff involved easily applied procedures for "buffering the increasing stress levels among care staff" (p. 68). They recommended further longitudinal work to see how stress level reduction worked over a period of time.

Researchers frequently rely on staff reports for information about nursing home residents with dementia. It was found in a study by Reid and Chappell (2000) that nurses generally tend to underestimate the severity of dementia, often confounding it with the client's functional and behavioral status, especially when this status is adequate. It is suggested that cognitive data are best collected using approved research methods, rather than relying on nurses' assessments, as such subjective judgments have less empirical value.

EARLY ADJUSTMENT IN THE NURSING HOME

Stillwell and Salamon (1990) see the early period after nursing home admission as a critical time for successful adjustment. This is an important issue for the staff of the home to understand, and can also become a key element in planning in-service training for this period. The effort here would be to alter stereotypical thinking about personality attributes, about the meaning of dependent and independent behaviors. These authors state, "Any individual staff member may be unable to articulate how a particular decision to respond or not was reached, where whether to respond or not was related to certain aspects of the interaction between the resident and the staff member" (p. 84).

Qualitative analysis shows that a Certified Nurse's Aide (CNA) can have a positive effect (quantitative analyses are not yet available) (Yeats, Cready, Ray, DeWitt, & Queen, 2004). However, steps for implementing these teams of managers, nurses, and aides include being sure that management *wants* these teams, as well as training the managers, nurses, and aides in how to use them and to provide them with the information to make good decisions. It is also necessary for them to meet regularly with staff, to interact with them, and to provide feedback. The authors note that this can result in better coordination of resident care, more awareness of staff absenteeism and lateness; in general, it leads to better understanding of nursing home policies. These self-managed work teams (SMWT) can have an effect on early adjustment in the nursing home.

A nursing home is a place where there are reduced options for maintaining an environment the older person can control. If a nursing home staff can keep some options open for the older person who has recently had to make the change to this environment, the possibility of a better adjustment is enhanced. On the other hand, if the staff encourages dependency by always being the decision makers, this affects the residents' autonomy as adults; the need for security can tip in the direction of further decline in the residents' competency (Zarit, Dolan, & Leitsch, 1996).

THERAPY OPTIONS

Duffy (2000), referring to the work of Bergin and Garfield (1994), says that much of the research into individual therapy with nursing home residents in the recent past indicates that theoretical approaches are less responsible for outcome effectiveness than are common elements of therapeutic process. Probably a variety of theoretic approaches can work, with a focus on type and intensity of the therapeutic relationship as a pivotal force in producing change in older residents. He points to the importance of the therapeutic alliance that develops between the client and the therapist as the most important aspect, although it may not be discussed as such. He says, "It is, in fact, essential to take the time to develop a relationship with older clients, and not restrict therapeutic interventions to purely technical approaches that involve little time and attention" (p. 75).

There were few reports in the literature of psychotherapy with elderly clients in nursing homes until the latter part of the 1980s. Lambert (1983) said, "Psychotherapy of the institutionalized elderly is subject to certain constraints: cognitive deficits, memory clouding or loss, physical debilitation, and relatively short time spans" (p. 55). However, even under such constraints, therapy can be empowering and can equip the resident to survive and even succeed in the institution. Fortunately, many other therapists since then have broadened the spectrum of arenas and disorders for which therapy has been described. For example, Rosowsky (2000) has described interventions for those with personality disorders who are residents of nursing homes. She indicates that such clients would, typically, have had few intimate relationships, a history of conflicted relationships, poor anger control, a history of problems with caregivers (see Teofila, described in chapter 5), and difficulty accepting dependence on others—all of which behaviors would have an effect on their new care providers in the institution. Personality disorders, she says, *are* amenable to help.

The therapist in the nursing home can address the variety of problems associated with dementia, disorientation and/or agitation, suicidal thoughts associated with severe depression, counseling the elderly dying client, and the recommendation of using psychopharmacology in the treatment of mental disorders.

Disorientation, and even depression, if considered as symptoms rather than psychological diagnoses, can be treated in some of the same ways. In every case, assessment to determine what the physical or psychological contribution is, and whether it is accompanied by sleep disorders and other medical symptoms such as appetite disturbances, guilt, agitation, suicidal thoughts, and so on, is necessary. Because depression is such a common symptom accompanying

institutionalization, a wide variety of individual and group psychotherapy approaches have been tried and are available: supportive
psychotherapy, insight-oriented psychodynamic psychotherapy,
and cognitive-behavioral therapy, among others.

As Liptzin (1986) stated, "Understanding the basic characteristics of nursing homes is a prerequisite for the study of mental illness
there" (p. 43). One of several areas he recommends for more objective research attention is the comparative value of specific management interventions such as psychosocial treatment approaches
versus psychotropic medications. There is such limited epidemiolog-
ical data to date for mental health disorders in general, in nursing
homes, as well as inadequate diagnoses and record keeping that
the basis for long-term policy change recommendations is seriously
lacking. It was only in 2000 that Victor Molinari's seminal volume,
Professional Psychology in Long Term Care, was published. In the
following chapters of this section, and in still later chapters, a philosophy of hope is echoed. We reinforce the idea that the elderly, no
matter where they reside, are open to change. Methodologies will
be outlined, including techniques for the most serious cognitive
impairments and Alzheimer's disease, for populations least likely to
be included in treatment strategies up to now.

As Duffy (2000) said, "Little emphasis has been placed on the
process of psychotherapy with older adults. Even less research has
been done in LTC settings, even though the nursing home has become a major setting for psychotherapeutic services" (p. 74). If
therapists of diverse clinical backgrounds do become interested in
providing help to older adults in institutions, then the practice of
psychotherapy for this cohort will surely advance theory and development in an underexplored realm.

A study that deals with longevity and health care expenditures
(Yang, Norton, & Stearns, 2003) found that spending on inpatient
care in the last year of life declines with age of death, but inpatient
expenditures are roughly constant across all ages for those not close
to death. During the last year of life, there is a decrease in inpatient
expenditures and an increase in nursing home expenditures so that
total health care expenditures look roughly constant by age. The
authors also noted that "the longer one lives, the less is spent on
inpatient care during the last year of life" (p. S10).

REFERENCES

Abramson, J. A., & Mendis, K. P. (1990). The organizational logistics of running a dementia group in a skilled nursing facility. *Clinical Gerontologist, 9*(3/4), 111–122.

Amirchanyan, A. A., & Wolf, D. A. (2003). Caregiver stress and noncaregiver stress: Exploring the pathways of psychiatric morbidity. *Gerontologist, 43*(6), 817–827.

Bergin, A. E., & Garfield, S. L. (1994). *Handbook of psychotherapy and behavior change.* New York: Wiley.

Brody, C. M. (1987). *Women's therapy groups: Paradigms of feminist treatment.* New York: Springer.

Brody, E. M. (2004). *Women in the middle: Their parent-care years* (2nd ed.). New York: Springer.

Brown-Watson, A. V. (1999). *Still kicking: Restorative groups for frail older adults.* Baltimore: Health Professional Press.

Burton, L. C., Zdaniuk, B., Schulz, R., Jackson, S., & Hirsch, C. (2003). Transitions in spousal caregiving. *Gerontologist, 43*(2), 230–247.

Corder, P. C., & Hernandez, M. (2004). Consumer discourse in assisted living. *Journals of Gerontology, 59B,* S58–S67.

D'Andrea, J. A., & Cassidy, E. (2000). Assessment of psychotherapy. In V. Molinari (Ed.). *Professional psychotherapy in long term care* (pp. 1–28). New York: Hatherleigh.

Duffy, M. (2000). Individual therapy in long term care. In V. Molinari (Ed.). *Professional psychology in long term care* (pp. 73–89). New York: Hatherleigh.

Evers, W., Tomic, W., & Brouwers, A. (2002). Aggressive behavior and burnout among staff of homes for the elderly. *International Journal of Mental Health Nursing, 11,* 2–9.

Golant, S. M. (2004). Impaired older persons with health care needs occupy U.S. assisted living facilities: An analysis of six studies. *Journals of Gerontology, 57B*(2), S68–S79.

Kramer, B. J. (2000). Husbands caring for wives with dementia: A longitudinal study of continuity and change. *Health and Social Work, 25*(2), 97–107.

Lambert, C. A. (1983). Psychotherapy of the elderly: Case #21, on meeting Peter Pan. *Journal of Geriatric Psychiatry, 16*(1), 51–55.

Lee, J., & Carr, M. B. (1993). The empowerment of women residents in the nursing home. *Women and Therapy, 14*(1–2), 187–203.

Liptzin, B. (1986). Major mental disorders/problems in nursing homes: Implications for research and public policy. In M. S. Harper & B. D. Lebowitz (Eds.). *Mental illness in nursing homes: Agenda for research* (pp. 41–55). NIMH, Rockville, MD: U.S. DHHS, Pub. No. (ADM) 86-1459.

Macpherson, R., Eastley, R. J., Richards, H., & Mian, H. (1994). Psychological distress among workers caring for the elderly. *International Journal of Geriatric Psychiatry, 9,* 381–386.

Molinari, V. (2000). *Professional psychology in long term care.* New York: Hatherleigh.

Proctor, R., Stratton-Powell, H., Tarrier, N., & Burns, A. (1998). The impact of training and support on stress among care staff in nursing and residential homes for the elderly. *Journal of Mental Health, 7*(1), 59–70.

Qualls, S. H. (2000). Working with families in nursing homes. In V. Molinari (Ed.). *Professional psychology in long term care* (pp. 91–112). New York: Hatherleigh.

Rantz, M. I., Hicks, L., Grando, V., Petroski, G. F., Madsden, R. W., Mehr, D. R., et al. (2004). Nursing home quality, cost, staffing, and staff mix. *Gerontologist, 44*(1), 24–38.

Reid, R. C., & Chappell, L. (2000). Accuracy of staff assessment in research: Dementia and environmental characteristics. *Journal of Mental Health and Aging, 6*(3), 237–248.

Rosowsky, E. (2000). Interventions for older adults with personality disorders. In V. Molinari (Ed.). *Professional psychology in long term care* (pp. 161–177). New York: Hatherleigh.

Ruckdeschel, H. (2000). Group psychotherapy with nursing homes. In V. Molinari (Ed.). *Professional psychology in long term care* (pp. 113–131). New York: Hatherleigh.

Schmidt, M. (1990). *Negotiating a good old age.* New York: McGraw-Hill.

Semel, V. G. (1986). The aging woman: Confrontation with hopelessness. In T. Bernay & D. W. Cantor (Eds.). *The psychology of today's woman* (pp. 253–269). Hillsdale, NJ: Erlbaum.

Stillwell, N. C., & Salamon, M. J. (1990). Complaining behavior in long-term care: A multifactorial conceptualization. *Clinical Gerontologist, 9*(3/4), 77–89.

Tappen, R. M., Williams, C. L., Barry, C., & DiSesa, D. (2001). Conversation intervention with Alzheimer's patients: Increasing the relevance of communication. *Clinical Gerontologist, 24*(3/4), 63–75.

Tornatore, J. B., & Grant, L. A. (2004). Family caregiver satisfaction with the nursing home after placement of a relative with dementia. *Journals of Gerontology, 59B*(2), S80–S88.

U.S. Department of Health and Human Services, National Center for Health Statistics. (1999). Unpublished data from the 1999 *National Nursing Home Survey, Table 3.* Washington, DC.

Washburn, A. M., Sands, L. P., & Walton, P. J. (2003). Assessment of social cognition in frail older adults and its association with social functioning in the nursing home. *Gerontologist, 43*(2), 203–212.

Williams, K., Kemper, S., & Hummert, M. L. (2003). Improving nursing home communication: An intervention to reduce elderspeak. *Gerontologist, 43*(2), 242–247.

Yang, Z., Norton, E. C., & Stearns, S. C. (2003). Longevity and health care expenditures: The real reason older people spend more. *Journals of Gerontology, 58B*(1), S2–S10.

Yeats, D. E., Cready, C., Ray, B., DeWitt, A., & Queen, C. (2004). Self-managed work teams in nursing homes: Implementing and empowering nurse aid teams. *Gerontologist, 44*(2), 256–261.

Zarit, S. H., Dolan, M. H., & Leitsch, S. A. (1996). Interventions in nursing homes and other alternative living centers. In I. H. Nordhus & G. R. Vandenbos (Eds.). *Clinical geropsychology* (pp. 329–343). Washington, DC: American Psychological Association.

Chapter 4

Reminiscence Groups With Women in a Nursing Home

Claire M. Brody

Over a period of three years, a series of reminiscing-type group sessions were conducted once per week with women in a New Jersey nursing home. Contrary to common stereotypes about the hopeless affect and lack of meaning in the lives of elderly nursing home residents, group participants showed a capacity for emotional survival and vitality that belied these stereotypes. This was revealed through a willingness to use life review to explore ways of relating more directly to their current reality, especially the elements that nourished them. Recognizing these traits and the proclivity toward emotional health that underlies them could be highly significant for professionals involved in program-planning for this population.

Sanders, Brockway, Ellis, Cotton, and Bredin (1999) describe many ways that mental health can be enhanced in a nursing home, among them, promoting dignity, independence, intimacy, and a sense of purpose and meaning. It involves collaboration with a variety of providers, as well as staff and families. It requires more than just working together; it involves "mutual respect and accommodation of differences" (p. 342), as well as sharing of information and frequent meetings. All of this can influence the overall mental health of a particular institution.

In one study (Klausner, Clarken, & Spielman, 1998), the researchers found that reminiscence therapy proved helpful in reducing major depressive symptoms and disability in elders. There was an association between hope, hopelessness, and suicidal ideation in these depressed adults. The group format allowed the depressed individuals to express current feelings and to recollect prior depressive experiences, both positive and negative, in a supportive and caring environment. "Simple reminiscence," as a coping style that an individual resorts to in response to stress, is determined by Puentes (2001) to have many positive outcomes for older adults in a nursing home setting. There were many problems recruiting subjects for a study such as the one detailed below, but there also is the possibility of greater understanding of the relationships among coping styles, anxiety levels, and reminiscence.

Excerpts from sessions are provided, along with comments on session process and content. It has been said that "The use of reminiscence as a means of therapeutic life review has become a standard of long term care therapeutic technique" (Duffy, 2000, p. 85). Although this can be narrative and a factual remembering of life events, it can also be an evaluation of these experiences. There can be a blurring of the boundary between past and present. Whereas the events may have taken place in the chronological past, their *meaning* is in the "psychological present" (p. 85). Reminiscing in a group "can enhance cohesion by illuminating common experiences shared by the group members" (Ruckdeschel, 2000, p. 126).

RECENT LITERATURE ON REMINISCENCE GROUPS

Life review therapy as an effective strategy both for addressing psychological problems and enhancing the quality of life for older people has been well documented. The study by Atkinson, Kim, Ruelas, and Lin (1999), however, was one of the first to examine Asian-American and Hispanic-American elders' attitudes toward facilitated reminiscence groups. The findings were that "Chinese-American elders are as favorably disposed toward life review therapy as European-American elders, and Mexican-American elders may be even more inclined toward sharing past experiences and resolving problems in life review therapy than are either Chinese-American or European-American elders" (p. 79). Elders from all three groups consider ethnic and cultural factors to be important when they consider participating in facilitated reminiscence, even though there are cultural prohibitions against sharing intimate problems in both Chinese and Hispanic cultures.

"Reminiscing groups" were initially intended to utilize life review methods such as those described by Butler (1963), Havighurst and Glasser (1972), and Goodman (1988), among others. Butler has described life review as a universally occurring process wherein there is a progressive return to consciousness of past experiences that can be purposefully utilized. Just as there has been a resurgence of interest among younger people to discover their roots and reclaim meaningful elements of their past, elders also appear to have an abiding interest in reviewing their histories. It was with a sense of optimism and open-mindedness, therefore, that this nursing home reminiscing group project was started. Although scrapbooks, old photo albums, letters, and other memorabilia can also be used to elicit memories, in the taped sessions to be presented here, structured life review sessions were used for reviewing milestones in the life course. Conversations often focused on food and holiday goodies associated with the memories.

It is difficult to compare research findings on reminiscence groups because of the diversity of the participants and the differences in methodology. Nevertheless, the studies that have been done with nursing home populations using life review or reminiscence as themes for group meetings have found a reduction in depression, and improved cognitive functioning as well as psychological well-being. In a fairly well controlled study Taft and Nehrke (1990) conducted with men and women aged 65 and over in a skilled nursing home facility, the authors relate the outcome of a life review–type of reminiscence group experience to "improved ego integrity," conceived as a resolution of Erikson's eighth and final developmental stage. They also suggest that this life review technique can be incorporated into individual therapy with the elderly as well. Molinari (1999) says that life review is particularly salient for older adults since aging may trigger a natural developmental crisis that can be resolved by gaining an overall perspective on one's life. He suggests that it is best performed in small group context, and he describes a "model" program.

M. J. Stones, Rattenberg, Taichman, Kosma, and L. Stones (1990) suggest that nursing home clients suffering from mild depression will derive the most benefit from participating in a reminiscing group where the intent is to raise the general well-being (happiness) of the participants. These authors also note that rigorous design and rationale for selection of participants in these groups had not appeared in the literature up to this time. Their own controlled study found that those residents in a "midrange level of happiness" appear to profit the most. However, provision must be made in the post-group experience for some form of "environmental facilitation," that is, continuity and replacement of these interventions by happiness. Otherwise, gains achieved may not be maintained. Research done by Webster (1998) confirms that one reason older adults with a positive model of self are happier than those with a negative model of self is that if one views attachment figures as accessible, caring, and supportive, and oneself as worthy of that kind of attention, it predisposes one to be happy. He says, "Feeling independent and in control may bolster self-esteem and related concepts such as happiness" (p. 322).

It is said that what is underreported in reminiscence literature are some of the cultural aspects of older people's pasts—aspects of the self that are sloughed off (Rubinstein, 2002). Rubinstein says, "Reminiscence is a cultural product and . . . for elders, one of its most important roles is as an element of the present-day self" (p. 154). In general, "reminiscence functions as one of a number of media that are fundamentally part of the aging self" (p. 163).

Ruckdeschel (2000) describes common themes for reminiscence in nursing homes. Adjusting to institutional life might be one. Sharing a room with a stranger; having to eat at prescribed times; being seen in a depersonalized way (as in terms of the medical illnesses residents have); leftover conflicts and problems; and maintaining a sense of control in the face of declining abilities are other themes. For these and other problems, a group is a place where one can be seen as a whole person, with a range of life experiences that sometimes overlap someone else's. Ruckdeschel also says that coping with losses, as through illness or death, is also a common issue. "The group members may share their feelings about their own and each other's declining health, confronting their fears, expressing concern, and offering support for one another" (p. 116). Sometimes, she says, expressing their feelings of loss and appreciation for a group member who has died may offer reassurance that they, too, will be missed when they die. When group members address issues of loss and death, they may also be working through general existential issues of meaning in life. Many of these themes were common to the groups described here.

The cohesiveness of the group and the empathy elicited in one member for another are the most notable goals achieved. Through reminiscing, they succeeded in reclaiming some of their autonomy. This has also been said by Lee and Carr (1993), who claim it is this barrier to empowerment that nursing homes often represent in their institutional constraints. In considering the mental health needs of residents in nursing homes, it is through working on their self-esteem and peer networking that women, especially, achieve some control over their lives.

THE PROJECT

Eight groups, each composed of five to eight women, were conducted over a period of three years. The shortest length of time any group met was for six weeks; one group continued for six months. Each group was designed to provide the participants with an opportunity to review key experiences of a lifetime. As the therapist, I usually suggested a life marker theme for the discussions, but sometimes a group member offered one.

The nursing home where the group meetings took place is a private institution that also accepts Medicaid clients, so the residents included elderly men and women from varied socioeconomic and cultural backgrounds. In the suburban location of this home, a large percentage of the residents were Caucasian, as were all of the group members.

The therapeutic recreation program at this nursing home is somewhat more elaborate than in other, comparably financed, institutions. After intensive interviews, evaluations, and consideration of the needs and desires of each resident, an individualized program is developed. The regularly scheduled nursing home activities might include word and memory games, recorded stories and discussions, current events presentations, residents' council, drama group, monthly newspaper, and others. These activities are graded and adapted based on an individual's mental and physical status and previous interests and skills. Stated goals of each resident's recreation program include enhancing a sense of achievement and renewing self-worth. There is encouragement for a withdrawn resident to participate and socialize. It is in the context of these goals that the women were selected by the recreation staff to participate in the reminiscing-type groups. The residents' agreement to participate was also required.

In several instances, despite encouragement by staff members, some women were too threatened, withdrawn, or fearful to chance participation in the groups and these needs and feelings were respected. Groups homogeneous for gender (women) were chosen because there are more females than males in nursing homes and also because in their early years, women were socialized to share and talk about their feelings more than the men of their generation. The recreation staff consulted with me in deciding which women to put together in a given group.

Often in these residential settings there can be an opportunity to combine reminiscing groups with life-history writing projects or other therapeutic or expressive activities. In this nursing home setting the half-hour weekly meetings offered the residents the only chance in their structured schedules to explore a lifetime of stored feelings. The group also became the place to deal with problems of current living. Incorporated into discussions of life marker events were basic themes of dependence and independence, friendship, secrets, and trust; occasionally themes of separation and isolation were brought up.

What evolved with the groups was a more eclectic experience than that described in earlier writings about reminiscing groups in non-residential settings. The women in the groups described here varied widely in their physical and cognitive abilities and in their capacity for sustained communication. I functioned as leader/participant, albeit a somewhat directive one, using a form of directed memory-jogging to elicit responsiveness. At the start of a new group, women who might have been sitting next to each other in the recreation room for weeks or months, but who had never more than smiled or commented on the temperature of the coffee served, would find themselves sitting together in the group and being encouraged to talk about themselves and their early lives.

Because group members had been removed from family relationships for varying lengths of time, the process of creating a new and meaningful social network through the group was a slow one. Trust had to be established before this process could occur and before a degree of spontaneity could develop. As the leader/therapist, I found that continuous prodding was often necessary for a group member to respond at all. My function was, therefore, to promote and facilitate meaningful intragroup communication. As the participants saw and heard about each other, the desire emerged to join in the discussion, although this often took many weeks to occur. (Note the comparative length and detail of the responses of the women in the third session reported.)

Each group used a version of life review in which life landmark themes focused their memories on their histories and feelings: starting school, graduations, going to work and/or getting married, children leaving, loss of loved ones, old age. Starting school appeared to be one of the landmarks from early childhood that was readily remembered. With most of the women it had some strong affect associated with the event, along with fairly specific details. The residents' acquired passivity is an important force in the nursing home environment; the emotional energy elicited by recalling such a life marker as "starting school" was significant in overcoming this passivity.

There was no doubt that problems with attention and memory affected group process. But this project, even with its limited success, highlighted the need for new approaches to working with these problems in nursing home groups. Because of the residents' cognitive limitations, their lack of sophistication about small group process, and the fact that their usual initial affect when response was expected was of helplessness and dependence, I found it necessary—and ultimately useful—to take an active role in helping group members remember. This was accomplished through questions, verbal prodding, use of humor, and sometimes with my own personal relevant recollections. It was also rare for spontaneous cross-group comments to be made, especially in the first few sessions with a new group. Another way I dealt with this difficulty was to make brief statements on a subject relevant to the day's theme, for example on feminism, comparative child-rearing practices, or the changing role of women in our culture.

I attempted to engage all group members in response, in turn, when discussing a particular issue. Not remembering or being confused is sometimes accepted and not confronted in the nursing home environment; the effort to remember or clarify thoughts is, therefore, essential in these groups. I used as many opportunities as possible to reinforce a sense of worth in the residents. The recollection of past achievements, whether in higher schooling or any other part of life, was always affirmed.

In an attempt to foster memory skills, I encouraged group members to learn and remember each other's names. I set this seemingly simple memory exercise as a primary task to affirm each member's sense of self in the group as well as to enhance the possibility of keeping contact and communication going when they are not in the group. In addition to starting a session by recapping what was said the previous week, I often repeated what a participant said or clarified a vague statement. The repetition also served to reinforce the importance of the contribution and to assure that everyone heard what was said, because an individual member's voice quality, sight, or hearing might be poor.

The reader might question my degree of direction in the groups on the one hand, and the "equality" of my participation as a group member on the other. However, the resulting responsiveness led group members to feel more connected with their own experience, and ultimately to an increase in self-direction. The outcome of these group sessions suggested movement in the participants toward reclaiming their autonomy.

The opportunity to make choices and a sense of control have been found to be related to measures of well-being among populations of older people (Crose, 2000). As Crose explains, older people grew up at a time when there were clearly defined gender roles. Even women who worked outside the home still did most of the work within the home. So "an institutional environment in which others take care of all their needs may represent a significant and distressing loss of control" (p. 377). This is true for women more than for men. Where women can make none of the decisions regarding meals, schedules, laundry, and housecleaning, it is especially difficult. For men, who are used to having food served and other chores performed by the women in their family, it is less difficult.

Although this is not illustrated in the excerpts below, the focus would sometimes shift to current problems of living in the institutional setting—for example, "dealing with someone I don't like" or "getting the courage to ask for something," despite the risk of rejection or failure. One resident longed for a cup of yogurt on her lunch tray and never considered the possibility of asking for it—and getting it! After some encouragement, she voiced her request and obtained positive results, enhancing her sense of worth and control over her life, as well as modeling behavior for others in the group.

The group members were encouraged to touch each other's hands as a symbol of being connected. An ambulatory member who communicated minimally with everyone in the nursing home took it upon herself to push another member's wheelchair back to the recreation room each week as a first sign of her emerging capacity to socialize. After several weeks, the evolution of this type of interaction reflected a feeling of hopefulness and a willingness to pursue the contacts that nourished her.

Excerpts from transcribed group sessions are provided in order to highlight some of the key themes that were discussed above, illustrating the quality of the interaction in these groups. The excerpts are taken from meetings of three different groups, each with six women, aged 69 to 93. They had been in the nursing home from one to five years. All but three were American-born; two were born in Ireland, one in Germany. Their education levels ranged from grade school not completed to high school plus secretarial or teacher training. The cognitive levels ranged from mild impairment to serious memory deficit and confusion; one woman was blind. All participants were mobile enough to spend three to six hours every day in a recreation room environment, either able to walk unaided or to sit in a wheelchair. About two thirds of them had been married and most of these had children.

THEME: REMEMBERING NAMES

Learning names of group members fosters memory skills, enhances the possibility of further communication among residents, and helps establish a sense of self within the group. In the first session, the participants also get an idea of what they will be doing and who the leader is. An atmosphere of openness and acceptance of their cognitive and physical limits is conveyed. (Note: " . . . " indicates a break in continuity in the excerpt.)

Therapist: Today we have a new group and everyone has to try to learn everyone's name. Can you hear me, Ellen? Is my voice loud enough? (Ellen nods.) We're going to go around and try to remember everybody's name. My name is Claire. Do you know where that voice is coming from, Edna? (Edna is blind.) I'm the leader of this group.

Edna: I can hear.

Therapist: You can hear me, O.K. This is Mary on my left, and Marie over here. Then this is Helen, sitting opposite me. Edna doesn't see, so I'm describing where people are; and Natalie is sitting opposite me, too; and Ellen is over there. Ellen (who is in a wheelchair), I'm going to move you over there, a little closer because you look like you're sitting in the balcony; we want everyone sitting in the orchestra in this group ... It's going to be hard remembering this many names, but it sounds like a wonderful group to me. Let's go around again. I'm Claire.

Marie: I'm Marie (Each member introduces herself.)

Therapist: Wow! I have a group where everybody says their own name, and let me tell you, sometimes I have to help people with it. (Skip to the end of the session.) This group is going to come together every week and we're going to talk about ourselves and our lives, everything that we can remember that happened to us. Now, the things you can't remember, you don't talk about; you just talk about what you do remember. Next week we're going to first try and remember everyone's name. Do you think if you see these women sitting in the recreation room, you might remember their names? Mary, whose name do you remember in this circle?

Mary: I know her face, but ...

Therapist: That's Ellen. Do you remember anybody's voice, Edna? Do you remember my name, Edna? ... I only told it to you once, so that's no surprise.

Edna: Mary? (to Claire)

Therapist: No, I'm Claire.

Ellen: You're Claire.

Therapist: That's right! Very good memory; you remember well. Natalie, do you remember anyone's name?

Natalie (with much hesitation): Helen.

Therapist: That's right! It is Helen. That's very good. Do you remember my name?

Natalie: It's Claire.

Therapist: That's right. See if you can remember it next week when we come together again. Now, Helen, whose name do you remember here?

Helen: (with much hesitation this time): I don't think so . . .

Therapist: Now, try hard . . . I want Helen to try. Do you remember who the nice woman sitting opposite you is; the nice person who cannot see? . . . Remember, that's Edna. See if you can remember that next week. Now, if you see Edna sitting here one day, you walk up to her and say, "Hi Edna. I'm Helen." Will you remember Helen, Edna, if she says hello, that she's from your group?

Edna: Oh yes, I'll remember.

Therapist: Of course you will . . . Well, I think we're going to stop now. Next week we're going to try to remember anything we can from when we were five or six. You can be thinking about that. Don't tell me now; we'll wait for next week.

THEME: STARTING SCHOOL

Recalling key experiences helps to focus memory, affirm achievements, and preserve ego integrity. When the therapist uses questions, verbal prodding, humor, and repetition she helps the group members recall what was said in previous sessions as well as call forth long-forgotten memories. Remembering "starting school" leads to remembering other small bits of life data such as teachers and friends. Sometimes one group member's recollection is confabulated by another member's, and she may take this memory for her own. Inaccurate memories or contradictions—or such confabulations— are not necessarily remarked on by the therapist, but occasionally a participant will reclaim her own experience by correcting another group member's inaccurate statement regarding her life:

Therapist: Last week, if you remember, we talked about when we were little girls. Remember, we tried to recall something about when we were six or seven or eight, when we just began school. Remember what you told us, Mary, about starting school? Did you have to walk to school? (Mary shakes head affirmatively.) You did. You do remember that?

Mary: Yes.

Therapist: Was it far?

Mary: Yes, it was.

Therapist: You all know that Mary grew up in Ireland. She didn't go to school in this country. And you had to walk to school. Was it maybe a mile?

Mary: Not that far. It was more.

Therapist: It was more than a mile. Each way. You had to have long legs and strong knees, I guess . . . What about you, Helen, what do you remember about starting school? Was it a neighborhood school?

Helen: Yes, it was a neighborhood school.

Therapist: Where did you grow up? Do you remember the name of the city where you grew up?

Helen: New York.

Therapist: New York City.

Edna: Me, too.

Therapist: You, too. And Ellen, where did you grow up?

Ellen: In Ireland.

Therapist: Another person who grew up in Ireland. We'll get to that in a minute. So, Helen, you grew up in New York City. Which borough?

Helen: In the Bronx. Way up near Bronx Park.

Therapist: Way up near Bronx Park. Was it far from a school where you lived?

Helen: No, near a school.

Therapist: Helen, do you remember how you felt when you started school?

Helen: Yes, I was very fond of school.

Therapist: So you didn't cry the first day?

Helen: No, no.

Therapist: Some children cry. Anybody, did you cry the first day? Marie, you?

Marie: I cried, after I ate my lunch. Because we had to take our lunch with us; we lived about 10 blocks.

Therapist: Ten blocks, then you couldn't walk home for lunch.

Marie: I cried for my lunch at home. I just didn't think that was lunch, that's all.

Therapist: Edna, what do you remember about starting school; where did you live?

Edna: Up in the Bronx, near Bronx Park.

(Note: Edna seems to be parroting what Helen said earlier.)

Edna: I could walk to school . . . I liked school. And then I went to high school and college.

(Note: It is not certain that Edna did go to college; however, the therapist does not contradict her.)

Therapist: We have some pretty smart women here. (To Natalie, who is getting a little restless) I'll get to you, Natalie; I didn't forget you sitting there. Mary, did you like school? Did you learn how to sew and make things? Did you learn embroidery?

Mary: Embroidery, knitting, crocheting.

Natalie: I learned sewing, and mending, and crocheting, too.

Therapist: I think those were very important skills to learn.

(Note: By calling up some of their first adult skills, the therapist acknowledges the value of these skills. Although they may have lost these skills because of physical and mental impairments, they had them once, and they can affirm this here.)

Therapist: Helen, when you were growing up, and going to school, did you think about what you wanted to be when you finished school?

Helen: I wanted to be a teacher and I became a teacher.

Therapist: Did you go to college to become something special, Edna?

Edna: Just to learn.

Helen: That was a good reason.

(Note: This is one of the few times in this session that another group member, not just the therapist, comments on what someone says.)

Therapist: Did you work at something afterwards, Edna?

Edna: I can't think; I'm 90 years old.

Therapist: That's old, but if you are having a hard time remembering it, you can try harder. You have plenty of time. A job that you worked at once? (a short pause).

(Note: Not remembering something is accepted, but a further effort to remember is encouraged.)

Edna: I worked for the Bell System—for the telephone company.

Therapist: There, we found that out.

Edna: For 50 years.

Therapist: You must have been an expert with telephones.

Edna: I was a secretary there; I did shorthand and stuff.

Therapist: Let's find out what kind of work everyone else did around here. Did you have a job at one time, Marie?

Marie: Yes, I did. I worked for Union Carbide. I started there and finished there. I operated a comptometer. You know, it adds and does other kinds of things.

Therapist: A calculator?

Marie: No, a *comptometer.*

(Note: Marie is one of the most cognitively intact members of the group. She knows the kind of machine she means and she has the capacity to assert her knowledge, which is unusual in this group.)

THEME: REMEMBERING PETS

The third excerpt is from a group that has been meeting weekly for about three months. Note the developing camaraderie among the members: their occasional ability to remember bits of data about the lives of other members, their empathy with feelings of sadness or sickness, and the greater spontaneity of the reminiscence. In this meeting, there are many more instances of participants responding to and interacting with other members, along with the therapist's interjections. The member who tells the longest, most detailed stories is Emma. She is 93!

Therapist: Kay, you weren't here last week. Were you in the hospital for a couple of days? I think you were.

Emma: Did you have a baby?

Therapist: Did you have a baby! She's pulling your leg, Kay, she's just making a joke. I guess you weren't feeling well for a couple of days, but you're back.

Kay: I forget; how long was it?

Therapist: Not too long, maybe a week at the most. You were here two weeks ago but last Thursday we missed you. Let's see what we should talk about today. Does anybody have a good suggestion? We always get good suggestions. Something that you would like to think about, something from the past that you would like to remember more about. We've talked about friends, and we've talked about family, and we've talked about where we used to live and we've . . . yes . . . you were going to say something, Emma?

Emma: I had a wonderful little pet that I found that was lost.

Therapist: Oh, pets, that's a good topic. You see, I knew if I waited three minutes somebody would come up with something. The subject is now pets. Did you have a little dog; did it have a name?

Emma: Yes, I named it Sport.

Therapist: Sport. Oh, leave it to Emma. You know we discovered last week, in case anybody forgot, that Emma is 93 years old (lots of exclamations). And Ann, you were the one who did the arithmetic and figured it out. She figured out how old you were, Emma, when we told her the year you were born.

Emma: 1894.

Therapist: You see what I mean? There you are, 1894 . . . (Two group members enter late and are introduced.) I'm very glad to see you, Mary; you missed last week. You came back. Well, let's remind each other what our names are.

Therapist: I'm Claire and you're . . . Charlotte, Emma, Gertrude, Mary, Kay, and Ann. You know what our subject is today? It's pets. We got started just a couple of minutes ago talking about what pets we remember. Even if you didn't have one, you must have known someone who had a pet. And Emma started us off by telling us she had a dog named Sport. You sure come up with good names, Emma. Now, did you know what kind of a dog it was? Was it a big dog?

Emma: It was a little tan dog.

Therapist: What kind of a dog was it?

Emma: Just a mutt.

Therapist: Just a mutt . . . Gertrude, did you have a pet, a dog or a cat or a . . .

Gertrude: A dog. Misty. (She spells it.) M-I-S-T-Y.

Therapist: Was it a girl dog or a boy dog? It's hard to know from the name.

Gertrude: I think it was a boy. He was a real tramp. (She trails off).

Therapist: He had lots of friends in the neighborhood? Was it your dog alone, or did it belong to the whole family? Was it your very own dog?

Gertrude: Well, the family's.

Therapist: Sort of the family's . . . Was it the kind of a dog you had to let out to take its own walk in the morning, or did you have to take it for a walk?

Gertrude: I had to take it.

Therapist: You had to take it for a walk.

Gertrude: He was lazy.

Therapist: So this was a dog you had to take out; it sounds like it was your dog. And did *you* have to walk your dog, Emma?

Emma: I had to walk that dog. And you know, I was near his neighborhood where he lived one day, and all the people lived in tenement houses in Weehawken. It was Easter or near Easter—it was a Sunday morning. I went out for a walk, and I just happened to take him where it was his home. He was lost.

Therapist: Oh, I see, you had a dog who had been lost and he had been with you for a while.

Emma: Yes. That was his home at one time, because when we found him he had a leash on.

Therapist: So what did he do when he saw the house where he used to live?

Emma: The next day he was gone, we never saw him again.

Therapist: He went back to where he was born. Well, you had him for a while anyway, and his name was Sport.

Emma: I was heartbroken, but he must have had a good home. And I cried.

(Note: "I cried . . . " is a perseverative phrase used by Emma, not necessarily denoting sadness.)

Therapist: Let's see if Kay had any pets. Kay, did you have any pets?

Kay: I'm alone.

(Note: Kay seems to be responding to Emma's sad story, but she cannot relate to Emma directly.)

Therapist: Yes, you're alone, I know, but when you were a little girl, did the family have a dog? They had a grocery store. Didn't they have a cat to catch the mice? (Laughter from Kay.) Grocery stores always had cats in the window.

Kay: My mother couldn't have pets; she had allergies, she had asthma.

Therapist: She had asthma, so who caught the mice in the grocery store?

Kay: I didn't hear about that (Laughing).

(Note: In responding to the humor, Kay seems more connected to what is said.)

Therapist: You didn't hear about the mice.

Emma: Did I ever tell you the story about the canary I had?

Therapist: I think you did, but if you want to tell it again we'll listen.

(Note: Emma is the most talkative in the group and often interrupts or repeats stories told before.)

Therapist: Well, let's see what you remember, Ann? Did you have any pets?

Ann: I never had a pet.

Therapist: You never had a pet, not even a bird. How about a fish?

Ann: No, I didn't have anything.

Therapist: No fish, no cats.

Gertrude: But you had a lot of children there. Your brothers and sisters, that was enough to feed.

(Note: Here, Gertrude is remembering some of Ann's life data.)

Therapist: Mary, did you have a pet when you were growing up?

Mary: At 12 years old . . . I had a little piggy.

Therapist: A piggy! Oh, Mary must have lived in the country. I know, you lived near Ossining, no not Ossining, someplace in upstate New York. I can't think of the town.

Mary: Elmira, New York.

(Note: Not only is Mary's memory for place of birth intact, but she feels free enough in the group to correct the therapist.)

CONCLUSIONS

Although it is hard to quantify the results of these group sessions, some positive changes were seen in the participants. Over the course of time there was more interaction noted among group members, and occasionally the self-confidence level of a given participant rose to the degree that she could express her feelings about the therapist or another group member directly. Some relationships did emerge and continued after the group meetings ended. It was hoped that as the women became better acquainted with one another they would share various experiences through verbal exchanges in the periods between the group meetings. There were reports from nursing home staff that this was beginning to happen. Staff members noted that a participant's way of relating to them—as with openness and feeling—evolved. Even when no obvious change was seen outside the group setting, the willingness of the participants to pursue life review and remain in the group, despite physical and cognitive hardships, highlighted their desire to find ways of relating to the realities of their lives. This level of courage and the ability to reclaim even a part of their autonomy through reminiscing is a model that professionals might explore further.

As mentioned earlier, group cohesiveness and empathy for others were the most notable goals achieved. When the same group of women continued meeting for more than six weeks, communication also became more open and supportive. One member might help another remember something or, occasionally, be supportive for another having difficulty remembering.

This seemed to indicate an implicit understanding on the part of the woman taking the helping role that her contribution was as valid as support from me, the authority figure. When this happened, I modified my directive approach, and the encouragement I offered would be directed to the helper, not to the needful member, letting her know that it was all right for her to continue this exploration of her new, more independent role.

Older women have been said to be in multiple jeopardy for stigmatization: ageism, sexism, and negative perception of their infirmities, especially when the latter includes depression. Nursing home residents are often plagued by serious and multiple medical and psychological problems, and thus the women's lack of power and their dependency syndrome can be the targets for help, even at this time in their lives. The group experience described above, led by a feminist therapist, attempts to address these issues. In the broadest sense, this project pointed up the untapped strengths that can become accessible to elderly institutionalized women, and by extrapolation, to men. They learn that they can still give something meaningful to others, which reinforces their own sense of hope, and that they can adapt positively to what is stereotypically thought of as the last rest stop on the way to the grave.

Wink and Schiff (2002) conclude, on the basis of empirical studies of life review and models of the self, that life review can be thought of as "as a purely psychological phenomenon and solely as a function of personality and immediate life experiences" (p. 59). The data, instead, suggest that "the process of life review may also be facilitated or inhibited by the larger historical and cultural contexts for one's life" (p. 59). Life review is thus one way (but not the only way) for successfully adapting to older adulthood by reorganization of the self. What this chapter suggests, therefore, is that reminiscing-type group sessions in a nursing home *can* affect and help dispel lack of meaning and hopelessness in the lives of those who live there.

REFERENCES

Atkinson, D. R., Kim, A. U., Ruelas, S. R., & Lin, A. T-M. (1999). Ethnicity and attitudes toward facilitated reminiscence. *Journal of Mental Health Counseling, 21*(1), 66–81.

Butler, R. (1963). The life review: An interpretation of reminiscence in the aged. *Psychiatry, 26,* 65–76.

Crose, R. (2000). The impact of culture and gender on mental health. In V. Molinari (Ed.). *Professional psychology in long term care* (pp. 373–400). New York: Hatherleigh.

Duffy, M. (2000). Individual therapy in long term care. In V. Molinari (Ed.). *Professional psychology in long term care* (pp. 73–89). New York: Hatherleigh.

Goodman, R. K. (1988). A geriatric group in an acute care psychiatric teaching hospital: Pride or prejudice? In B. W. MacLennan, S. Saul, & M. B. Weiner (Eds.). *Group psychotherapy for the elderly* (pp. 151–164). Madison, CT: International Universities Press.

Havighurst, R. J., & Glasser, R. (1972). An exploratory study of reminiscence. *Journal of Gerontology, 27*(2), 245–253.

Klausner, E. J., Clarken, J. F., & Spielman, L. (1998). Late life depression and functional disability: The role of goal-focused group psychotherapy. *International Journal of Geriatric Psychiatry, 13*(10), 707–716.

Lee, J., & Carr, M. B. (1993). The empowerment of women residents in the nursing home. *Women and Therapy, 14*(1–2), 187–203.

Molinari, V. (1999). Using reminiscence and life review as natural therapeutic strategies in group therapy. In M. Duffy, *Handbook of counseling and psychotherapy* (pp. 154–165). New York: Wiley.

Puentes, W. J. (2001). Coping styles, stress levels, and the occurrence of spontaneous, simple reminiscence in older adult nursing home residents. *Issues in Mental Health Nursing, 22*, 51–61.

Rubinstein, R. L. (2002). Reminiscence, personal meaning, themes, and the "object relations" of older people. In J. L. Webster & B. K. Haight (Eds.). *Critical advances in reminiscence work: From theory to application* (pp. 153–164). New York: Springer.

Ruckdeschel, H. (2000). Group psychotherapy in the nursing home. In V. Molinari (Ed.). *Professional psychology in long term care* (pp. 113–131). New York: Hatherleigh.

Sanders, K., Brockway, J. A., Ellis, B., Cotton, E. M., & Bredin, J. (1999). Enhancing mental health climate in hospitals and nursing homes: Collaboration strategies for medical and mental health staff. In M. Duffy (Ed.). *Handbook of counseling and psychotherapy with older adults* (pp. 335–349). New York: Wiley.

Stones, M. J., Rattenberg, C., Taichman, B., Kosma, A., & Stones, L. (1990). Effective selection of participants for group discussion intervention. *Clinical Gerontologist, 9*(3/4), 135–143.

Taft, L. B., & Nehrke, M. F. (1990). Reminiscence, life review, and ego integrity in nursing home residents. *International Journal of Aging and Human Development, 30*(3), 189–196.

Webster, J. D. (1998). Attachment styles: Reminiscence functions, happiness in young and elderly adults. *Journal of Aging Studies, 12*(3), 315–330.

Wink, P., & Schiff, B. (2002). To review or not to review? The role of personality and life events in life review and adaptation to older age. In J. D. Webster & B. K. Haight (Eds.). *Critical advances in reminiscence work: From theory to application* (pp. 44–60). New York: Springer.

Chapter 5

Mothers and Daughters: Caregiving and Adjustment Issues

Claire M. Brody

MYTHS AND REALITIES

This chapter is an overview of a lifetime's relationship between mothers and daughters. In working with women, young or old, it is always clear that their view of their mothers and of motherhood is central to the adjustment they make. Whether in their original families, in their mid-life years and, finally, when they find themselves living alone or in a nursing home, the affect and optimism—or lack thereof—they bring to their later years is related to the models provided by their mothers for caregiving skills, love, and autonomy. As Bumagin and Hein (2001) said, "The baby-boom generation, larger than any of its predecessors, has increased the number of both potential recipients and potential providers of care" (p. 3).

Alice Walker (1983), in her beautiful book, *In Search of Our Mothers' Gardens*, says,

> Who were these saints? These crazy, loony, pitiful women? Some
> of them, without a doubt, were our mothers and grandmoth-
> ers . . . some of them moving to music not yet written. And they

waited. They waited for a day when the unknown thing that was in them would be made known; but guessed, somehow in their darkness, that on the day of their revelation they would be long dead (pp. 232–233).

Walker reminds us of Virginia Woolf's (1929) comment in her book, *A Room of One's Own*, that in order for a woman to write she must have two things, certainly: a room of her own (with keys and lock) and enough money to support herself (Walker, 1983). Walker goes on to say, "Through years of listening to my mother's stories of her life, I have absorbed not only the stories themselves, but something of the manner in which she spoke" (p. 240). Nevertheless, women still have conflict when they become more independent and autonomous and reflect the cultural roles for which they were prepared. A daughter's personal myth of her mother is shaped by the patriarchal society's realities.

Elaine M. Brody (2004) says, "What are often called 'traditional' values hold that the provision of help to the disabled family is a family responsibility and, in particular, is the role of the women in the family" (p. 69). These values have been in existence for a long time, and before the number and proportion of older people in society, and since before the life spans extended to the degree they have now. It was also since before the dramatic drop in the birth rate, which further affected the number of "women in the middle" who were overburdened. This was also despite the "new" values that held that women were to have roles that were more egalitarian with men.

Women have long been buffeted by changing values and expectations, as E. M. Brody (2004) so aptly explains, and though they may have been out of step with their time, they redoubled their efforts and felt guilty about not doing enough to care for aging parents, while at the same time working to support the economic status of the family. As Brody says, values in regard to family care of elderly parents have not eroded and are still powerful, even among women who are nontraditional.

Brody continues, "The women of the youngest generation (now the 'women in the middle'), strongly favored shared roles, but they were even more emphatic than their mothers or grandmothers about filial responsibility. Their emphasis on 'grandfilial responsibility' will need to be monitored as the dependent, very old population continues to increase, and as some grandchildren even may become responsible for two generations of elderly—their parents and their grandparents" (pp. 80–81).

Peters-Davis, Moss, and Puchno (1999) conducted a study about children-in-law in caregiver families. They found, overall, that the differences between daughters and daughters-in-law (DILs) were not significant. They also state that society has the expectation that children will be responsible and caring toward their elderly parents. A sense of obligation may engender guilt, but it is not greater for the DILs than for the daughters! The sons-in-law (SILs), on the other hand, feel it is the daughter's role (or their wives'); they are once-removed from our society's expectations. The authors make the further point that in our culture, the parent-in-law/daughter-in-law tie is less clearly delineated than in, say, Japan. There was more satisfaction with the caregiving role of the daughters than the DILs, and less concern about the impingement on the daughters' long-term family intimacy, possibly because they had many years to adapt to the intrusion on their privacy and personal space. More research in this area is recommended.

Archer and MacLean (1993) reported in a study of sons and husbands of chronically ill elderly women that what made a difference for *them* (and different from women in the same roles), was that they maintained outside interests. These sons and husbands were then able to distance themselves emotionally—even if just for a short time—from the burdens of caregiving. The authors suggest that participating in a group with other caregivers (male and female) would also prevent them from feeling overwhelmed by their caregiving duties.

A study done in China by Sun (2002), and this author's visit to China in 2003 indicate that there are many demographic and social changes going on in that country. Even though in the past, the Chinese were noted for their Confucian model of respect and care for the elderly, as a result of national policies (one child per family), and also because the Chinese population is aging at an unprecedented rate, they will undoubtedly see even further changes. It can be expected that the status of the elderly in regard to method of support (financial aid, in-kind gifts, and assistance in daily living) may be further eroded, both socially and in individual families.

The effect will be experienced both by the elderly parents and the children. Urban families will face different issues than rural ones.

As a result of Sun's study, it would appear that intergenerational support rests both on the elderlys' needs and on the children's capacity. The provision of help to parents is not uniformly distributed among siblings and often depends on geographic proximity. As China is still a developing country, there is no state-sponsored social security system, and the family network remains the main source of support. Those living closer to parents tend to help with daily tasks; those living further away tend to provide financial transfers. There has also been a dramatic drop in families living under one roof in urban areas, which makes it more difficult for families to provide sources of aid to their elderly, and social institutions must be developed to substitute for family support systems. This may eventually conform to the mutual aid model, wherein the relatively healthier, more economically well-off elderly help other needy ones. The vast pool of human resources, the author says, will have to be tapped.

Herman (1989) refers to Doris Lessing's (1970) character of Martha Quest, who deals with the issue of interference by her mother and her need to separate from her. When Martha finally effects this separation, it is accompanied by guilt, which, in turn, affects her attempt to live her own life. Herman states, "A daughter's hostility directed against her mother will often spring from her experience that maternal intervention, whether covert or overt, is thwarting her potential growth" (p. 275). Whether this is seen as destructive interference will depend on the personalities of the two grown women and on the wider cultural norms. Shere Hite (1990) has written about mothers and daughters and whether daughters perceive themselves as like or unlike their mothers, and their feelings of ambivalence, anger, or resentment about their mothers. As a model for themselves, some women identify more with the power that their fathers had. Unresolved identification conflicts are often projected onto women's caregiving tasks in their interactions with their mothers, fathers, or husbands in later life.

One more "myth" is that in later life the roles of mother and daughter are always reversed; the aging older woman steps back into a state of dependency on the younger one. It is as if the ever-present need to be taken care of re-emerges (Neisser, 1967). One could question whether this is a myth or simply inevitable reality in our present-day culture. There are mothers who remain healthy and independent and do not need additional care.

Although refuted by more recent studies, Neisser (1967) claimed that another myth often held by older women is that the aging process would be slowed down if their daughters paid more affectionate attention to them. Specifically, he said that the elderly woman's emotional response to the loss of her spouse is the key issue here, and is often not assuaged by even the best daughter. The daughter's reciprocal response is often that if she were more devoted to her mother, the mother would keep from growing old. One myth that has prevailed, according to Neisser, is that aged mothers are neglected by their adult children. Rather, what might be lacking is communication, in general, as well as understanding. The degree of attention a mother expects is undoubtedly related to the way she treated her own mother.

Caplan (1989), in her book *Don't Blame Mother*, also tackles the "perfect mother" myth. She sees it as being responsible for the barrier between mother and daughter, because both need to fill traditional feminine stereotypes; that is, mothers think they must shape their daughters to get married, whatever else they do. This perpetuates anguish for them both, keeping them divided. In this way they do not notice that it is societal expectations that make the problem. Instead, they blame themselves and each other. She enumerates nine myths that keep this mother-blaming alive. They range from "perfect mother" myths, which make a mother's good efforts seem inadequate because they are imperfect, to "bad mother" myths, which highlight a mother's failings and even make some of her strengths or neutral points seem harmful (p. 69).

Chodorow (1989) criticizes certain recurrent themes in feminist writings of the 1970s, namely that mothers are totally responsible for the outcomes of their mothering practices and that mothers are the "agents of their daughters' oppression" (p. 81). In reviewing writings of Adrienne Rich (1976), Dorothy Dinnerstein (1976), Nancy Friday (1977), and others who theorized that mothers *can* be perfect, she says they also imply that daughters' needs are legitimate and must be met. While focusing on conditions of patriarchy, under which "bad mothering" takes place, they suggest that if these patriarchal constraints were removed "perfect mothering" would take place. She states that in the "fantasies of motherhood" described by these authors, mothering, sexuality, aggression, death, and isolation often merge in different cultural interpretations, so that myths are formed and perpetuated.

As Chodorow points out, both nineteenth–century cultural ideology about motherhood and post-Freudian psychological theory blamed mothers for any failing in their children and idealized possible maternal perfection. In most recent times, as women's life roles have come to include being part of the paid labor force and some women have chosen not to become mothers, they have been blamed once again, this time for "maternal deprivation." Thus, as Chodorow states, blame and idealization of mothers are two sides of the same belief in the all-powerful mother. Chodorow argues for moving beyond these fantasies about perfect mothering to a new theory of childhood and child development, wherein a child's inevitable rage against caregivers will be shared between men and women; that the girl–child as well as the boy–child will be accorded the right to "agency and intentionality" in response to environmental pressures.

E. M. Brody (2004) refers to the daughters-in-law who become principal caregivers as the "proxy primaries," and whereas there are many who do not assume the role of primary caregiver, there are many who do. In the future, because there will be fewer daughters who assume this role when there are fewer adult children, there will be more daughters-in-law who assume the care of their husband's parents. If this is culturally dictated, or through some special circumstance this may be necessary, and there will be wide variation in the degree of involvement of these daughters-in-law.

A daughter's personal myth of her mother involves seeing their relationship in the context of the patriarchal society's realities. If the mother modeled a repressive or depressive response to unfair burdens, if she played out a traditional housewife/caregiver role, if her educational or social expectations were curtailed by her original or second family, if she experienced a sense of loneliness or abandonment in her early childhood years, then these experiences could result in the daughter's flawed view of motherhood. A very special effort would have to ensue for the daughter to "re-image" her concept of herself in relation to her mother and herself. Often, this recasting of her image is played out for the older woman in connection with her relation to her mother-in-law, if her own mother is no longer available.

Esther

Esther, now age 92, came to this country from Greece as a young girl. She had grown up in a patriarchal extended family. Her own marriage experience largely mirrored that of her original family, although she was different because she had worked and was also a housewife while her children were growing up. Many years later, when she revisited her early environment, both she and her husband reflected upon their changed outlook. In the nursing home women's therapy group, she presented herself as a participant more open to new ideas and new information, tolerant of differences. Yet she had needed her husband's help in confronting her traditional mother-in-law at an earlier time in her life.

Esther: You know mothers-in-law and daughters-in-law, they can't live together . . . I went back to Greece when my husband's mother was 100 years old. A very nice old lady, and my husband was so happy. But my poor mother-in-law saw me in a summer dress, and she said to my husband, "I love your wife but I don't like her to dress up with short sleeves and skirts above her knees." My husband said, "I like my wife to dress the way she does!" And she stopped. Because she was 100 years old, she thought you should wear long sleeves when you go to church—cover yourself.

WOMEN, CAREGIVING, AND AGING

When grown daughters (adult women) are asked why they want to give care to their mothers, the most commonly stated motive is a feeling of love and affection (E. M. Brody, 2004). The daughters perceive this as an important foundation of the moral obligation between parents and their adult children. Brody says that the most negative and pervasive effect of the numerous caregiving roles that women play bare the emotional strains, based on studies cited from the '70s, '80s, and '90s. Among the symptoms she mentions are depression, anger, anxiety, and emotional exhaustion. Even more than these effects, however, are the restrictions on the caregiver's time and freedom, the demands of various responsibilities, and the difficulty in setting priorities.

A study was conducted offering a psychoeducative group program for caregivers of demented persons (Hebert et al., 2003). It demonstrated a significant effect on behavior problems in demented persons. This two-hour weekly training program decreased caregivers' reactions to disruptive behavior and burden, and, by extrapolation, institutionalization was affected for the demented person. Any improvement in coping behavior on the part of caregivers will have an important effect on the disruptive behaviors.

Daughters often feel they are "paying back" their mothers for earlier care the daughters received. Many daughters—or surrogate daughters, as in the case of Teofila, below—report reasons of both desire and obligation for providing the care. Mancini (1989) makes the point that "obligation" as a variable in caregiving is not often recognized in the literature on this subject, whereas at one time "obligation" was a given in American culture. An additional point is that the mother can often vent her anger more easily at the daughter who is doing the primary caregiving because she also sees her as the most instrumental in bringing about the nursing home placement.

A study was done by Musil, Youngblut, Ahn, and Curry (2002) comparing the stress in grandmothers versus that in mothers. The number of grandmothers who have grandchildren living with them has increased markedly in the last 20 years, and there are more African-American than Caucasian families where this is true. The grandmothers who have grandchildren living with them reported more overall stress than the mothers did. Unemployed mothers reported more negative perceptions of their children and more difficult interactions with them, even though the grandmothers seemed to find that employment (or not) was unrelated to their stress. It might be related instead to their having less energy for the task, and to the unanticipated changes they have to make in their lives. They are also more depressed than the mothers. More research is recommended by these authors to determine what accounts for the grandmothers' greater stress. It would be important to compare the mothers and grandmothers who are also taking care of elderly parents.

Campbell and Martin-Matthews (2000) also have explored the gender issue in caregiving. They say that although "obligation" moves many women to assume this role, men's overall involvement is more complex, with sociodemographic, employment, and family structure variables included. In the case of men, commitment to care, legitimate excuses, and commitment by default (where there are no female relatives better situated) are often involved. For example, if the men have young children as well as distance constraints, these can be used as legitimate reasons for limited caregiving. These authors say there is a "need to study many and diverse obligational and motivational factors" if one is to understand men's filial care in the "traditional gender ideology" (p. 75). J. N. Laditka and S. B. Laditka (2000), who describe many of the same family scenarios, confirm that daughters are more likely to give elderly parents more care than sons.

A study by Franks, Pierce, and Dwyer (2004) looked at normative, individual, and contextual characteristics of being *primarily* responsible for an ill parent. They were not found to expect to provide primary care for their parents and, overall, they did not expect a significant level of involvement in this care. It also was found that the number of siblings (sisters, specifically) in a family affected their expectations regarding primary care. Among the influences on expectations, the authors proposed, was the provision of primary care for *their* parents (the grandparents), setting the stage for future caregiving. This study also found no difference by gender among primary caregivers in a family. This is borne out by other research on sons' involvement in caregiving (see associated literature by Campbell and Martin-Matthews [2000] above).

Teofila

Teofila, age 89, had entered the nursing home from a hospital rehabilitation program after her third serious fall resulted in a broken hip. She had been widowed for about 10 years, had no children and, except for one niece, had no relatives who were either available or willing to take on regular contact with her.

Teofila had come to this country as a teenager, had worked and had been very independent and socially involved, active in both community and political life. She also had painted, done creative writing, and traveled abroad a great deal on her own. Now, the more frail and debilitated she became, the more angry and cantankerous her disposition, so that she alienated home care workers to the point where nursing home placement was the only viable option. At this point her niece took on the role of surrogate daughter, visiting her regularly and becoming her only link with remaining family members and the outside world that she had so reluctantly relinquished. However, the niece did this full of her own ambivalence and out of a sense of obligation. Of the large extended family Teofila had once been part of, only this one person made herself available for her.

In the case of Teofila and her niece/caregiver, both obligation and desire were clear variables. The obligation stemmed from historical intrafamilial factors: the niece felt she was carrying forward the prior family role obligation of *her* mother, Teofila's older sister. The niece also was acting out of a desire to get closer to a family member she remembered from childhood as someone who, like herself, had been a loner, felt different, ostracized, had been a renegade.

Teofila responded to the nursing home environment much as she had to the home care workers—with rage and orneriness. She blamed her niece for placing her in the nursing home. She resisted group involvement, but responded well to a short period of individual sessions with a student social worker and to aides that her family paid to provide her with some additional personal care. She found her loss of independence and her almost totally curtailed mobility unbearable, and seemed determined to defeat any efforts to make her quality of life better.

Caregiving daughters or their surrogates often have competing demands, which vary with the ages and stages of the family life cycle, according to S. J. Brody (1986). The demands of parent care on some older women increase at a time of life when their capacity to provide it is declining. Some daughters in their middle years or early stages of aging are able to take on this task, but others may be experiencing concomitant interpersonal losses that make it more difficult to deal with an elderly mother—for example, widowhood, chronic illness, lower energy level.

E. M. Brody (2004) reinforces the idea that placing a parent in a nursing home is often described by adult children as the most powerful decision they ever make. Even if family relations are basically warm and the necessity for placement is recognized, feelings of abandonment and rejection may be experienced by the daughter and the mother and, in turn, affect both mother and daughter. When the elderly person is in a state of intense anxiety about such potential placement, the psychological phenomenon of separation is experienced again, with whatever associations there were from an earlier period of the elderly person's life. Nursing home placement also carries the overtones of the forthcoming ultimate separation: death. This occurs, of course, in the face of the guilt-inducing cultural injunctions against placing an elderly parent in a nursing home, regardless of the real need to do so.

Alice

Alice, age 78, had only recently moved to the nursing home. She had agreed, very reluctantly, to leave the small apartment where she had lived independently since the death of her husband about five years before. Because of Alice's increasing physical problems, her daughter, who had several small children, had to "rescue" her—that is, take her to the doctor or the hospital with increasing frequency, and with considerable inconvenience to her own family. A nursing home placement seemed to offer the most practical solution. The daughter made the arrangements with misgivings and guilt.

Once in the nursing home, Alice expressed resentment about the daughter's involvement with her own family. She was cranky with staff and refused to become involved in any group or recreational activities. In fact, she chose to eat most of her meals by herself, in her room. "I didn't need anyone else when I lived alone, and I don't need anyone else now," she said. "Except my daughter!" Although her daughter visited several times a week—probably more than when Alice was well and living in her own apartment—she continued to demand more frequent visits, and assigned the daughter errands and shopping tasks. Once-per-week individual therapy sessions gave her an opportunity to vent her anger, but she resisted making any move to become more involved in the social life of the nursing home.

Once the placement has occurred, there ensue all the problems associated with daughters visiting, phoning, providing linkage to the larger family outside, and so forth. Although this attention has the expected strains attendant on these new roles, it does confound the myth that daughters—or their surrogates—overcome their ambivalence by their attention. Individual and group therapy can improve such situations and resolve some of the strains. In the future, with demographics in flux, it can be expected that growing numbers of adult children will have parents in long term care facilities, barring the possibility that some dramatic scientific discovery will prevent or cure some of the major disabling diseases of aging, such as Alzheimer's, which in turn could cause a sharp drop in the nursing home population.

According to E. M. Brody (2004), women have always been responsive to social values. She says that although a majority of the middle generation of women is in the labor force, the strength of their attitudes about filial responsibility is compelling evidence that the old values remain strong. This makes them particularly vulnerable to the stress and conflict of role overload.

According to demographic trends (U.S. Department of Health and Human Services, 1998), by 2050 life expectancy will be 83 years. There were 3.1 million older people, representing four percent of the population in 1900; that number rose to 34 million older people in 1999 (i.e., one in eight persons was considered older). Not only is this increase accounted for by improved welfare programs, but by better nutrition, antibiotics, and ways to prevent epidemic diseases. The number of elderly is projected to increase to 70 million by 2030, or 20 percent of the total population. By the year 2000, older men were much more likely to be married (74 percent of men versus 43 percent of women). In relation to caregiving, more wives were likely to care for husbands, with an accompanying increase in need for care of the disabled spouses.

The falling birth rate has also affected the ratio between young and older generations, so that older people have fewer children responsible for parent care. With many more children having parents who survive until the children reach maturity, and parents surviving to have great-grandchildren, the very old people will have adult children who are also old. Of the "sandwich generation" (those aged 45–55, the baby boomers), 70 percent have at least one surviving parent and four out of 10 have children still living at home. According to the Center on Aging Society in 1999, two-thirds of caregiving daughters of the elderly were aged 45–64, and more than 15 percent were over 65! Medical breakthroughs may alter the picture, with chronic ailments like AIDS, Alzheimer's disease, and arthritis increasing the number of elderly requiring care, although these diseases may become more chronic than acute. Thus, women can expect to spend more time caring for an aging parent than for a dependent child. An older woman can expect to require help from her daughter and/or to be the caregiver of such care in later middle age to *her* mother.

Haggan (1998), summarizing work by other researchers, says there is an ever-increasing need to counsel adult children about their caring for disabled and chronically ill older parents. He says that "their adult children have (not) been socialized to optimally

cope with the intergenerational issues involved with increased longevity and fewer caregivers" (p. 333). He suggests ways to counsel
these adults to deal with issues such as dependency, loneliness, and
communication, as well as financial, occupational, marital, and end-
of-life matters.

THERAPY GROUP THEMES

In the therapy groups with women in the nursing home, discussed
in chapter 4, there are allusions to mother/daughter relationships
connected to a variety of the themes. The following are excerpts
from statements women made in group therapy sessions. (Note: All
of the nursing home participants in the groups were moderately
impaired for cognitive functioning.)

Regarding children helping to support parents:

Therapist: Can you remember something from when you were
    25?

Edna, age 92: My father left home and traveled around the
    world . . . and I was helping to support my older parents when
    I was 20. Nowadays, there are hardly any children who do this;
    mostly it's parents who support children! . . . You couldn't get
    married if you had parents to support . . . our parents were a
    responsibility to us . . . now families seem to be younger.

**Regarding separation issues and independence, even as a
grown woman:**

Maria, age 85: My mother didn't like me to travel. She said,
    "What do you have to go so many miles away for?" She never
    liked us to travel too far from home. And I said, "I'll be all
    right." . . . They didn't want me to go too far . . . I might end
    up in the hospital.

Another example:

Therapist: We're talking about remembering, about when you
    were 50. Did you go anywhere special, take any trips when
    your children were grown?

Ethel, age 86: My children didn't leave home until very late;
    they stayed with me, and kept me company . . . they didn't get

married until much later. . . . They were a little hesitant about leaving, for fear I would be left alone; so they stayed with me. . . .

Another example:

Therapist (to Anastasia, age 90): When did you make that trip to Europe?

Anastasia: In my forties. I didn't go too far from my mother's house. . . . She had her own home, but we lived close to her so we could take care of her.

Regarding working and looking after elderly parents:

Therapist (to Anastasia): Did you have children you looked after?

Anastasia: I looked after other people's children, and I worked, although I stopped working before it was time to retire (at 65) because my elderly mother needed me at home. . . . She'd say, "I miss you and I want you home." So I stopped working.

Times are clearly changing in terms of women's power in society and in their roles as senior members of the population. Women who are reaching middle and old age in the twenty-first century indeed have lived different lives from those in prior centuries—different even from those reaching 60 and older in the 1990s. As E. M. Brody (2004) reminds us, a continuing increase in the elderly population is not to be viewed negatively. "Each new cohort of older people in past decades has been progressively healthier, better educated, and has enjoyed higher incomes and more leisure" (p. 324). We can also expect that this will impact the younger generation of caregivers, as well; many more children will get to know grandparents and great-grandparents, and parents can raise children without fear that the children will be carried off by epidemics. In addition, older people who are a source of financial and emotional support for young grandchildren will be there to supply those and other resources to families.

REFERENCES

Archer, C. K., & MacLean, M. J. (1993). Husbands and sons as caregivers of chronically ill elderly women. *Journal of Gerontological Social Work, 21*(1/2), 5–23.

Brody, E. M. (2004). *Women in the middle: Their parent-care years* (2nd ed.). New York: Springer.

Brody, S. J. (1986). Impact of the formal support system on the elderly. In S. J. Brody & G. E. Ruff (Eds.). *Aging and rehabilitation: Advances in the state of the art* (pp. 62–86). New York: Springer.

Bumagin, V. E., & Hein, K. F. (2001). *Caregiving: A guide for those who give care and those who receive it.* New York: Springer.

Campbell, L. D., & Martin-Matthews, A. (2000). Caring sons: Exploring men's involvements in filial care. *Canadian Journal on Aging, 19*(1), 57–97.

Caplan, P. (1989). *Don't blame mother: Mending mother–daughter relations.* New York: Harper & Row.

Center on Aging Society. (1999). Analysis of data from the 1999 NLTCS-Beta Release Version 3.0. Washington, DC: Author.

Chodorow, N. (1989). *Feminism and psychoanalytic theory.* New Haven, CT: Yale University Press.

Dinnerstein, D. (1976). *The mermaid and the minotaur: Sexual arrangements and human malaise.* New York: Harper Colophon.

Franks, M. M., Pierce, L. S., & Dwyer, J. W. (2003). Expected parent-care involvement of adult children. *Journal of Applied Gerontology, 22*(1), 104–117.

Friday, N. (1977). *My mother, myself.* New York: Knopf.

Haggan, P. S. (1998). Counseling adult children of aging parents. *Educational Gerontology, 24*, 333–348.

Hebert, R., Levesque, L., Vezina, J., Lavoie, J-P., Ducharme, F., Gendron, C., Preville, M., Voyer, L., & Dubois, M-F. (2003). Efficacy of a psychoeducative group program for caregivers of demented persons living at home: A randomized controlled trial. *Journals of Gerontology, 58B*(1), S58–S67.

Herman, N. (1989). *Too long a child.* London: Free Association Books.

Hite, S. (1990). "I hope I'm not like my mother." *Women and Therapy, 10*(1/2), 13–30.

Laditka, J. N., & Laditka, S. B. (2000). Aging children and their older parents: The coming generation of caregiving. *Journal of Women and Aging, 62*(1), 189–204.

Lessing, D. (1970). *Martha Quest.* New York: NAL-Dutton.

Mancini, J. A. (1989). *Aging parents and adult children.* Lexington, MA: Lexington Books.

Musil, C. M., Youngblut, J. M., Ahn, S., & Curry, V. L. (2002). Parenting stress: A comparison of grandmother caretakers and mothers. *Journal of Mental Health and Aging, 8*(1), 197–201.

Neisser, E. G. (1967). *Mothers and daughters.* New York: Harper & Row.

Peters-Davis, N. D., Moss, M. S., & Pruchno, R. A. (1999). Children-in-law in caregiving families. *Gerontologist, 39*(1), 66–75.

Rich, A. (1976). *Of woman born: Motherhood as experience and institution.* New York: Norton.

Sun, R. (2002). Old age support in contemporary urban China from both parents' and children's perspective. *Research on Aging, 24*(2), 337–359.

U.S. Department of Health and Human Services, Administration on Aging. (1998). *A profile of older Americans: 1998.* Washington, DC: Author.

U.S. Department of Health and Human Services, Center on Aging Society. (1999). Unpublished data (quoted in E. M. Brody, 2004, *Women in the middle: Their parent care years*, p. 40, New York: Springer). Washington, DC: Author.

Walker, A. (1983). *In search of our mothers' gardens*. San Diego, CA: Harcourt Brace Jovanovich.

Woolf, V. (1929). *A room of one's own*. San Diego, CA: Harcourt Brace Jovanovich.

Chapter 6

Working With Alzheimer's Disease Residents of a Nursing Home

Claire M. Brody

This chapter outlines a project to involve women nursing home residents with Alzheimer's disease in a therapeutic endeavor. Other innovative programs for evaluating such clients and diverse new management strategies that have been used in a variety of settings are also described.

FINDINGS FROM THE LITERATURE

The cost of Alzheimer's disease (AD) is high, although reliable estimates are not available, according to Bloom, de Pouvourville, and Strauss (2003). Costs are also likely to rise in this country, as will policy initiatives, from basic science research to end-of-life care. In the United States, estimates of the cost of AD range from $5.6 to $88 billion per year, because of study design and quality of methodology, as well as indirect costs. Long-term care and family costs are the most important determinants of the overall cost. Also, costs increase with disease severity and a decline in any activity of living. When those with mild or moderate AD severity are considered, the cost goes up; the costs of care at home are higher than in a nursing home.

In predicting costs, Gaugler, Kane, Clary, and Newcomer (2003) found it was important to incorporate both care recipient and caregiver function and service-use patterns when targeting programs to prevent or delay institutionalization for people with dementia. Care recipient demographics, such as age, race, medical status, and living alone were all important predictors of the time to institutionalize. Important caregiver variables are shifts in their own instrumental tasks performance.

Gottlieb (1990) and other researchers noted evidence that rehabilitative strategies can preserve the assets remaining and improve at least short-term functioning for persons with severe cognitive decline. With this in mind, after a review of recent literature, in the following pages I will propose a project for a group with moderate cognitive deficit. Some of the procedures used could be adapted for differentially diagnosing the level of cognitive functioning, with the objective of forming more homogeneous groups of residents, if this is desirable. Gottlieb describes three major phases (mild, moderate, and severe) of AD, in order to place clients in a homogeneous group for rehabilitation purposes. There is an expected progression within these phases. These differentiations are still applicable today.

Very Mild Cognitive Decline: Forgetfulness phase with little decline in competence.

Mild Cognitive Decline: Early confusional phase, with objective evidence of memory impairment and concentration deficits.

Moderate Cognitive Decline: Late confusional stage, with diminished ability to recall recent and current events and deficits in recalling personal history.

Moderately Severe Cognitive Decline: Early dementia phase, with severe memory deficits and disorientation common. The person may still recall his or her own name and children's names and may require no help with eating or toileting.

Severe Cognitive Decline: "Middle mentia" phase, where the person retains limited knowledge of past events, but cannot describe any recent events. This is the stage when treatment for "wandering" can be tried (see McGrowder & Bhatt [1998] below).

Very Severe Cognitive Decline: Late dementia phase, where Gottlieb believes that stage appropriate rehabilitation strategies
may prolong preservation of retained assets and improve
short-term functional outcomes.

Kasi-Godley and Gatz (2000) state that over the last 20 years
there has been an increased understanding of the different varieties
of dementia: Alzheimer's disease and vascular dementia, including
multi-infarct dementia. From conducting their clinical interviews and
observations, they conclude that there are differences in symptomatology, subjective experiences, behavioral disturbances, personality changes, disturbances of affect, and multiple cognitive domains
(language, problem solving, judgment, visuospatial abilities). They
suggest a variety of psychosocial interventions for individuals with
dementia, including psychodynamic approaches, reminiscence and
life review therapy, supportive groups, reality orientation, memory
training, and cognitive/behavioral approaches. They conclude that
whereas different interventions target particular factors and place
emphasis on different goals, all of the suggested approaches help
those with mild impairments more than those with more advanced
levels of the condition, with significant overlaps among the approaches.

Some approaches do better at promoting interpersonal and in-
trapersonal functioning (reminiscence and life review therapy, support groups). Others deal with reducing confusion in disoriented
individuals (reality orientation), and there does seem to be an increasing convergence of memory training and behavioral interventions. Again, these authors point out that individuals in the early
stages of dementia appear to respond to most principles of learning,
whereas those with moderate impairment may still respond to reinforcement, but show less sensitivity to *schedules* of reinforcement.
"In later stages of dementia, techniques cannot rely on the individual's active participation" (p. 776). Types of behavioral problems that
can be addressed include wandering, agitation, self-care, and depression.

Nomura (2002) refers to Bender, Bauckham, and Norris (1999)
when talking about the "therapeutic purposes" of reminiscence. For
people with dementia it is not therapy because people are referred

who do not perceive they have a problem. At the same time it provides a "historical identity" while it allows people to "rework troubling parts of their lives" (p. 290). People generally enjoy being listened to and respected, although in Nomura's study there was no significant effect of the reminiscence group on Alzheimer-type dementia in terms of cognitive functioning. However, in the group for people with vascular dementia, rather than being stimulated by the materials, goods, and tools that were used, the group's reminiscing was invoked and mediated through social interaction with other members. This has been confirmed by the groups that I have led.

It has been said (Bergener, Hasegawa, Finkel, & Nishimura, 1992) that no one should be surprised at the variability in the estimate of dementia reported in surveys throughout the world. Dementia is, rather, a "continua" (p. 66). Different observers place "cut points" at different positions on the continuum both in diagnostic criteria and in the diagnostic instruments used for case detection. As of 1992, these authors continue, there were no sociodemographic or environmental correlates of prevalence that were without refute, other than age itself.

In referring to "Angie" who lives in an assisted living facility (ALF), I cite her (C. M. Brody, 1999) as an example of a client with whom a therapist might not ordinarily choose to work because of her poor prognosis. Over about a 10-year period of working with her, her dementia went from early stage to moderate impairment, and she eventually lost the power of speech altogether. The therapist did not abandon her, accepted her declining abilities, and communicated with her largely nonverbally. In fact, when she was finally transferred to a "good" nursing home, the director could not understand why the therapist proposed to continue her weekly visits if Angie, in fact, didn't talk! (See Duffy's [1999] comments below.)

In a study in Italy by Paaza, Sofarizzi, and Mastroianni (1996), there was an improvement in memory test scores as a result of neuropsychological training on memory performances in the early stages of degenerative dementia with those who had mild memory impairment. This confirmed work done earlier by Yesavage, Lapp, and Sheikh (1987). The improvement was in visuoverbal memory for the population studied; with this training, older subjects with cognitive slowing down might show improvement of selective attentive capabilities and visual memory.

Zarit, Femia, Watson, Rice-Oeschger, and Kakos (2004) recently described a program of treatment in a nursing home that deals with the common problem of memory loss. The 10-session group program, which also provided information about memory loss, offered resources for those coping with it and their partners, in an emotionally supportive atmosphere. In early stage dementia, people are facing inevitable decline, and they find it helpful to talk with peers who are in the same circumstances. It also helps the caregiving dyad function as a team to communicate more effectively. They learn coping strategies for memory loss and experience grief and loss together, while learning about the disease and treatment options. "The structure of the group, which provided time for the dyad to be together and time when they were apart with their peers, was a key to the success of the program" (p. 268). The group was able to discuss long-standing family problems that could be worsened by AD. Other problems that could be discussed include the decision to leave a job, trying medication for memory loss, finding ways to continue to feel useful, and, in general, discussing one's illness with family and friends.

For the Alzheimer's symptom of "wandering" as a management problem in an institutional setting, McGrowder and Bhatt (1988) suggested creating a "wanderer's lounge." This simple remedy also served to reduce the use of physical and pharmacological restraints. It was hypothesized that in addition to providing respite for the more alert nursing home residents from the invasiveness of the afflicted residents, it also increased the cognitive functioning of those with whom it was tried. The program included a $1^1/_2$- to 2-hour daily session of sequenced introductions to each other, warm-up exercises, a scheduled activity such as a discussion, refreshments, dancing, or quiet time. Over a period of four years, of those who continued, there was an increased level of participation in "higher level" institutional activities, decreased screaming, greater continence, sleeping rather than wandering at night, and more friendly interaction with peers. In another, more recent procedure for dealing with "wandering," Sanders, Brockway, Ellis, Cotton, and Bredin (1999) suggested that a behavioral data collection system be set up to determine what antecedent conditions consistently preceded wandering behavior. They indicate that a program needs to be flexible, and that observations need to be explained to both resident and family.

Moye, Karel, Azar, and Guerrera (2004) found that most adults with mild dementia could also participate in medical decision making as defined by legal standards. However, according to Dobalian

(2004), those with dementia may have difficulty reasoning about treatment options. In these cases, it would be best to focus on whether demented persons can describe salient reasons for a specific choice; they also should be helped, the authors state, to focus on the implications of the choices for future states. Strategies to compensate for their problem with verbal recall, processing, and planning can be devised. This also applies in end-of-life care decisions about "Do Not Hospitalize" orders. These are effective services for promoting patient wishes for medical services in nursing homes. (Further research is needed to determine why nursing homes do not always comply with these orders.) Dobalian discovered that hospitalized residents with "DNH" orders appeared to be "sicker" than non-hospitalized residents, but no particular pattern was evident in relation to health status.

Solomon and Jennings (1998) also studied AD in the terminal phases of the illness, and said, "We argue that palliative and hospice care are appropriate treatment options for Alzheimer's patients under certain conditions and especially during the terminal phase of this disease when life-prolonging medical technology offers little meaningful benefit to the patient" (p. 134). At this phase, pain relief for some of the associated physical problems is of primary concern.

Gilley, Wilson, Bienas, Bennett, and Evans (2004) conducted a study in which they assessed depressive symptoms in persons with dementia. Two factors were explored that may contribute to the development of depressive symptoms in AD: the individual's lifelong pattern of emotional responses, and temperament, presumably reflecting the cumulative effects on brain chemistry. In fact, the premorbid personality and cognitive impairment level, along with age and gender, were found to reliably predict depressive symptoms. This study will need to be replicated.

E. M. Brody (2004), writing about "special care" units in nursing homes, said that although there is no consensus about the definition of an "Alzheimer's unit," the criterion generally is a homogenous group of residents with a dementing illness who are segregated from those who are intact cognitively. Special training for staff, therapeutic environmental modifications, and an increased number of activity programs should be included. It is just such a program that will be described here.

Davis and colleagues (2000) conducted a study of dementia programs in a variety of residential care facilities. Although the results are controversial, they suggest that smaller facilities offer some unique possibilities, including a more homelike setting, lower cost, and more flexibility. However, the United States system of care for older persons is still evolving, with a trend toward residential care homes serving increasing numbers of older persons with dementia. Formerly, many of the latter would have been placed in nursing homes with special care units (see E. M. Brody's definition, above), or special dementia programs. At this time, there is no clear-cut difference between the programs in the larger and smaller facilities.

The U.S. Congress Office of Technology Assessment (OTA) report (1987) emphasized the necessity of including measures of cognitive ability in surveys of elderly, long-term care populations. It is just as true today. Behavior descriptors alone, although pointing to severe disabilities, could apply to some persons who do not have true dementia. Often, the staff of a nursing home does not distinguish between cognitive impairments caused by dementia disorders and those due to other factors, such as hearing and speech impairments, emotional withdrawal, acute and chronic diseases, and so forth. This report also suggests that despite a growing movement in nursing home care to provide special units within a given institution for the treatment and care of dementia patients, an estimated 60 to 74 percent of nursing home residents with dementia are in "traditional mixed units" (p. 256). It should again be noted that this estimate was as of 1987.

Fernie and Fernie (1990) suggest that in organizing group programs in a nursing home it is better to have "minimally heterogeneous" groups. That is, it is preferable to put mildly confused with mentally alert residents than mildly confused with very confused residents. Additional variables to consider, specifically for AD clients, would be their prior experience with groups, their ability to communicate verbally, adequate hearing and vision, and cooperativeness. These authors recommend reminiscence themes, as well as groups that involve new activities. Maintaining consistent starting times and having more than one 30- to 45-minute meeting session in a week are also suggested. There is an emphasis on group trust and bonding and encouragement to participate. Just as in the groups I describe here, these therapists point to the importance of acknowledging new members by name and noting absent members in order to reinforce their value to the group. Remembering names can be facilitated by use of name tags. Members who tend to monopolize the group discussion are steered toward helping roles with other persons who have more difficulty participating. As these authors state, "passivity can be contagious; one member's apathy can, in turn, affect the motivation of others" (p. 131). A leader needs to use active encouragement for silent members. (See chapters 3 and 4 for the use of some of these techniques with heterogeneous groups.)

When considering the organizational logistics of running a dementia group in a nursing home, we must take into account its "system" and personnel, as well as the characteristics of the residents (Abramson & Mendis, 1990). First, the administrator of the institution must support the treatment plan because this, in turn, will affect the nurses, aides, and other personnel who will be involved. The goals of the group treatment, and how achieving these goals will enhance the facility, must also be clear. The degree to which group members are cognitively impaired is a very significant variable and will affect the overall goals of the group, as well as particular goals for individual members. Collaboration between the medical staff person, the psychologist, social worker, occupational and physical therapists, nurses, and aides is also essential for the success of the program. They stated that the overall needs for the *group* should reflect the composite needs of each individual. Depending on whether it is the early, middle, or late stage of the disorder, different therapeutic interventions will be required. All relevant staff members should provide assessment input. Not only is assessment needed for prospective members, but it is also needed to define an individual's limitations and abilities in the group.

Duffy (1999), writing in his own edited book, has been the model for most of my recent work with people with dementia. He advocates using whatever means possible to "reach the person behind the dementia," including subvocal and nonverbal strategies (see C. M. Brody's [1999] description of "Angie"). He says that speech communication theorists, often more expertly than mental health workers and psychologists, have a sophisticated classification to understand the various ways in which people communicate. Thus, in working with clients with dementia, a simple pat on the shoulder, or holding hands, is a way of communicating interest and concern. Duffy notes studies that show continuity in emotional life at the same time that there can be a decrement in logical thinking and language. He also says that the premorbid securely attached persons seem to do better in older life even under the conditions of dementia. He talks of the rich, idiosyncratic character that lurks just beneath the surface and commends therapists to be curious about it, and to do what they can to forge strong therapeutic relationships without necessarily relying on verbal strategies. "Touch" is one nonverbal strategy he suggests.

Ongoing communication among the institution's staff members is required in order to continually revise and define new goals for the individual group members. A therapist whose group activity revolves around exercising declining cognitive skills needs to integrate this activity with other forms of treatment being carried out by other staff specialists. I agree with Abramson and Mendis that dementia clients function best in small groups that are relatively stable (four to six members for each group leader). Details of the ideal number of members per group, method for replacement of dropouts, the basis for determination of member appropriateness, and so forth, should be worked out in advance. Persons with dementia respond well to repetition and consistency, which should be considered when deciding where and when to hold meetings. Cooperation for this is essential from the administrator and those staff who will be affected. Some of the most ideal concomitants of a therapy group may simply not be possible in any given nursing home.

A program specific for use with Alzheimer's disease residents in a nursing home is described in detail by Zarit, Zarit, and Rosenberg-Thompson (1990). The environment is open and homelike, with controlled access and egress so that minimal use of medication and restraints is necessary. Behavioral treatment approaches described include, first, the use of problem solving by staff to "identify antecedents and consequences of targeted behavior, and general alternative responses," (p. 48) to reduce disruptive and other problem behaviors. The authors note that because clients who are active cause fewer problems than ones who are inactive, providing programs to involve them is advantageous. Using role-playing techniques that did not confront the client's (faulty) view of reality was helpful, especially where the focus was on the staff's attempt to accept the feelings or metaphorical import rather than literal meanings that the resident was communicating.

Nomura (2002) also describes in detail working in reminiscence groups with people with different kinds of dementia. The participants clearly expressed feeling that such groups helped them to connect their past and their present. In the *Alzheimer Care Quarterly*, Van Haitsma and Ruckdeschel (2001) describe a variety of programs for dementia in nursing homes. The programs generally fall into four categories: those that focus on individualization of care, ones to promote functional independence, ones utilizing technology of various sorts, and ones that utilize alternative therapies. The programs to be described here probably fall into the category of "alternative therapies" but they are also individualized and utilize enhancement of residents' psychosocial quality of life. The authors state that some approaches work with certain people and not with others; some also work better with those clients who have limited impairment. The vast majority of techniques have had few well controlled studies, but the outline of possibilities can be useful.

Maloney and Daily (1986), working with a dementia population in a nursing home, outline an approach with a philosophical base that includes

> respect for each resident's wisdom, life experience and individual-ity; [it is] non-judgmental, non-parental, affectionate, friendly, warm; [there is] genuine interest in the resident, respect for each resident's choice not to attend . . . the meeting; [an] expectation of appropriate behavior, appreciation of the expression of feelings while avoiding pressure to express them; recognition that each time a resident has participated in conversation or an activity, that they [sic] had made an effort to communicate beyond the barriers created by their sensory losses. This approach is main-tained regardless of the resident's behavior—before and after group meetings.

Reminiscing is used as a way of getting residents who otherwise were passive and uninvolved in their surroundings to interact with peers, to gain self-esteem from contributing to the group, and to gain a sense of contact with less feeling of isolation. This view is still relevant today. These authors use sensory stimuli objects while asking questions such as "What does this remind you of?"; "Have you ever eaten this before?" Stimuli might be tactile, auditory, visual, gustatory, olfactory, vestibular—all of which might increase the resi-dent's level of alertness. Sensory stimulation/sensory integration means using two or more stimuli simultaneously. What they call "re-motivation therapy" implies a structured, theme-centered format. Supplies for this kind of stimulation were mostly common household objects with no expense entailed—for example, nail files, lip balm, body lotions, kitchen utensils, and so on. These authors observed that physical contact—touching, rubbing hands, hugging between residents and staff—was an aid in establishing trust.

E. M. Brody (2004) says that the absence of increased nursing home use that was predicted earlier has multiple determinants. One of these determinants was the increase in home health care use from 1985 to 1995 and the increased use of assisted living as a substitute for nursing home placement (see chapter 9 on assisted living facilities). As a result, nursing home residents are older and more functionally disabled. As Brody explains, "Though nursing home care is usually thought to be a permanent plan, lasting to the resident's death, long-stay residents constitute only one of several different populations in these facilities" (p. 292). These disabled people move around frequently among institutions of various types (hospitals, rehabilitation centers) for many months before they become permanent residents of long-term stay facilities and eventually die there, or are moved to a hospital for terminal care. This often results in frustration, disorganization, and emotional strains on family members.

According to a recent report in the *AARP Bulletin* (Basler, 2004), residents in a San Francisco nursing home are "suing to get out in the world" (pp. 3ff.)! It is just one indication of how some older people are desperately trying to avoid going to or remaining in nursing homes. A class action suit—one of the first in the country—claims that whereas it costs less to maintain someone disabled in the community (about $130,000 less per year), disabled people who prefer that arrangement need not be institutionalized. Mainly, though, it takes the *wishes* of older persons into account in determining which placement would be better.

I tried a format similar to one used by Maloney and Daily with less confused residents—that is, introducing a theme that would lead the group through a progression of memories from childhood to old age. However, it was not sufficient to structure the sessions with direct questions or to elicit memories from silent members. What often was obtained with this confused population were rambling or repetitive verbalizations. There was still the difficulty of maintaining continuity from one week to the next if only one session per week was held. For this reason a more activity-oriented session was devised, with reminiscence a backdrop for the focus on "doing." Although groups for members with lesser or greater deficits than the group described below could be formed, the tasks described were used over a period of six months with a somewhat heterogeneous group that included women who had "Moderately Severe Cognitive Decline," according to Gottlieb's (1990) description.

What is most significant about this outline of Alzheimer's development is that "treatment" strategies are suggested for *all* phases of the disease, including the stages when nursing home care is most often prescribed. Even at this point it is possible to improve functioning and preserve assets.

SMALL GROUP ACTIVITIES

Four nursing home female residents with moderate cognitive decline and confusion met for a half-hour with the psychologist-therapist once per week. A relatively secluded area or closed off part of the dining room was used. They sat in a circle around a small table (no more than four or five feet in diameter).

Group members and the group leader introduced themselves by first name, but there was no emphasis on members recalling each other's names after this, as it was in the groups described in chapter 4. Each week a different activity was tried. As suggested by S. J. Brody and Pawlson (1990), these activities were largely intended to reinforce over-learned activities and to enhance the clients' feeling of control. In light of the usual equivocal diagnosis of Alzheimer's that preceded any individual group member's selection for this group, there was a wide variation in skill levels and attention capacities. A slightly better differential diagnostic picture was often achieved by the level of performance in these activities. In retrospect, initial use of these activities to differentiate the members might have resulted in a more homogeneous group. Some of the techniques used with these four women in the nursing home are discussed below.

Identifying Smells

The therapist brings a bottle of perfume to the meeting. The perfume has a fairly identifiable flowery smell. Each group member is allowed to sniff the bottle and then is asked questions that lead to increasing levels of cognitive functioning: (a) if they *can* smell something, (b) whether they *like* the smell, (c) what it reminds them of (hints are offered: a favorite flower, plant, food), and (d) if a memory is evoked, to share it.

Word Association

An index card is given to each participant, with a single word on it in bold letters—for example: house, dog, baby, car. Each person is then asked to make up a sentence, or to say something she associates with the word. If it is easier for the member to draw something instead of saying it, she can do this (paper and pencils are available in the center of the table). A second phase of this activity is initiated a few minutes later. Each member is asked to recall the word to which she was associating. Encouragement and hints are provided if group members have difficulty recalling the word. (They often do have such difficulty and prompts are helpful.)

Drawings of "Happy" and "Sad" Faces

A page with two drawings on it is presented—one with a "happy" face, and one with a "sad" face (see Figure 6.1). Each member, in turn, is asked to differentiate the faces by the two moods (for appropriateness of choice). Then, associations to the two faces are elicited from each person: "What does this face remind you of?" "Whose face in the group looks 'happy' or 'sad'?"

FIGURE 6.1   Drawing of "happy" and "sad" faces.

Drawings of "Male" and "Female" Heads

A single page with schematic drawings (no facial features) of a "male" and "female" head, with a stereotypical article of clothing, is provided for each member (see Figure 6.2). Each person is asked to fill in as much of the face of each figure as she wishes. If a feature—for example, the mouth—is left out, the therapist will prompt by asking, "What's missing?" Members are encouraged to work only on their own drawings. When each person is finished, she is asked to identify the drawing as someone familiar, or someone of whom it reminds her, and to say something about that person. Sometimes the discussion that ensues can revolve around gender differences.

Occasionally, the gender of the two drawings is indistinguishable by the features added. Sometimes the features are put in upside down, with disregard of cues provided by the clothing; sometimes one face is completed and the other is not, or there is obvious difficulty with one particular feature. All of these detail omissions are undoubtedly of psychological and/or neurological significance, but until more data are collected, interpretation is reserved. In any event, it does point up here the wide variation in levels of cognitive intactness that can be incorporated into one therapeutic activity.

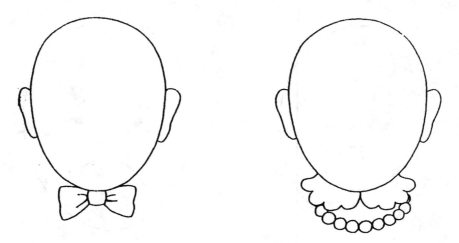

FIGURE 6.2   Drawing of "male" and "female" heads.

A schematic drawing of a whole human figure, without any features, is given to each member of the group (see Figure 6.3). With the instruction, "Dress it," they are asked to complete as much of the figure as they would like. When all members have finished, discussion is encouraged about their own drawings, questions can be asked about each other's, and a focus can evolve based on material provided in the drawings. For example, one woman added very explicit sexual organs to her naked male figure and there was heated

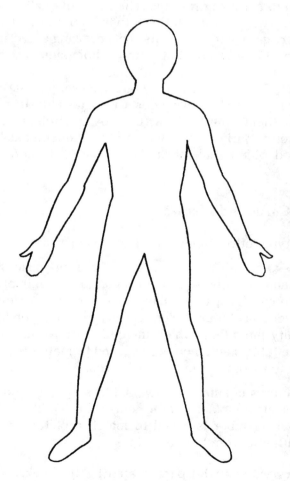

FIGURE 6.3 Drawing of a whole human figure.

response to her daringness, as well as some sharing of sexual fantasies.

House, Tree, Person

Three blank pieces of paper are provided, one at a time, and each member is asked to make the best picture that she can of a house, a tree, and a person. (This is similar to what is requested in the House, Tree, Person Projective Test.) Associations are obtained from each person to her own drawings. The range of quality of the drawings is usually wide, although the activity is not intended for those with severe cognitive impairments. This drawing exercise can often aid in composing a group that is more homogeneous for level of deficit.

If, in fact, the objective at the start of a group of AD clients is to make the group more homogeneous, then a task for the participants might be for them each to draw (or copy) a circle, then a square, then a diamond. Marked difficulty with the diamond has been found to be a good differential diagnostic measure of moderate cognitive deficit.

Matching Cards and Pictures

Pre-school type lotto or matching picture cards are provided.

(1)   An array of four cards with different basic shapes (for example circle, square, hexagon, triangle) is placed in the center of the table. Each member has in front of her a selection of four to eight cards (depending on level of difficulty intended), which include the ones in the center of the table. Each member is asked to match the ones in the center from her own set of cards.

(2)   Pictures of animals, flowers, birds, or common household objects are placed in the center of the table. One at a time, each member is asked to match a picture in the center with one from her set.

The four women who participated in the weekly small group activities showed some progress over the period of approximately three months. The two members who had more pronounced symptoms of Alzheimer's showed no exacerbation of their confusion and memory loss. Along with the two other moderately impaired women, they benefited from the socialization and the focusing of their attention on "doing." This succeeded better than the type of meeting where their inclination toward rambling verbalizations would have been enhanced. It seemed clear that participants with different levels of deficit could be incorporated into one group if the group was small enough.

CONCLUSIONS

The need will increase for qualified therapists sensitive to persons with Alzheimer's disease's special needs and the realities and circumstances of their lives. More diverse methodologies (short-term or problem-centered therapy, small groups, and so forth) and locations for therapy (community settings, long-term care facilities, home) will need to be considered. Therapists who view impairments in the elderly as potentially reversible, and not as inevitable destiny, are imperative. Because there also was evidence from some of the small-group activities with Alzheimer clients (e.g., drawings of shapes and figures) that performance might be a good differential diagnostic measure for assessing cognitive deficit, further research along these lines would be valuable, and not only to establish more homogeneous groups, but to work on diverse methodologies, as well.

The growth in number of nursing home beds (U.S. Department of Health and Human Services, 1999) from 25,000 in 1200 homes in 1939, to over 1.6 million in 18,000 facilities in 1999, is accounted for by the number of vulnerable older people (as well as the number of retarded persons over 65) who reach advanced old age, and by the increase in federal programs making funds available (E. M. Brody, 2004). Brody points out that the amount of social support in the family is a critical factor in avoiding nursing home placement, as well as related factors such as characteristics of the potential family members who could take care of these older people, instead. Additionally, she points out how truly difficult it is for families to cope with behavioral disturbances that such older persons often exhibit (as in dementia). There is thus no one reason for institutionalization;

it is multiply determined. Often it is when there is no other possible solution that it takes place.

REFERENCES

Abramson, T. A., & Mendis, K. P. (1990). The organizational logistics of a dementia group in a skilled nursing facility. *Clinical Gerontologist, 9*(3/4), 111–122.

Basler, B. (2004, June). Suing to get out in the world. *AARP Bulletin, 3*, 11–12.

Bergener, M., Hasegawa, K., Finkel, S. I., & Nishimura, T. (1992). *Aging and mental disorders: International perspectives.* New York: Springer.

Bloom, B. S., de Pouvourville, N., & Straus, W. L. (2000). Cost of Alzheimer's disease: How useful are current estimates? *Gerontologist, 43*(2), 158–164.

Brody, C. M. (1999). Existential issues of hope and meaning in late life therapy. In M. Duffy (Ed.). *Handbook of counseling and psychotherapy in older adults* (pp. 91–106). New York: Wiley.

Brody, E. M. (2004). *Women in the middle: Their parent care years* (2nd ed.). New York: Springer.

Brody, S. J., & Pawlson, L. G. (Eds.). (1990). *Aging in rehabilitation.* New York: Springer.

Davis, K. J., Sloane, P. D., Mitchell, C. M., Preisser, J., Grant, L., Hawes, M. C., Lindeman, D., Montgomery, R., Long, K., Phillips, C., & Koch, G. (2000). Specialized dementia care programs in residential care settings. *Gerontologist, 40*(1), 30–42.

Dobalian, A. (2004). Nursing facility compliance with "Do Not Hospitalize" orders. *Gerontologist, 43*(2), 159–165.

Duffy, M. (1999). Reaching the person behind the dementia: Treating co-morbid, affective disorders through sub-vocal and nonverbal strategies. In M. Duffy (Ed.). *Handbook of counseling and psychotherapy in older adults* (pp. 577–589). New York: Wiley.

Fernie, B., & Fernie, G. (1990). Organizational group programs for cognitively impaired elderly residents of nursing homes. *Clinical Gerontologist, 9*(3/4), 123–134.

Gaugler, J. S., Kane, R. A., Clary, T., & Newcomer, R. (2003). Caregiving and institutionalization of cognitively impaired older people: Utilization of dynamic predictors of change. *Gerontologist, 43*(2), 219–229.

Gilley, D. W., Wilson, R. S., Bienas, J. L., Bennett, D. A., & Evans, D. A. (2004). Predictors of depressive symptoms in persons with Alzheimer's disease. *Journals of Gerontology, 59B*, P75–P83.

Gottlieb, C. (1990). Rehabilitation and dementia of the Alzheimer's type. In S. J. Brody & L. G. Pawlson (Eds.). *Aging and rehabilitation II: The state of the practice* (pp. 255–271). New York: Springer.

Kasi-Godley, J., & Gatz, M. (2000). Psychosocial interventions for individuals with dementia: An integration of theory, therapy, and a clinical understanding of dementia. *Clinical Psychology Review, 20*(6), 755–782.

Maloney, C. C., & Daily, T. (1986). An eclectic group program for nursing home residents with dementia. *Physical and Occupational Therapy in Geriatrics, 4*(3), 55–80.

McGrowder, L. R., & Bhatt, A. (1988). A wanderer's lounge program for nursing home residents with Alzheimer's disease. *Gerontologist, 28*(5), 607–609.

Moye, J. G., Karel, M. J., Azar, A. R., & Guerrera, R. J. (2004). Capacity to consent to treatment: Empirical comparison of three instruments in older adults with dementia. *Gerontologist, 44*(2), 166–175.

Nomura, T. (2002). Evaluative research on reminiscence groups for people with dementia. In J. D. Webster & B. K. Haight (Eds.). *Critical advances in reminiscence work: From theory to application* (pp. 289–299). New York: Springer.

Paaza, F., Sofarizzi, V., & Mastroianni, F. (1996). A rehabilitative program for mild memory impairments. *Archives of Gerontology and Geriatrics, 5*, 51–55.

Sanders, K., Brockway, J. A., Ellis, B., Cotton, E. M., & Bredin, J. (1999). Enhancing mental health climate in hospitals and nursing homes: Collaboration strategies for medical and mental health staffs. In M. Duffy (Ed.). *Handbook of counseling and psychotherapy with older adults* (pp. 335–349). New York: Wiley.

Solomon, M. Z., & Jennings, D. (1998). Palliative care for Alzheimer's patients: Implications for institutions, caregivers, families. In L. Volicer & A. Hurley (Eds.). *Hospice care for patients with advanced progressive dementia* (pp. 132–134). New York: Springer.

U.S. Congress Office of Technology Assessment (OTA). (1987). *Losing a million minds: Confronting the tragedy of Alzheimer's disease dementias.* OTA-BA-323. Washington, DC: U.S. Government Printing Office.

U.S. Department of Health and Human Services, National Center for Health Statistics. (1999). Unpublished data from the *National Nursing Home Survey, Table 3*. Washington, DC: Author.

Van Haitsma, K., & Ruckdeschel, K. (2001). Special care for dementia in nursing homes: Overview of innovations in programs and activities. *Alzheimer's Care Quarterly, 2*(3), 49–56.

Yesavage, J. A., Lapp, D., & Sheikh, J. I. (1987). *Mnemonics as modified for use by the elderly.* Hillsdale, NJ: Erlbaum.

Zarit, S. H., Femia, E. E., Watson, J., Rice-Oeschger, L., & Kakos, B. (2004). Memory club: A group intervention for people with early stage dementia and their care partner. *Gerontologist, 44*(2), 262–269.

Zarit, S. H., Zarit, J. M., & Rosenberg-Thompson, S. (1990). A special treatment unit for Alzheimer's disease: Medical, behavioral and environmental features. *Clinical Gerontologist, 9*(3/4), 47–63.

Part III

Issues of the Elderly in the Community

Chapter 7

Caregiving: An Overview With Clinical Examples

Miriam E. Lemerman

A CONCERN OVER TIME

Until several generations ago, it was customary in Europe and the United States for the elderly to be taken care of by their children. In some homes, the elderly were taken in as a matter of course. Multigenerational families were not an anomaly. This has been a prevalent family pattern for hundreds if not thousands of years. However, societal patterns evolve and change. Our workforce has grown to be more technically oriented since World War II. Women have joined the workforce in unprecedented numbers. Fewer people have been available to take care of the frail elderly in their own residences or in the homes of family members. Therefore, there has been a significant expansion of assisted living facilities, senior residences, and nursing homes to care for senior citizens who had formerly lived with their now deceased spouses, on their own, or with their children.

I would like to thank Joseph Martino, Jr. and Diane Miller for their sharing of thoughts and feelings, Judith Rubin Florek for her practical and enthusiastic assistance, Dr. Vicki Semel and Dr. Claire Brody for their understanding and guidance, and my mother, Lillian Lemerman, who has been my teacher in caring.

Elderly people living on their own share the basic needs of all of us. Cooking, cleaning, and taking care of themselves in all ways from eating nutritionally to being properly clothed are basic and essential activities. Sociability is another crucial dimension for seniors. People tend to do better physically and mentally when their lives include human connections. Many elderly individuals lack these connections; they have no children, no friends, and relatives are out of touch. These are the elderly about whom the community must be especially concerned.

Various caregiving arrangements exist today for the elderly. Some seniors reside with their families. Some elderly live on their own but have family or friends close by to supervise and/or care for them. Paid workers are sometimes brought into the home on a full-time or part-time basis to care for the elderly and infirm.

THE FAMILY CAREGIVER

All of the above caregiving situations are commonplace in our society. This chapter, however, concentrates on caregivers who are not monetarily compensated for their help, focusing primarily on family members taking care of an elderly relative. Their role of assisting the elder with the basic requirements of daily living is compounded by the emotional demands of ministering to someone who, in the past, took care of them. The complex interpersonal history of the caregiver and senior becomes entwined with emotions provoked by the elder's loss of independence and freedom. As a result of these complicated dynamics, anger and frustration are often experienced by the cared-for and caregiver alike.

A question, among many other questions for our age is: "Who is taking care of the caregiver?" Very often the caregiver is a working woman or man who is the son or daughter of an elderly parent. Typically, business and/or professional duties occupy this individual's day, and activities and concerns relating to spouse and/or children occupy the evenings and weekends. Where is the time for the caregiver? His or her needs also have to be met. Doctor's appointments have to be kept; food shopping has to be done. What about quality time with one's family and friends? Many of these activities are all too often placed on the back burner or are tremendously curtailed when the component of caregiving comes into play.

Lives of expanded responsibilities are common among an increasingly vast number of people. Chryss Cada (2000) has offered statistics that reveal a growing care gap:

> Twenty-two percent of the American people have eldercare responsibilities while raising their own families, according to information from Work/Family Directions, Inc., a Boston-based consulting firm. By 2020, there will be 15 million Americans who are 85 and older, and by 2050, 22% of the population will be 65 and older. With so many people waiting longer to have children, a growing number of folks between 40 and 60 are ending up in the so-called "sandwich generation" (para 7).

Caregiving in the home entails a labor-intensive, emotionally absorbing, and often physically taxing one-on-one relationship between the senior and the caregiver. Basic tasks can be accomplished through an umbrella situation whereby siblings in one family divide up the work. One may do the grocery shopping; one may pay the bills; another may act as dad's nurse, seeing that he's bathed and takes his medications. If there are more siblings, the tasks sometimes rotate. This scenario, however, constitutes the ideal situation rather than the norm. In many families, the responsibility of taking care of an elderly parent falls solely upon one of the children—usually a daughter who is single, divorced, but, in many cases, a married daughter or daughter-in-law. The caregiver of an elderly man is very often his elderly wife.

There are many levels of supervision and assistance that are involved in the caregiving enterprise. When an elderly person is mentally competent and is physically able to perform the tasks of daily living (toileting, bathing, feeding, and so forth), the caregiver does not have to provide hands-on assistance. Instead, the caregiver's role may be to procure outside services for specific purposes such as helping the senior with public or municipally sponsored transportation. Sometimes such services are not available or financially feasible. The caregiver then must pitch in to help the senior with these chores or do the chores for the senior. The list of tasks can be extensive. There is grocery shopping and there are appointments with doctors. Often, there are maintenance issues to manage. The senior may need to be helped with basic housekeeping or with hiring cleaning help and craftsmen. Some seniors can manage their own finances; others require assistance with their paperwork and their money management. How labor-intensive and stressful these responsibilities can be for both senior and caregiver!

A DELICATE BALANCE

It is not surprising to see workshops and seminars offered to caregivers. One such workshop is entitled "Caretaking for an Elderly Individual: Managing Your Emotions" (Albert Ellis Institute, 2003). This workshop focuses on emotional aspects of caregiving, such as the anger, frustration, and depression often experienced by the caregiver. The workshop's goal is to address psychological issues and help to alleviate the impact of stress associated with caring for the elderly.

Given the emotional strain and physical effort of the caregiving role, it is important for the caregiver to seek help wherever and however available. Ask other family members to partake in the day-in, day-out caregiving duties and let family and friends pitch in. When there are adequate funds, hire a housekeeper or an aide. Take advantage of available resources, either within the community or at the elder's home, to enrich his or her life with activities while being supervised by others. The caregiver must arrange relaxing times for him- or herself. This leisure time may include rest, sports, bridge, reading, or just lolling in front of the television. It is imperative that some time be set aside for the caregiver, not just to provide an opportunity for rejuvenation before attacking the next list of caregiving duties, but so that the caregiver can have a life of his or her own, too.

Sometimes, when caregiving becomes too much, it is important for the caregiver to see a therapist and discuss the many issues that bubble up over a lifetime of connectedness. Participating in a therapy group with other caregivers can also be of great value in reducing the sense of aloneness and isolation that often surfaces.

Caregivers often rely upon outside resources to assist in their tasks. There are community agencies that provide supervised day-care for ambulatory older adults. Local churches, synagogues, community centers, and municipal and county governments sponsor these agencies. Senior centers provide activities, meals, and comfortable settings where seniors can congregate and socialize. These resources provide an excellent vehicle for the elderly to engage in structured, meaningful, and sustaining activities.

When a senior lives in his or her own home or with family members, the caregiver's role becomes more expansive. The elder's living environment must be carefully and continuously inspected to ensure that it is safe. Floors must be checked to make sure that rugs are secured. Stairways must be provided with double railings so the senior can go from level to level with support and assuredness. Home maintenance includes preserving structural quality as well as maintaining the cleanliness and order of the premises. If the senior can't do it alone, assistance must be provided by outside help (if financially feasible) or directly by the caregiver, friends, or relatives.

What about sociability for the senior who cannot or will not attend functions in the community? The housebound senior benefits from visits by family, neighbors, and friends. The elder certainly derives stimulation and pleasure from the relationship with the caregiver (although not always, and not all the time). Some seniors do not appear to desire or need much attention. As long as they are well tended and physically comfortable, they seem satisfied. Much depends on the senior's character. Some people are accepting and uncomplaining about no longer having the life of yesteryear. They may mourn the loss of their past, but they have no desire to establish new friends, relationships, and interests. The caregiver must learn when to encourage and when to let up. Elders can't be pushed to do something that they don't want to do. One must learn to "follow the contact." If the senior wants to reach out and socialize or converse, respond in kind. If the elder would rather remain quiet, don't try to force conversation. If not pushed or pressured, the senior may voluntarily become more conversational. Learn to respect silences. They can be restful for both parties. Instead of feeling infantilized by being cajoled into conversation, the senior will feel respected. The need for insulation and following the contact is an approach that stems from the writings of Nagelberg and Feldman (1987).

A MULTI-TALENTED CAREGIVER . . . A SENSITIVE COMMUNICATOR

The ideal caregiver is clearly a multi-talented person. Physical duties such as bathing, toileting, and even diapering are required when the

senior is frail. On another level, psychological insight and percepti-
vity are needed to recognize and provide the appropriate level of
attention, encouragement, quiet respect, and response.

One of the hallmarks of our time is verbalization. We hear words
all day on the radio, television, cinema, and DVDs, in addition to
our conversations. We tend to place great value on speech and feel
we must always be a participant, a "talker." One of the delights of
being a caregiver is that it may provide us with an opportunity to
be with someone without constantly talking—just being. Giving the
senior his or her "space," giving both parties the opportunity to just
be with one another, could move the relationship to a whole new
level—perhaps a greater level of intimacy and, for the senior, relaxed
and freer exchange.

Another point to keep in mind is the protection of the patient's
ego. For example, rather than saying, "Why can't you climb those
steps? I'm sure you could if you tried," the caregiver might instead
ask, "What makes those steps so difficult?" Place the focus on the
inanimate object (the steps) and take the focus off the person. Ask
object-oriented questions (e.g., "How was breakfast?" "What's the
weather report?") instead of asking questions that focus on the
senior's frailties (e.g., "Are you still feeling sick?" "How is your
back?"). Avoid ego-invading questions that could result in the elder
closing down and the ultimate diminution of communication.

When dealing with an elderly parent, one can often see that
certain behaviors and attitudes are not necessarily genuine. They
are cover-ups for feelings that may not be sanguine, feelings the
senior finds hard to tolerate and more difficult to express. Zukerman
(2003), in an informative book called *Eldercare for Dummies*, lists
ten ways that the elderly hide their feelings and recommends ways
to deal with self-deceptions. "Don't rush to expose your elder's self-
deceptions. If they help her cope and do no harm, leave well enough
alone" (p. 333).

One of the key roles of the caregiver is communicating with the
elder's physician and other health care professionals. Procedures
for obtaining necessary medical appointments must be accurately
followed. Diagnoses and treatment, as explained by the doctor, must
be clearly understood and noted. Naturally, the patient should be
encouraged to communicate directly with health care professionals.
At times, however, a back-up person may be needed to get the

correct information. My 89-year-old mother recently needed to make an appointment with a physical therapist. When she phoned the office, she was put on hold and, later, was prompted to answer questions via a recording. Because this seemed daunting to her, I completed the task. According to the Internet citing of CareGuide, Care for Caregivers—Communicating With Your Aging Parent's Physician (1996–2004, para 7), one must sensitively choose one's interventions.

When a physician reviews medication dosages and prescription adjustments, the process is often made more understandable when the caregiver is there to ask questions and request clarification. Within the intricate world of medical care, there are some situations that the patient can independently handle and there are other situations when the presence of a caregiver, with a "second set of ears," reduces anxiety and improves the likelihood of successful treatment.

When caregivers do not live near the person for whom they are responsible, elder care becomes much more difficult. "Approximately seven million Americans are involved in providing care for another person who may live over one hour away" (CareGuide, Care for Caregivers—Long Distance Caregiving: The Basics, 1998–2003). Extended travel time produces added physical and emotional stress for the caregiver. In a long-distance situation, friends or family members can sometimes be enlisted to help with daily tasks. If funds are adequate, one option is to hire a geriatric care manager to coordinate and schedule nurses and/or aides and handle various other aspects of care. This care manager might, for example, be in charge of hiring a housekeeper to manage the household, purchase food, prepare meals, and be responsible for basic maintenance. A geriatric care manager has a list of approved workers with the necessary qualifications to care for an elderly person in a healthy, well-kept environment. Geriatric care managers can be found through a variety of sources, including word-of-mouth, recommendations from reliable peers, and clergy (see resource listing at the end of this chapter).

A multitude of emotions come into play when hiring outside assistance for an elderly parent. The parent may resent the fact that a family member is bringing in a stranger and feel that the family member should be doing all the work him- or herself. The parent may resent the expenditure of funds. All these reactions can cause guilt for the caregiver. Feelings of guilt may eventually pass, but in the interim caregivers need to take care of themselves. If they have always deferred to others, they need to be very careful not to get sucked in and swallowed up. They must, even at an advanced middle age, learn to stand up to the situation. The physical and emotional consequences of capitulating to a parent's demands could be grave.

When one's parents begin losing their physical and/or cognitive abilities, there is often a tendency to over-respond to their needs. One must be careful not to infantilize the parent by helping "too much." If the senior is capable of making a cup of coffee or folding laundry, let him do it. It proves he is still "in the ballgame." One could consider checking with the parent to determine if assistance is desired. The idea of using the parent as a consultant works as an insulator of that person's ego. Being viewed as a partner enhances the relationship between caregiver and senior. These ideas are adaptations of Spotnitz's modern psychoanalytic theory as adapted by Nagelberg and Feldman (1987).

Many aspects of our own character come into play when we step into the role of caregiver for an elderly parent. A giant shift in the universe occurs when a parent becomes the recipient, rather than the initiator, of decisions. Children, either consciously or unconsciously, gain an enhanced sense of their own mortality as they begin to deal with their parent's diminishing hold on life. Tensions often surface when an elderly parent grows closer and closer to death. Thoughts of family inheritance may come to mind. If one person has assumed the role of primary caregiver, other siblings may wonder if their lesser participation may diminish their share of the inheritance. Recommendations for solving communication problems emanating from situations such as this are expertly discussed by Kievman and Blackman (1989).

It is compelling to contemplate what will happen to the caregiving role as people live to older and older ages. Clark and Weber (1997) state as follows:

> In 1900, about 3.1 million persons or roughly 4% of the population were aged 65 years and older. By 1990, the number of elderly persons had reached 31.2 million or 12.6% of the population. It is projected that in 2040 the elderly portion of the total U.S. population could total 22.6%. (para 6)

Because people are living longer and their grandchildren are having fewer children, an imbalance will ultimately take place between the number of family members able to assume the caregiving role and the number of seniors who need to be cared for. Our government may eventually have to assume more responsibility for seniors by establishing more extensive facilities, agencies, and services to satisfy their basic needs.

Today, most elderly who live at home are cared for by their children. Such caregiving is generally voluntary and based on love, devotion, obligation, or some combination thereof. Currently, 26 states have statutes that consider it adult children's duty to provide for their indigent parents (Maker, 1999, para 7). By law, once the obligation of caregiving has been assumed, it must be continued. "In New Jersey, any person who has assumed continuing responsibility for the care of an elderly person is subject to criminal liability for the neglect of such person. The crime in New Jersey is one of the third degree" (New Jersey Stats Ann. 1995 § 2c:24-8 [para 7]).

The pressures of caregiving often take their toll. A gamut of emotions is aroused by the caregiving role, from loving and nurturing affection to murderous rage. It is natural to experience all kinds of feelings. Many individuals have been trained to suppress their negative emotions. Not only do they find them difficult to discuss, but also they can scarcely acknowledge even to themselves that they are experiencing them. Seeing a therapist and/or being involved in a group with other caregivers can be very helpful. Hearing others express their joy, their rage, their sadness and grief, their fear and worry, their fatigue and isolation, can be inspiring and validating (Clark & Weber, 1997).

When the end approaches and an elderly parent slips into the final hours or days of letting go, the toll on the caregiver is usually great. He or she may be flooded with many feelings. These feelings are often mixed: a combination of loss, anger, grieving, love, and possibly a strong feeling of relief and release from the tether of a connection that has become besieged with the struggle of illness or the gradual relinquishing of life. A full description of caregivers' reactions and the actual physical aspects of dying are clearly noted in an excellent book called *How to Care for Aging Parents* by Virginia Morris (1996) and her more recent ones published in 2001. The kaleidoscope of emotions in the caregiving role for all of its challenge and pain can also result in great pleasure and a sense of renewed bonding. One caregiver, Denise, relates her story (both negative and positive aspects):

My mother does not say that much. She has never been that demonstrative. Sometimes, when she takes my arm to walk or when she places her hand on mine, she will say, "What would I do without you?" It is a sense of connectedness that is warming to me. It also leaves me with the feeling, "More, I want more." Although in reality it has not been an ideal relationship, perhaps too much mutual dependency, we have enjoyed closeness and a companionship over the years that are rich in sharing and mutual support. To be able to be there for her, to feel that now I am the competent one and to nurture her with warmth, is very gratifying. And yet there are times when the many feelings that I experience can be very difficult. I can feel anger when I am tending to her needs and I would rather be free to read a book. I can feel anger when the feelings of limitations in my own life are keen and I realize that there will be no daughter there for me. Every once in a while I think about an aunt of mine who grimly proclaimed one day that she was "in her dotage." I wonder for a moment, "What will be in store for me when I am this age?"

The feelings can be intense. The feelings are natural, angry ones, sad ones, mixed ones and loving ones. The angry feelings are not acted upon. They are experienced as feelings. Therefore, for me, they are manageable. I do not feel compelled to act when I have one. Other people in my geriatric caregivers' group very often feel more action-prone or deal with their feelings by denying them or trying to blot them out.

Sometimes it seems very lonely. The repetition of tasks or the limited socialization with one's friends will give one an enclosed feeling. And yet, given the situation, I feel fulfilled when I am with my mother. I enjoy seeing her retain her independence while living in her own home. I enjoy the good feeling of being her daughter, her close friend. She has an aide who comes into the home several days a week, drives her to appointments, and prepares some meals. This young woman is well suited to her role and she and my mom have bonded. To help our mother to stay in her own home rather than sending her to a facility is a commitment that my family and I have worked towards because it fulfills her wishes. As the major caregiver, I feel that at a certain point, we will need more home coverage than we have now. Our mother is in agreement as she acknowledges her increasing frailty. We will get additional help so that we can take care of her needs as well as taking care of our own as healthy caregivers.

Elaine is the daughter of an 88-year-old mother who is a resident of an assisted living facility. Although the daily tasks of care for her mother are under the surveillance of the facility, Elaine feels it is necessary to be involved and keep an eye on things daily because she is disappointed in the way the facility is managed.

My mother is an independent lady. If she doesn't feel well, she is reticent to inform the authorities. Once when I hadn't seen her in three days, she was becoming quite ill and was dehydrated. No one on the staff had picked up on it. I was furious. It was another reason to be more vigilant. Watching her grow older and frailer makes me very sad. Several months after entering the facility, she had a heart attack. When she was scheduled to leave the hospital, I wanted her to go to a rehabilitation facility. My daughter was about to have her baby and it was to be induced the day after my mother's release from the hospital. My mother insisted on returning to the assisted living for recuperation, claiming that she would be taken care of there. I scheduled a private duty nurse to come and be with her while I went to my daughter's to care for her older children. The nurse never showed up at the assisted living until 2 days later. It was one of those times when I realized, "You can do what you can do. You will never make it perfect." Though I will do my best for my mother, "I can't fix it." That is a truth that I am learning to accept.

Daniel, a bachelor, returned to the family home when his parents grew old and frail. He describes his situation as follows:

My mother fell and broke her shoulder. But she was still able to manage. And then a few weeks after the New Year, she broke her hip. After the hospitalization, she was placed in a nursing home for rehabilitation. I would go and visit her twice a day, once in the morning and once in the evening. Sometimes I would take her outside to be in the fresh air. Once, when we returned from our expedition (the leaves had been particularly pretty), she looked up at me and said "Thank you." Once, before she was moved to the nursing home, she said, "We need to do this. You need to have a life too." We understood one another very well. Taking care of her at home and then at the nursing home—this was something I wanted to do. As I told her, "You took care of me when I was young. Now it's my turn."

These sentiments are echoed by many caregivers who derive pleasure from the reciprocal act of caring. As fulfilling as caregiving may be, it is also inevitably stressful. Much more needs to be done within our healthcare system to increase funding for outside assistance. Being a caregiver is a challenge, an opportunity to create closure in the parent–child relationship, a chance to be fulfilled by giving back to one's parent. However, for those who have no outside relief, it can be a heavy burden. As we continue to evaluate our Social Security system, Medicare, and our traditional health systems, studies are needed on the caregiving factor and how improvements can be made. Think of the money saved when a senior stays at home rather than going to a facility where Medicaid picks up the tab. Think of the humanity for the senior and the caregiver's need for support and respite. Our country should assume greater responsibility in the specific area of eldercare.

Betty Reid Mandell (2003), a retired professor of social work at Bridgewater State College, in Bridgewater, Massachusetts, has indicated several areas that need to be addressed in the caregiving area, including our system of work, the concept of flexible hours, paid family leave, and a system for respite for the caregiver. We need to strive toward a widespread system of home health aides, sponsored by the government and paid reasonable wages by the family. Indeed, the issue of eldercare is increasingly critical in the twenty-first century.

REFERENCES

Albert Ellis Institute. (2003). *Caretaking for an elderly individual: Managing your emotions.* Retrieved June 11, 2004, from www.rebt.org/workshops//february

Cada, C. (2000). *Caring for yourself, your children, your parents: Survival tips for the sandwich generation.* Retrieved August 23, 2004, from http://www.health district.org/HWlibrary/sandwichgeneration.htm

Clark, J., & Weber, K. (1997). *Challenges and choices: Family relationships—Elderly caregiving.* Retrieved June 13, 2004, from University of Missouri–Columbia, Department of Human Development and Family Studies Web site: http:// muextension.missouri.edu

Care for caregivers—communicating with your aging parent's physician. (1996–2004). Retrieved September 4, 2004, from CareGuide.com

Care for caregivers—long distance caregiving: The basics. (1998–2003). Retrieved September 4, 2004, from CareGuide.com

Kievman, B., & Blackman, S. (1989). *For better or for worse: A couple's guide to dealing with chronic illness.* Chicago: Contemporary Books.

Maker, J. (1999). *The duty of care adult children owe their elderly parents.* Retrieved June 11, 2004, from www.Keln.org

Mandell, B. (2003). The future of caretaking. *New Politics, 9*(2), 34 [entire issue]. Retrieved June 13, 2004, from http://www.wpunj.edu/newpol/issue34/ mandell34.htm

Morris, V. (1996). *How to care for aging parents.* New York: Workman.
Morris, V. (2001). *Talking about death won't kill you.* New York: Workman.
Morris, V. (2004). *Talking about death.* Chapel Hill, NC: Algonquin Books.
Nagelberg, L., & Feldman, Y. (1987). The attempt at healthy insulation in the withdrawn child. In H. W. Spotnitz, *Psychotherapy of Preoedipal Conditions* (pp. 175–187). Northvale, NJ: Jason Aronson.
New Jersey Statutes Annotated § 2c:24-8. Minneapolis, West.
Zukerman, R. (2003). *Eldercare for dummies.* Indianapolis, IN: Wiley.

RESOURCES

Alzheimer's Disease Education and Referral Center
P.O. Box 8250
Silver Spring, MD 20907
800-438-4380

American Association of Homes and Services for the Aging
901 E St., NW, Suite 500
Washington, DC 20004
202-783-2242

American Association of Retired Persons (AARP)
601 E. St., NW
Washington, DC 20049
202-434-2277
800-424-3410

American Cancer Society
1599 Clifton Rd., NE
Atlanta, GA 30329
800-227-2345
404-320-3333

Children of Aging Parents
1609 Woodbourne Rd.
Suite 302A
Levittown, PA 19057
800-227-7294
215-945-6900

Eldercare Locator
800-677-1116

National Association of Meal Programs
101 N. Alfred St., Suite 202
Alexandria, VA 22314
703-548-5558

National Mental Health Association
1021 Prince St.
Alexandria, VA 22314
800-969-6642

National Self-Help Clearinghouse
25 West 43rd St., Room 620
New York, NY 10036
212-354-8525

Chapter 8

Housing and
Community Options

Jennifer L. Rutberg

Housing is not only a treatment modality in itself, it is a foundation for living. Without housing, food, and safety necessities, full participation in and positive results from therapy are unlikely (Maslow, 1943). This chapter describes the importance of suitable housing and services, the therapist's role in identifying and obtaining them, and a basic method for decision making regarding appropriate living environments and services. It also includes options for housing and supplementary services found in many areas in the United States. The summary suggests approaches for discussion with elderly clients and their families. Several case histories are presented, and one community's informal continuum of care is described.

ENVIRONMENT

Case: Clara

Clara had moved into low-income housing 30 years ago. She had several family members who also rented in the same building, which she had felt would be ideal during her "golden years." Now Clara was 97 and life was far from ideal. The building superintendent noticed that her apartment was not clean. He told her relatives that either they needed to clean her apartment or hire someone to do it.

Her relatives complained to their county welfare case managers, stating that it was not their responsibility to take care of her and that she should go to a nursing home. One of the case managers suspected that the family was taking money from Clara. She referred the case to the Division on Aging, which sent an outreach worker to Clara's apartment. Clara agreed to have someone come in to clean, but denied having problems with her family.

The "cleaning service" was actually the Home Friends, a Division on Aging–funded program contracted to the local hospital. The coordinator of the program worked extensively with Clara, identifying areas that Clara found difficult in her life. These areas included health care and nutrition. The coordinator noted that Clara seemed to be afraid of her relatives but unwilling to speak against them. They supposedly bought her groceries for her, yet there was little food in the house and she had visibly lost weight. Adult Protective Services assessed but could not act, as Clara was competent and denied having problems. The coordinator assigned a Home Friend to Clara for the purposes of cleaning, grocery shopping, and monitoring. Clara started going to the doctor at the hospital's geriatric assessment center and attending the hospital's medical day center. These steps improved her health and her nutrition, but she remained quiet and had no real friends, even at the medical day center.

Over the course of several months, the family members became frustrated, openly stating to the Home Friend and the driver of the medical day center bus that they were going to "start taking care of" Clara and "get paid." Adult Protective Services met with Clara again, to no avail.

A great-niece of Clara's broke in her door one night and took several items. She was arrested by the police while trying to sell the items and later convicted. She claimed that she deserved the items because Clara had lived too long. When Clara's other relatives openly agreed, Clara finally decided to change her life. She had formed a strong trusting bond with the Home Friend. In consultation with Adult Protective Services and the medical day center, the coordinator proposed to Clara that she move in with the Home Friend. She consented.

Tasks were divided among the involved agencies. The social worker at the medical day center arranged delivery of a hospital bed and a specially sized lift recliner (Clara was 4'10" tall) to the Home Friend's house. Adult Protective Services paid for furniture movers. The Division on Aging located a local church with volunteers to help pack and unpack, as well as provide a large enough support group that the family would be reluctant to challenge. The Home Friend coordinator stayed by Clara's side the entire time for reassurance.

Clara lived with the Home Friend for several months before passing away. She blossomed; she made many friends at the medical day center and participated fully in the activities. She gained weight. She began singing at church again and talking with the children there. Shortly before her death, she told her friends at the medical day center and at her church that she had not been so happy since she had been a little girl.

Clara's situation is an example of environment affecting the ability of a senior citizen to live a full life. Although she could benefit from improved health care and nutrition, she could not begin to enjoy her life until her living environment was safe and secure.

The practicalities of life may be a barrier to the client effectively working in therapy. The care issues of the moment may even be exacerbating past conflicts or wounds. Example: An 82-year-old woman is in therapy due to nightmares and feelings of fear and anxiety, beginning about six months ago. She shares that her childhood was one of deprivation and hunger. Her daughter is very embarrassed, disclosing that her mother has suddenly begun taking sugar packets and rolls from the diner where they have lunch once a week. Upon further investigation, it turns out that six months ago, she had a successful hip operation. However, she cannot stand up long enough to cook, and her slow walking puts her at risk of missing the bus ride home on supermarket trips from her senior building. Her daughter has observed her slowness and tries to cheer her mother up by enthusing over the operation's success. Mom does not want to sound like she is complaining or to upset her daughter, so she says nothing. Now her life has become a reenactment of the deprivation of her childhood, and she is unconsciously repeating the survival tactics that served her then. How can this client focus on confronting and resolving past issues that cause her nightmares and anxiety when her energy is occupied with trying to obtain groceries and fixing a meal?

In such situations, the therapist's role can be:

- to refer to social service agencies, case managers, or other appropriate sources that can assist with the more practical issues of nutrition, personal care, home safety, housing, and so forth,

- to ensure that any referrals or suggestions are emotionally acceptable to the client before being put into action (or it is likely that the referral or service will fail),

- to work with the client and any involved family/caregivers on their mutual communication and expectations,

- to advocate and assist the client in making his/her needs known, and

- to help the client adjust to the changes that such services will bring.

If there is trust between the therapist and the client, the client may try to have the therapist choose and arrange for services or a housing change, or the therapist may try to do this out of a desire to help. However, this causes a fundamental change in the role of the therapist and the nature of the therapy itself. Providing a dual role of therapist and case manager can be confusing to the client and a barrier to therapy going forward. If the therapist is to take on this role, a strong structure and clear expectations can be most helpful.

Therapy and the support of a therapist can be invaluable during a period of dramatic change in an elderly person's life. Decision making frequently takes place during periods of crisis, and, as described in *My Mother's Voice*:

> People . . . expect definitive, fast decisions. Sometimes, decisions change and, often, initial decisions are emotional rather than carefully thought out. These are not conditions conducive to making the often muddy, emotionally charged decisions required. . . . (Callahan, 2000, p. 35)

In this time of change, the therapist can help the senior to retain or discover a sense of control, which has been shown to be essential for positive adjustment to a new situation, and possibly for life itself. Also, the therapist can help to mitigate the effects of previously integrated negative stereotypes of people in similar situations (e.g., people in nursing homes are all helpless or dying) (Langer & Avorn, 1987).

ASSESSING AND IDENTIFYING AREAS OF NEED

How does the therapist know when an elderly client is in need of practical assistance or adjustment in living situation? There are four main ways. First, go with the primary source—the client may tell the therapist directly. The client may state that a specific service is needed (e.g., "I need Meals on Wheels") or may describe a problem (e.g., "I can't clean my bathtub anymore"). Second, auxiliary sources may alert the therapist, such as a family member or physician (e.g., "His blood pressure is remaining high because he is not taking his medication"). Third, the therapist may become aware that the client is having difficulty engaging in the therapeutic process because of current environmental circumstances, as discussed earlier in the case of the mother who was unable to shop or cook, was reenacting her past survival methods, and was shocking her daughter by taking sugar packets and other small food items. Fourth, the client may have initiated or agreed to therapy to alleviate emotional issues caused or exacerbated by practical issues.

Regardless how it comes to the therapist's attention, the important piece is what to do with this information. As in any other aspect of therapy, things are not always as they appear. The client who asks for Meals on Wheels may need help with nutrition, but may benefit more from a nutrition site or day center where socialization will also occur. Medication may not be taken because of side effects, cost, or any number of other factors. The client may find it more emotionally acceptable to ask for practical assistance than to express grief, isolation, and loneliness, and requesting help or sharing a problem may be a way to "open the door" with the therapist. It may also be a tool for avoidance of difficult issues in therapy, a way to focus on other topics. The therapist's investigative and intuitive skills are essential here.

Case: Mrs. V

Mrs. V. lived with her son and new daughter-in-law. She had three other children, none of whom had contact with her. Mrs. V. insisted that her son should "kick that woman out" and spend more time with her. Her son refused. He accepted his mother's "threat" to move out. She moved to an apartment in a senior building.

Mrs. V. was physically and cognitively capable of managing her health care, medications, shopping, finances, and other business. However, she demanded that her son come to her apartment to perform these tasks. When he refused, she retaliated by sabotaging her health and finances. She began overspending and failing to pay her bills. She was a non–insulin dependent diabetic with controlled hypertension, and became increasingly noncompliant with her diet. Emergency room visits became frequent, with the hospital calling Mrs. V.'s son and expecting him to bring her home and take care of her, stating that "She just needs some of your attention."

Mrs. V. attended a senior center. In response to her increasing statements that she was depressed, they recommended that she try a therapist. She agreed but refused to go back after the first session. The therapist had listened to her, and understood that her actions (including participating in therapy) were designed to manipulate and control her son. In formulating the treatment plan together, Mrs. V. had realized that the therapist would not enable her.

In evaluating housing and service needs, a general guide is found in Mace and Rabins' (2001) *The 36-Hour Day*: "Analyze each task [of daily living] as thoroughly and objectively as possible, and decide whether the person can still do specific tasks *completely, safely*, and *without becoming upset*" (p. 46).

This advice is specifically directed at families dealing with someone affected by a progressive dementia, but it can be adapted for use with most seniors. What tasks can the client manage completely and safely? What tasks are most important to that client? How does the client feel about his/her current abilities and functional levels? What are the client's views regarding adaptations that can enable him/her to perform those tasks safely and completely, or about having assistance with those tasks? Clara would accept help in food shopping and cleaning, but would not make further changes until lasting trust had been established and options with family exhausted.

Mrs. V. wanted to be more impaired than she was for the purpose of manipulating her son, and refused to utilize the services of her senior center because she would be less dependent. Services and/ or housing must be both applicable to the need and acceptable to the client. Coste (2003) uses the following in *Learning to Speak Alzheimer's* to reinforce the necessity for seniors to retain a sense of control, the feeling of directing their own life course:

> Take away my license,
> but don't steal my independence.
> I will let you drive,
> But let me tell you
> Where I want you to go. (Coste, 2003, p. 32)

HOUSING TYPES

Although there is a great deal of variation by state, region, and county, as well as numerous unique specialty programs, there are several basic housing types available for the elderly in the United States.

- *Private houses or condominiums:* In addition to regular houses, condos, or townhouses that are available to the general public, many areas have developments open only to older adults. Qualifying ages vary, often starting around 50 for one member of a couple. Most communities have entry interviews or evaluations to ensure that new residents are healthy and active. Rules preventing other family members (such as grandchildren or adult children) from residing in the home are common. Services are usually limited to group transportation to trips, supermarkets, and local events, but other services available in the community can be brought in.

- *Apartments:* Most regular apartment buildings do not have services, although services can be brought in, depending on what is available in the area. "Senior buildings" or "senior apartments" frequently have services provided through the building management, but these vary widely from building to building. Services may include some meals, laundry, housekeeping, or personal care. There may be charges for these services. Buildings may or may not have apartments subsidized through the U.S. Department of Housing and Urban Development (HUD) or other programs. Frequently there are long wait lists, or a building may have a closed wait list.

- *Boarding homes:* Licensing of boarding homes differs among states. In New Jersey, there are three levels of boarding homes: Class A boarding homes provide rooms only; Class B provide rooms and some meals; and Class C provide rooms, three meals a day, and personal care assistance. Boarding homes may be all private pay or contract to provide accommodation to those receiving Supplemental Security Income (SSI) or other programs. Additional services may possibly be brought into the boarding home, depending on payor source and licensing. For example, in New Jersey, the Veteran's Administration has been able to provide psychiatric nurse case managers to boarding home residents, and home care can be brought into Class A and B boarding homes. Home care services cannot currently be brought into New Jersey's Class C boarding homes for SSI/Medicaid recipients, as Class C boarding homes are to provide those services, and external provision is considered a double-billing issue. Boarding homes may serve specialty populations, such as veterans, those involved in psychiatric care, or the elderly. Listings of boarding homes frequently can be obtained from the county government, usually through the county's Area Agency on Aging or boarding home licensing board.

- *Residential health care (RHCFs) or assisted living facilities (ALFs):* Each state has its own licensing for assisted living and residential health care facilities. These terms may also vary. Assisted living is designed to be a midpoint between independent living and nursing home, providing medication administration, personal care, activities, nursing and medical care, and meals. Often physical therapy, fitness centers, and religious services are also available on-site. Some have specialized sections or facilities for those with a dementia. Funding varies widely by state; some states have Medicaid provisions for assisted living residents. The major payor source for assisted-living, however, is private pay. Services beyond meals and housing may require additional payment.

- *Continuing care retirement communities (CCRCs):* These are communities for older adults. Seniors move in when they are healthy and require little care. As their needs increase, care is increased. Services are either brought into their dwelling (e.g., apartment, cottage) or the residents move to another section of the community. If the senior must move, difficulties can arise for couples as one is frequently more in need than the other one (e.g., should the couple be separated?). Not all continuing care communities provide the full spectrum of care, including dementia care or skilled nursing home care. Payment varies. Some CCRCs require a buy-in upon entry, and monthly rent. Others require rent only. Still others require a very large one-time fee upon entry, with no payment afterward, with the facility absorbing the financial risk of residents outliving what their money has prepaid.

SERVICES

As with housing, there are vast differences in what services are available from area to area. One place to start is the area Agency on Aging, which may provide services directly or contract programs out. In most areas, other services are offered by local private companies, hospitals, and not-for-profit organizations. The telephone yellow pages, community health nurses (through towns, counties, or hospitals), senior centers, and hospital social workers can be sources of referral.

Commonly found services include:

- Home care, which is usually provided by for-profit companies, by hospitals, or by community agencies

- Nutrition sites, which may be housed within senior buildings, senior centers, recreational programs, or houses of worship

- Medical and social day centers

- Senior centers, which can be independent or a function of local recreation programs, YMCAs, Jewish Community Centers (JCCs), and houses of worship

- Meals on Wheels or other meal delivery programs

- Community mental health programs for seniors

- Employment programs

- Counseling, support groups, and health education

- Companion services

- Continuing education, including via telephone and Internet

- Bill-paying assistance

- Protective services for seniors at risk for abuse or neglect

- Services for the visually and hearing-impaired

ONE COMMUNITY'S RESPONSE

Over the past 30 years, a comprehensive system of care for seniors has developed in a Jewish community in New Jersey. Starting with a nursing home and hospital in the early 1900s, this community has made provisions for health care and its elderly. As the population increased, senior housing and ancillary services became necessities. Several buildings were built for senior apartments, and services such as lunch and housekeeping began. The nursing home opened a medical day center and built ties with hospice services. A kosher Meals on Wheels program was created. A specialty social housing program was opened, complete with three kosher meals a day, laundry service, housekeeping, and recreational programs. The local JCC developed an extensive program for seniors. Vocational services were created for job training and employment for seniors and those who wanted to work with seniors (such as health care workers, van drivers, housekeepers, and companions). A mutual support and self-expression program for now-elderly Holocaust survivors was formed by Jewish Family Services. Transportation services were created. Community health nurses traveled to area synagogues and homes. An assisted living facility was opened. A counseling and case management program was brought into the senior buildings and a caregiver's resource center was created.

Together, these programs form a continuum of care for the area's seniors, from the most independent, who may be in need of employment and diversional activities, to those in need of full end-of-life care.

SUMMARY

Seniors involved in therapy may experience issues that impede their full participation in therapy. Such issues can involve housing, health care, food, personal care, and other basics of living. Adequate, reliable provisioning of these essentials can enable the senior to focus on psychotherapeutic needs. Assessing and arranging for such services, including housing changes, can be done by the therapist where structured within the client–therapist relationship or by appropriate case management or other staff with the therapist acting as emotional support for the client.

Any plan of supportive care and assistance for a senior should begin with the assessment. Services, including housing, should then be matched or adapted to the senior's need (as opposed to the senior having to adapt to a "cookie-cutter" list of what services are available). With this in mind, any plan of care must also be as emotionally acceptable as possible to the senior, or the plan is likely to fail or to precipitate other emotional issues.

Housing and ancillary services come in many varieties, each with its own rules and funding sources. This chapter has presented some of the basic types as a general guide. The listings in this chapter are designed to give the therapist directions for investigation of what is available in any given area.

REFERENCES

Callahan, S. (2000). *My mother's voice.* Forest Knolls, CA: Elder Books.

Coste, J. K. (2003). *Learning to speak Alzheimer's.* New York: Houghton Mifflin.

Langer, E. J., & Avorn, J. (1987). Impact of the psychosocial environment of the elderly on behavioral and health outcomes. In B. B. Hess & E. W. Markson (Eds.). *Growing old in America* (pp. 464–465). New Brunswick, NJ: Transaction.

Mace, N. L., & Rabins, P. V. (1991). *The 36-hour day* (rev. ed.). Baltimore: Johns Hopkins University Press.

Maslow, A. H. (1943). A theory of human motivation. *Psychological Review, 50,* 370–396.

Chapter 9

Therapeutic Activity Programs for Assisted Living Facilities

Benjamin W. Pearce

BACKGROUND

Many inquiries and subsequent admissions to retirement communities are triggered by a significant life event. For many seniors, requesting information about an "independent" retirement community can be, in fact, the first step toward declaring their own *dependence*. Many seniors investigate lifestyle changes as a result of some type of loss in their lives. They may have lost their spouse, their ability to drive or to take care of themselves independently, or perhaps experienced some other traumatic event. During times like this, it is human nature to grieve these losses, and through this process people have a tendency to re-evaluate their lives. It is natural at this stage to compare personal accomplishments and position in life to a mental image of what they thought it might be when they were younger. At age 40, when one comes to the conclusion that life has not met one's expectations, there is ample time to adjust priorities and get back on track. At age 80, however, the opportunity for change is limited. John Barrymore, Sr. once said, "A man is never old 'til regrets take the place of dreams." Research into seniors' attitudes and behavior suggests that anxieties related to future adverse health conditions are less important than fears about the loss of opportunities to be what they want to be (Wolfe, 1990). This is the time in life when the physical world may be perceived to be continually shrinking. Many face this time and the bereavement process alone as they re-evaluate their lives and are confronted with their own mortality. There is a natural tendency to focus on the limitations of one's life and all of the obstacles that aging presents. When sadness turns to depression, seniors are headed for trouble.

Much of the stress of this evaluation process becomes internalized, which can make elders very vulnerable to depression. There has been ample research to demonstrate the mind's capacity to influence physical health, both positively and negatively. If left unchecked, depression and despair can inhibit recovery from illness, lead to hopelessness, and even, ultimately, premature death. Researchers Manning and Wells, in the landmark Rand study at UCLA (1986), found that 50 percent of all depressed people are over the age of 65. They studied depressed versus non-depressed people and found that depressed elderly use four times the amount of health care dollars than non-depressed and had a 58 percent greater mortality rate within the first year of admittance to a skilled nursing facility than their non-depressed counterparts. As depressed people tend to stay in bed or seated most of the day, this inactivity makes them susceptible to urinary tract infections and pneumonia, which, if left untreated, can lead to kidney failure and death.

The reluctant admission to the retirement community is for many yet another reminder of their inability to live at home independently. Americans of this age group who struggled through the Depression years to ultimately achieve the American dream of home ownership derive much of their identity from their living environment. It is indeed a significant challenge for many to give up the home in which they have lived for many years and now identify with the new retirement "home," not to mention learning to function in a communal environment.

In such communities enrichment and activity programs are essential. For such programs to be effective, they must be sensitive to the emotional forces that motivate people in this age group and be designed to direct their focus away from their limitations onto productive, educational, and social activities with a positive emphasis to enhance or enrich their quality of life.

Today's senior apartments are full of activity. Residents attend college courses, play golf, travel, and remain active in their community-service organizations. Variety and respect for individual prefer-ence are keys to successful recreational offerings. Leisure interests are lifelong habits that each of us develops. We don't stop being interested in them merely because we become older or our address has changed.

A community's (life enrichment) activity/recreation director is instrumental in maintaining resident satisfaction. Involved residents are happy residents. The activity professionals should provide the opportunity to maintain a balanced leisure lifestyle. This means a program of offerings that includes potential for growth, educational opportunities, physical activity and exercise, social programs, cre-ative expression, and travel networks. In addition, the activity de-partment can be a bridge to the community via such offerings as intergenerational programs with children, fund raising, and the for-mation of active resident councils. The list is endless, should be highly individualized, based on the leisure interest survey conducted at the time of admission, and is limited only by the creativity of the program director.

Each retirement community should have its own activity "face," based on what residents like to do, what is important to them, and what they like to participate in and see. This "personality" becomes the community and is evidenced by the appearance of its newsletter, calendar, and even the holiday decor in common areas. The same basic picture holds true for assisted living communities and skilled nursing homes.

With the OBRA (Omnibus Budget Reconciliation Act) guidelines (U.S. Department of Labor, 1997), HCFA (Health Care Financing Ad-ministration), and in some cases JCAHO (Joint Commission on Ac-creditation for Hospitals Organization), and CARF (Certification Administration for Rehabilitation Facilities), skilled nursing units' recreational activity programs are being scrutinized more than ever. This trend can be expected across the continuum of care, as regula-tors look to assisted living communities as a more cost effective setting to deliver care. The old standbys of "birthdays, bible, bridge, and bingo" as the basis for programming activities fall short in this heavily regulated part of the continuing care retirement community. Because of these needs, the activity director must be a qualified recreation professional.

In seeking a recreation director for an assisted living facility, consider applicants who are Certified Therapeutic Recreation Specialists (CTRS). These professionals not only have a bachelor's level degree in recreation administration and activity programming for special populations, but also are nationally certified by the National Council for Therapeutic Recreation Certification (NCTRC). Those communities with assisted living and skilled nursing complements can eliminate the need for outside activity consultants, at substantial savings. Regulations concerning activity consulting vary from state to state. However, many states have specifically named therapeutic recreation specialists as qualified candidates for activity director. The CTRS is trained to perform activity assessments, programming, planning, documentation, evaluation, and supervision for the elderly and other special populations. This level of sophistication can add considerable depth to an enrichment program while meeting the needs of active, independent residents as well as the frail elderly who may be aging in place or in higher levels of care. Operators would be well advised to consider hiring a professional with a clinical background and a solid base knowledge of documentation and activity adaptations. A high energy level and empathy toward the elderly are key ingredients for the successful director.

Activity assistants can be individuals with high school diplomas or with 36 hours of activity therapy courses with some experience or interest in working with the elderly. Typically, more mature individuals who may have aging parents are better equipped to connect with the residents. However, people of any age with the right attitude, solid communication skills, and sincerity can earn the trust and respect of residents.

Currently, there are no industry guidelines for staffing ratios across all levels of care. The appropriate staffing complement for each community will need to be customized according to internal factors such as the resident profile, the extent of programming offered in the service package, number and abilities of volunteers, interests of the residents, and nature of the activities. External factors that may influence staffing include regulatory requirements, extent of programming offered by local competitors, geographic location of the community, proximity to entertainment sources, and transportation. For skilled nursing, the staff-to-resident ratio should be no less than 1:50. This puts a 99-bed home at one activity assistant and one director. The assistant can work Sunday through Thursday or Tuesday through Saturday, or rotate weekends off to provide activity programming seven days per week. A typical schedule will also include two late nights per week to provide for evening programs (Pearce, 1998). The staffing in retirement centers is adjusted downward. The activity director can work alone or with one assistant and have access to a van driver for community outings. Many smaller communities with staffing constraints have effectively used volunteers and entertainers, or offered courses and seminars to supplement evening and weekend programming. Table 9.1 details full time equivalents (FTEs) by resident population and is offered as a general guideline (Pearce, 1998).

Staff should be responsible for maintaining certification and the activity director needs to keep records of all in-service training provided to activity assistants, aides, and other nursing home staff, where applicable. All certificates pertaining to an employee's credentials need to be on file in personnel records or with the human resources director at the property for review by regulators. Based upon the hiring package, the Continuing Care Retirement Community (CCRC) may reimburse some tuition and continuing education toward the certification of its employees, particularly if the position certification is a regulatory requirement.

VOLUNTEER PROGRAMS

Typically, the activity director also performs the function of the volunteer services coordinator. This is not always an ideal situation,

TABLE 9.1 Activity Staffing Analysis (FTEs)

Residents	Independent (1:150)	Assisted Living Facility (ALF) (1:100)	Skilled Nursing Facility (SNF) (1:50)
< 50	0.5	1.0	1.0
51–100	1.0	1.0	2.0
101–150	1.25	1.25–1.5	3.0
151–200	1.5	1.5–2.0	4.0
201–250	1.75	2.0–2.5	5.0
251–300	2.0	2.5–3.0	6.0
301–350	2.25	3.0–3.5	7.0

as the activity director's time may be at a premium. Recruiting a volunteer to be the volunteer coordinator is often an option. Many residents have leadership skills and management experiences that may lend themselves very well to coordinate this function, needing only a nudge in the right direction to fill this position. Volunteers can provide activity programs, teach courses, assist with large functions, provide one-on-one activities to assisted living and SNF residents; some may even work in the business office or provide musical entertainment.

The volunteer recruitment process should start with a leisure interest survey upon admission. At that time, residents can be asked if they are interested in working in any number of areas or if they have a talent to share with their neighbors. If their response is affirmative, they are then asked to fill out an application, as would an employee, and, after receiving a thorough orientation, would be scheduled according to specific job descriptions provided by the activity director. This way, the activity director and the volunteer can clearly establish the expectations of each in this function. The more structure that can be provided to the volunteer, the better the outcome will be and the chance of misunderstanding regarding the role of each will be minimized.

Networking the neighborhood is another way to recruit volunteers. Place announcements in church bulletins, contact local high schools for community service students, call university recreation and leisure departments, gerontology and psychology departments, and schools of social services. Many programs require internships and the student intern is a wonderful asset to providing additional staff at little cost (ICR Research Group, 1991). Students can be offered a per diem salary, a vacant apartment, meals for each day worked, or even bus passes as possible incentives in return for being a full-time employee. Many communities hire temporary interns after graduation because these entry-level employees are already trained and familiar with the community operations and residents. If the activity director is a CTRS, he or she can act as a preceptor to many university therapy programs. These may include, but are not limited to, therapeutic recreation, gerontology, occupational therapy, and psychology student–interns.

In 1991, Marriott Senior Living Services and the United States Administration on Aging conducted a senior volunteer study in conjunction with ICR Survey Research Group of Media, which included 962 telephone interviews with respondents 60 years of age or older (ICR Research Group, 1991). This landmark study confirmed that there is a tremendous pent-up demand for volunteering opportunities among the elderly. The following highlights of the survey portray a spirit of volunteerism that is largely untapped by community operators.

- Over 41 percent (5.5 million) of the 37.7 million Americans 60 years of age and older performed some form of volunteer work in the past year. The 65 to 69 and 70 to 74 age groups had the greatest percentage of volunteers, 46 and 45 percent, respectively. Seniors over the age of 80 had the smallest percentage of volunteers, 27 percent.

- Fourteen million older Americans (37.4 percent) are potential volunteers who, if asked, are or may be willing to volunteer.

- Among current volunteers, 25.6 percent indicated they would have preferred to volunteer more time, if asked.

- Eighty-three percent of seniors said they performed volunteer services in order to help others, whereas 56 percent did it to feel more useful or productive. Slightly over one-half of those asked said they volunteered to fulfill a moral responsibility (52 percent) and almost one-third volunteered because they felt volunteering was a social obligation. One out of four seniors volunteered as a way of finding companionship, and only five percent volunteered to alleviate feelings of guilt.

- Most seniors (57 percent) volunteered their services to church or religious organizations, followed by social service agencies (32 percent), civic or cultural organizations (25 percent), schools or institutions (22 percent), and health-related organizations, such as the American Red Cross or the Alzheimer's Association (16 percent). Less than 10 percent indicated that they donate time to a political party or campaign.

The study goes on to explain that among potential volunteers, retirement communities replaced social service organizations as the second most preferred organizations for which to volunteer. This could be attributed, at least in part, to seniors' curiosity about their own senior living options. A well-organized community outreach program designed to promote volunteerism within the community can help to dispel the myths and fears among seniors about senior living. As volunteers become accustomed to the senior living community and make friends there, they begin to recognize the inherent value and benefits that may apply to their own lifestyle needs. Clearly, savvy operators who recognize the marketing potential of this form of community outreach may realize that the benefits of these programs may stretch well beyond the intended value to their resident population.

MANAGEMENT OF THE ACTIVITY DEPARTMENT

Organization of an efficient activity department begins with written, clear policies and procedures. Policy and procedure manuals are an OBRA and HCFA requirement. Activity department policy and procedure manuals need to be on file for review in the executive director's office, as well as in the activity office. Activity staff should review and update the manual annually. Policy and procedure manuals should also be included in the new employee orientation process to ensure consistent delivery of activity standards. The policy and procedure manual should generally include the following:

- A *philosophy or mission statement* for the community's life enrichment or recreation services.
- *Clearly stated objectives* for providing service to residents.
- *Organization of the department*, including detailed responsibilities of all personnel.
- *Staffing and personnel policies*, including employee orientation, in-servicing, job descriptions, staff meeting outlines, volunteer and student intern programs.
- *Scheduling* of activities, programs and staffing.
- *Documentation policies for activities* including SNF initial assessments, resident leisure interest survey, patient care plans, Minimum Data Sets (MDS), progress notes, and frequency and participation records.
- *Program descriptions:* Outline in-house activities, including program protocol information for each group provided by

the activity department. All outings should have an outing policy and emergency van procedures. For communities with Alzheimer's residents, an escort policy for safety needs to be in place.

- *Communication:* Monthly calendars, newsletters and other frequently distributed pieces should be planned, along with guidelines detailing when and where to post and a mailing list. Bulletin boards and decoration guidelines also should be included, as they are essential communication tools with the resident population.

- *Quality assurance plan,* which evaluates the participation and effectiveness of programs and the activity department in meeting residents' needs. This program should also include some form of resident satisfaction criteria.

RECREATIONAL ACTIVITIES IN THE ASSISTED LIVING FACILITY

There are two areas of particular concern to the retirement community administrator: in-house programs and community or out-of-house programs. Within each are shared cost activities and community provided activities.

In-House Programs

Residents of both the retirement center and the SNF should have completed either an initial assessment upon placement, or a leisure interest survey upon admission. These tools predict which in-house programs should be offered. The in-house programs offered on a monthly calendar should include the basics: physical activity, music, social groups, spiritual and educational programs, community outings, special events, personal parties, arts and crafts, movies, current events, and so forth.

Community Programs

In the residential component of the community, shared cost programs might include spa activities such as massage or fitness trainers. Many retirement communities utilize travel agents to provide reduced group rates for resident cruises. One community conducted a series of educational classes on the culture and history of the ancient Mayan Indians of the Yucatan Peninsula and the Caribbean (Stephens, Ackerman, & Catherwood, 1996), which culminated in a cruise and tour of the ruins in Mexico. It should be clear that the community accepts no responsibility for either the residents or employees while on activities that will take them out of the geographic vicinity and that they are taking these trips at their own risk. Casino and theater trips are also popular. In planning activities for independent residents, the best advice is to *listen, listen, listen.* The residents can be an excellent source of ideas and it is the responsibility of the activity department to act on those ideas and incorporate the residents' leisure interests into program offerings.

In-house recreation services might include a gardening club, bridge afternoons, movies, educational series, arts and crafts classes, and resident council. In an effort to capture residents' interests in learning, some communities have devised innovative continuing education opportunities. These programs include computer training, so that seniors can learn to communicate by e-mail and instant messenger (IM) with their adult children and grandchildren.

Today's senior "is a member of the most information-driven segment of U.S. society," according to David Wolfe, one of the foremost experts on the mature market. "They prefer news shows and documentaries to other TV viewing. They are big readers of newspapers and magazines. They travel to expand their horizons, rather than for the escapist reasons that widely motivate young people to travel. They are signing up at colleges and universities by the tens of thousands. They are creative about shaping their lives and are intellectually involved in life" (Wolfe, 1990, pp. 45–46).

On the average, older adults see themselves as more than 10 years younger then their actual age, according to the Marriott Senior Attitudes Study conducted by ICR Survey Research Group for Marriott Senior Living Services. "Within our society, older adults offer the greatest potential for volunteerism. They offer a tremendous amount of knowledge, proven experience and creative talent that is too valuable to ignore," the survey found (ICR Research Group, 1991, p. 1). Asked if they were bored with their lives, most said no (76.3 percent). Asked what they would do differently with their lives, 68 percent said they would do more to help society and 75 percent said they would get more education (ICR Research Group, 1991).

Many residents consider learning a lifelong experience. Communities that develop a course curriculum to address this need for stimulating, enriching programming will better serve the real interests of their populations. Ethnicity and cultural origins also provide a rich variety of activity programming potential. The activity director can, and, in fact, should look beyond Christmas to celebrating Chanukah and Kwanzaa. These programs can take the shape of week-long events, education, and parties. Often, celebrating the differences and uniqueness of individuals enables a community to become one, and more accepting of others. Courses might include special studies in religion, native art, and ethnic customs endemic to various geographic and cultural regions of the world. Monthly book or literary reviews are always well received. Classes also provide an environment in which residents can learn from each other; "textbook learning" comes to life when residents/students can discuss relevant personal experiences in a relaxed setting.

Classes should emphasize the fun in learning and cover subjects that promote personal growth and are of particular interest to older persons. They can be taught by volunteer instructors or, at the residents' expense, for a small charge. Residents will usually be willing to participate in the expense of special educational courses provided that the cost is generally held under $25.

Prior to admission, prospective or future residents might be invited to attend programs on subjects in which they have indicated an interest, enabling them to interact with residents and experience the companionship associated with community life. In many cases, the strength of a well-coordinated program can prompt prospects to move to a facility sooner than they may have initially indicated. By making these courses available to the public, the community facilitates a better understanding of the "active retirement living" concept. Once seniors from the community-at-large meet the residents and experience the high-caliber programs, any preconceived notions they may have had about institutional activities are put to rest. To help residents maintain strong relationships outside the community, they should be encouraged to invite their friends to attend the classes. The healthy interaction between residents and non-residents helps further spread the word about the positive attributes of retirement living.

Sample activity programming standards for independent/residential and assisted living communities can be found at the end of this chapter. Each community needs to develop planning standards of its own that reflect the information gathered during the leisure interest surveys of initial assessments (Pearce, 1998). Of course, actual programming will vary widely depending on the natural talents and creativity of each activity director. The point here is to encourage some formalized planning to aid the individual director in the development of the monthly calendar and annual budgets.

Operators with Medicare units must be goal oriented to meet the needs of each resident, as represented by the Minimum Data Set (MDS) (Center for Medicare and Medicaid Services, 2002) and the initial assessment mentioned earlier. The residents' needs are clearly defined on the patient care plan and activities in this documentation must incorporate residents' interests. For example, Mr. Smith is admitted with a diagnosis of congestive heart failure (CHF) and dementia to a SNF. He states in his initial assessment to the activity director that he used to enjoy gardening and in fact, after retiring from his law practice, was an award-winning horticulturist. The activity director writes a specific goal for Mr. Smith to participate in a horticultural therapy group once per week. Staff interventions might include providing Mr. Smith with a window garden in his room (per facility policy) or delegating him the responsibility to water plants in the common areas. Empowerment, choices, dignity, and respect are deserved by us all and must be represented clearly on the care plan.

The following program, coordinated in a care center in Phoenix, Arizona (Carda, 1989), provides another example of putting residents first in activities planning. This multilevel extended care facility had an Alzheimer's floor. The problem for the activity director was to mobilize the entire building (all levels) to participate in a holiday bazaar fundraiser. The activity director was well aware of the ability of her involved Alzheimer's disease and related disorder (ADRD) residents. She devised a long banner of paper and taped it to a tabletop. Then she added brushes, sponges, paint, and glitter and let the residents literally wander in and out, making their individual contributions to the "mural." After the paint dried, the mural was cut into smaller sections and given to bed patients to cut into 1" ×

3″ strips, then passed on to another floor to punch holes in one end. Next the strips went into shoeboxes to other residents who tied red and green yarn in one end and bundled them in bunches of 25 gift tags to be sold at the bazaar. This multilevel adaptation involved residents from all functional levels on every floor of the facility to complete the project. Sales of the gift tags reached over $300 for the resident council fund! Attached to the back of each bundle was a label stating "Made by the Alzheimer's residents of St. Joseph's Care Center." The care center was well represented to the community by this fundraising activity and received considerable media exposure. Ingenuity and the ability to adapt activities for the complex multilevel properties are two desirable traits for an activity director. The challenges in today's retirement communities are endless, and a versatile activity program must be ready for anything.

Everyone benefits from a big project; it has purpose, provides a sense of belonging, and creates a sense of accomplishment. Projects such as the gift tags, which involve the entire staff, can considerably enhance the effectiveness of an enrichment program. Projects that are conceived and well organized with a *purpose* will attract participation from the personal care assistants. If the activity director can devise creative programs designed to be interesting to other staff, it is amazing what can be accomplished. Activities that are meant to entertain or motivate just the residents or special interests of the residents are usually poorly attended. However, a big project that appeals to everyone has the potential to attract large numbers of participants, residents and staff alike. The following (Table 9.2) is a list of activities and suggested frequency for assisted living residents.

TABLE 9.2 Sample Activity Programming Standards: Assisted Living

Program Type	Typical Frequency
Slow exercise	3×/wk.
Bingo	2×/wk.
Birthday party	1×/mo.
Cards	1×/wk.
Movies	1×/wk.
Entertainment	2×/mo.

(continued)

TABLE 9.2 *(continued)*

Program Type	Typical Frequency
Crafts	1×/wk.
Sing-along	2×/mo.
Group discussion	1×/wk.
Religious services	1×/wk.
Pets	2×/mo.
Puzzles	3×/mo.
Kids	2×/mo.
Plants	6×/yr.
Walks around building	5×/wk.
Bulletin boards changed	1×/mo.
Newsletters (large print)	1×/mo.
Decorate	1×/mo.
Transportation	1×/wk.
One-on-one	7×/wk.

THERAPEUTIC PROGRAMMING

Purpose

- To preserve physical well-being as long as possible

- To encourage emotional self-expression without fear of failure or criticism

- To provide appropriate and meaningful cognitive and sensory stimulation

- To enhance remaining skills and abilities

- To encourage interaction with others and assist with relationship building

Goals

- To provide a sense of accomplishment without frustration

- To encourage skills that remain on any given day or at any given hour of the day

- To provide a sense of well-being and positive self-esteem

- To promote and facilitate physical movement, which will reduce resident agitation

- To promote an awareness of surroundings and other people within the environment

- To provide a vehicle for the expression of feelings

THERAPEUTIC ACTIVITIES

Improve Communication

The activities, staff, and the coordinator must all focus on the residents and practice active listening skills; eliminate distractions in the environment, like a TV or radio in the background, before attempting communication; treat each resident as an individual (do not speak to a group, but to each person in the group); do not interrupt the resident who is trying to make a point, no matter how confused it may seem; and get in front of the person at eye level when interacting with him/her. Remember, body language can convey tension and impatience to the resident. Use a relaxed expression and simplified visual and verbal cues to help.

Supervise the Activities—Don't Take Them Over

Activity coordinators should remember it is the process of active involvement that is important to the resident, not the finished product. Structure the activity so that it is challenging, not frustrating. The resident may need a step-by-step breakdown of tasks. Written instructions with one step on each page often help, if the resident is able to read.

Normalize the Activity Schedule

The schedule of activities should fit the normal daily routine. For example, an older adult in the community may enjoy morning or evening walks outdoors. A therapeutic walking program might be offered while residents are waiting for breakfast, or just after dinner. Along with this idea, the activity coordinator should normalize both what he/she wears and what the resident wears. Residents might get confused if the activities coordinator comes to the walking group in business attire instead of sportswear; dressing similarly helps set the stage for the activity. Conversely, the resident might not understand the aim of the program if he/she is wearing slippers instead of walking shoes. Post the schedule in the community, in the residents' rooms, in elevators, and give reminder cards to residents who may need them.

Create a Structured Environment

Residents with dementia can become agitated if the activity and the environment are not structured to match their level of functioning. If there is too much noise or not enough one-on-one communication in the program, or if the resident is not allowed free movement and an opportunity for physical activity, agitation may result.

Be Prepared to Offer a Diversion

If a resident becomes bored or agitated in a therapeutic activities program, attempt to divert his/her attention with a new task. Ideas to offer as diversion include magnets and a magnetic board, a pocketbook filled with things to rummage through, a pair of colorful socks with objects hidden inside, old jewelry boxes filled with costume jewelry, an old briefcase full of magazines, and wallets with items in every pocket.

Base Program Tasks on Residents' Functioning Levels

If the program tasks are too easy, the resident will complete them without a challenge and become bored. If the tasks are too difficult, the resident will become confused and frustrated.

Although One-on-One Programming Is Ideal, it Is Not Usually Practical

The activities coordinator should use small groups of five to eight individuals, providing one-on-one attention for each task within the group for the best effect. Attempts to get the residents to share objects and communicate with each other will enhance the therapeutic effects of the session.

Offer Opportunity for Movement and Stimulation

Merely attending a program may not be enough to benefit the resident. Exercise and movement help to relieve emotional and physical stress. Exercise can reduce illness and agitation. Maintaining or improving strength, flexibility and mobility skills are important goals that can lead to improving self-care. Therapeutic goals to improve fitness can promote the residents' sense of purpose while improving their health. For nonambulatory residents, chair exercises can be added to their daily routine.

Empower Residents by Providing Simplified and Structured Choices

The activity coordinator who offers two containers of paint and asks, "Which color do you prefer?" or "Would you like to walk outdoors or indoors today?" puts the resident in charge of the situation. The resident should be able to choose where to recreate and for how long.

The Best Therapeutic Programming Is Interdisciplinary

Site supervisors, personal care staff, and activity coordinators should use a consistent approach and work together so that the daily routine makes sense.

Universal Strengths

The therapeutic program should incorporate the universal strengths of persons with dementia that include:

Habitual skills: Require innate thought and call on the resident's life experience and long-term memory.

Primary motor function: Strength, dexterity and motor control. Break down into simple steps and get help starting and stopping.

Primary/sensory function: Experience sensations; aromatherapy, hand massages, soothing music, and snoezelen therapies such as soothing lighting, bubble towers, or aquariums.

Sense of rhythm and movement: Music, dancing, sewing, threading, folding, rocking, and swinging.

Remote memory: General versus specific memories; reminiscence group's memory boxes, old songs, old pictures.

Emotions: Residents still experience negative and positive feelings and need outlets for them. Encourage talking about and expressing feelings.

Sense of humor: Slapstick and simple humor work best. Physical humor that is easily understood is effective.

RELATIONSHIP-BUILDING

Another important component of an activity program is to encourage and foster the formation of relationships. Throughout the course of the day, residents come into contact with many different people. Fellow residents, family members, and staff represent a wide variety of opportunities for social interaction and the formation of close bonds. Look for common interests that residents share, such as cards, hobbies, sports, or political topics. This way, meaningful programs can be structured for small groups with similar interests or even just for two people, especially for newcomers. It is important that residents' needs are understood when relationship-building techniques are reviewed. Four important considerations are:

- **Intimacy**—The capacity to feel wanted and important within the environment.

- **Creativity**—The ability to express emotions through art, music, or discussions.

- **Need to leave a legacy**—The ability to feel one's presence has had an impact on others.

- **The need for life review**—A review process of one's life that finds meaning (use reminiscence techniques).

Many of the activities address these resident needs; however, it is through individual relationships that each resident develops comfort, stimulation, enjoyment, and security. Relationship-building should not be confined to the social portion of the activity program. Although large and small group events foster verbal communication among residents, they only address a small portion of the relationship-building need. The goal is to encourage and foster the creation of close relationships for all residents.

To foster relationships among residents with ADRD:

- Learn as much as you can about the disease.

- Learn as much as you can about each individual resident. Each piece of information will allow you to provide immediate comfort when a resident is upset and may help to effectively distract when agitation occurs.

  - Names of spouse, children, grandchildren, siblings

  - Past occupations or key life events

  - Birthplace and other places resident has lived

  - Favorite food or drink

  - Most cherished personal items

- Communicate clearly.

  - Get the resident's attention and maintain eye contact

  - Understand each resident's ability and limitations

  - Remember, the tone of your voice helps the resident to hear

  - Listen

  - Encourage and praise at every opportunity

  - Use Validation Therapy (see below)

- Pair compatible residents with each other during:

  - Large and small group activity events

- Meals

- Formal social gatherings (e.g., cookouts, parties)

- Be creative with residents who don't easily engage with others

  - A resident may withdraw from his/her surroundings. It is staff's responsibility to recognize the signs of withdrawal. When this occurs, staff should provide dedicated one-on-one attention to engage the resident. Many times a warm touch and comforting talk will be sufficient to encourage the resident to get involved. In other cases, a structured intervention plan may need to be designed. The plan should include a series of individual activities that condition the resident toward social interaction. The goal of the plan is to provide the resident with a dependable relationship that he/she recognizes, depends on, and can use to develop a sense of worth and personal value. Remind each resident how special he or she is to the other. Encourage the friendship. Make it a priority during the day.

SOCIAL ACTIVITIES

Social activities are intended to create an environment that

- Promotes positive relationships

- Improves the "self" concept of each resident

- Reflects normalized social behaviors

Many residents engaged in frequent social interactions prior to their dementia (ADRD). It is important to ensure that residents continue to experience these social interactions and enjoy the important benefits of renewed self-esteem and relationship-building. Social activities that involve more than one person, resident, staff, or family, offer an opportunity to create a "normalized" situation. It is understood that dementia diminishes one's ability to initiate activities or social interactions. We also understand that if we assist in starting these social contacts and take the lead in managing them, residents will participate and enjoy them. Social activities should enhance human interactions and provide an outlet for residents to enjoy familiar experiences. Experienced in a group (large or small), social activities help maintain social skills and promote a sense of accomplishment and bonding among residents.

It is staff's responsibility to ensure that each resident is given the opportunity to create his or her own individual home environment. Each resident has the right to be treated with respect, dignity, and freedom of choice. Staff must be sensitive to these rights when creating social activities, remembering, however, that each resident has the right to be engaged in social stimulation. It is also the resident's individual right to decline participating in a particular social activity that is not appealing; it is the staff's responsibility to identify other social activities that the resident will enjoy and that will provide proper engagement and stimulation.

EXAMPLES OF SOCIAL ACTIVITIES

- **Afternoon/ice cream socials:** Residents can be called together at a table and "invited" to a tea or afternoon social. Encourage the residents to set the table, fold the napkins, arrange the silverware, and set up the condiments. Encourage them to "dress up" for this special event. If necessary, arrange seating and provide topics for conversation. Have cookies, fancy cakes, and the "good" teacups.

- **Walks:** Each resident is walked a minimum of twice per day. Gather a small group of residents and invite them to take a walk or stroll. These strolls can be either inside or outside. If inside, comment on the artwork, look out of the windows and comment on the surroundings. Point out anything of interest. This may stimulate the residents to comment or share a memory. Even if the staff person fails to generate conversation, the walk is still important for the exercise and social interaction it provides.

- **Craft groups:** Plan a craft such as holiday decorations, room decorations, basket making, or anything the resident wishes. Tell the resident the purpose of the group and how to proceed. Encourage residents to interact. Initiate and stimulate the socialization, if necessary. For example, say, "Mary, isn't Joan's basket beautiful?" Or "Mary, your design is very pretty; can you show Joan how you did that?" The activity leader may need to try several different topics to get conversation started.

- **Talk groups:** A social activity can be created with real or "invented" sorting tasks or projects. As an example, a group of residents could cut pictures out of a magazine of children, birds, dogs, cats, flowers, and so forth, and put these pictures in albums. Simultaneously, staff can suggest topics to discuss, perhaps related to the pictures. All residents should be encouraged to add their thoughts to the discussion. Often the activity leader will need to prompt the residents.

- **Other social activities include:**

    - Table games such as bingo or cards
    - Intergenerational visits (e.g., youth groups, Boy/Girl Scouts, religious groups)
    - Pet/animal visits
    - Cookouts
    - Spelling bees
    - Outings
    - Parties

Group projects and other social activities should offer opportunities for resident discussion and reminiscence. For instance, while the residents are making scrapbooks, the caregiver should ask about people and stories that the pictures bring to mind. Staff constantly should be engaging all residents and encouraging them to talk with each other. In all activities, staff should *praise!* Social activities are situations residents probably avoided before coming to a residential facility because they were unable to manage these situations with their progressing dementia. Now, with staff help, they can interact without fear of failure. Assure participants that *there is no wrong answer or statement.* Help them feel successful again in a social situation.

PHYSICAL ACTIVITIES

Residents benefit from regular and appropriate exercise. Within the activities program, schedule physical stimulation that is intended to

- Provide an outlet for energy
- Provide a method of maintaining muscle strength and joint flexibility
- Enhance cardiopulmonary function
- Strengthen coordination
- Allow for fun and group interaction
- Create a positive outlet for what might otherwise be socially unacceptable behavior

Exercise programs, walking groups, and sports activities should be a part of the daily schedule. Care should be taken to design these activities for both the frail and stronger residents. Props such as balls, scarf elastic bands, and flags add visual stimulation to the physical exercise and help maintain residents' interest.

Guidelines for Leading an Exercise Program

- Always consult the individual's physician before starting any exercise program.
- Limit the total exercise period to about 15 minutes and watch for signs of overexertion.
- Avoid using exercises that require residents to hold their breath too long or stamp their feet energetically, as these may cause strain or overexertion.
- Use periodic rests as an opportunity for talking and reminiscing.
- Do the exercise at the same time each day.
- Keep exercise in the same order to reduce confusion.
- Start and end active exercise with a short period of stretching.
- When giving instructions:
    - Avoid distinguishing between right and left

- Move into each exercise slowly, using simple instructions
- Break instructions into appropriate steps
- Demonstrate how to do the exercise
- Gently help the person begin the movement, if necessary
- Monitor progress and stop if the individual seems to tire or lose interest.

VALIDATION THERAPY

Validation Therapy, developed by Naomi Feil, ACSW, is a positive and reassuring method for interacting with disoriented and confused residents (Feil & DeKlerk-Rubin, 2002). For years, it was thought that "Reality Therapy" was the best way of relating to confused residents. Reality Therapy suggests that when a resident talks as if things that occurred in the past are actually happening in the present, a resident should be corrected and reoriented to understand the current reality.

An Example of Reality Therapy

A resident is trying to get out to go to meet her mother. The resident says, "I am going to meet my mother at the store." Using Reality Therapy, a staff person might say, "You are 87 years old; you know that your mother is not still living."

Such a Reality Therapy response is not helpful. It is counterproductive to contradict or correct the Alzheimer's resident, and reminding the resident of a sad or unpleasant event, such as the death of a parent, is often upsetting and even painful. Some residents have been known to hear the news as though it just happened and they experience the grief again. Further, as their memory is poor, they might not remember the response and may raise the issue again. This may cause them to be upset over and over again.

Validation Therapy is a better way of handling these issues. Validation Therapy suggests that every feeling a person has needs to be expressed and acknowledged. Residents' feelings are critical to their self-esteem. Validation Therapy acknowledges and encourages their feelings and interests. It asks staff to "go where the resident is" and treat whatever the resident is thinking or feeling as important. Meeting residents in the moment and, therefore, validating their feelings, is critical.

Examples of Validation Therapy

A resident is standing by the front door saying, "I need to go and meet my mother." A staff person, knowing her mother is deceased, says, "I'd like to meet her. Can you tell me about her? Does she have big blue eyes like you?"

This example offers the resident an opportunity to have her feelings and her thoughts about her mother acknowledged. Validation Therapy engages the resident in a pleasant conversation that helps her recall happy memories. Often, Validation Therapy distracts residents from the original concern and helps them engage in a happier thought or conversation. Validation Therapy requires creative thinking, compassion, and patience.

As another example, a resident says, "I have to get to work. I have to get to my job." Using Validation Therapy, a staff person might say, "What kind of work do you do? You were a carpenter? Did you build furniture or cabinets?"

A resident says, "I have to meet the school bus; my children are coming home." Using Validation Therapy, a staff person might say, "How many children do you have? Are they boys or girls? What are their names?"

Residents should not be expected to behave in any preconceived way. Staff must be nonjudgmental and accept any physical and intellectual losses that exist or develop. Validation Therapy asks staff to respect the resident's intuitive wisdom and interests and provides an essential endorsement of the resident as a unique individual.

Examples of Verbal and Nonverbal Validation Techniques

Verbal

- Listen carefully to the words used by residents.
- Repeat their key ideas by paraphrasing or summarizing.

- Ask the extreme (i.e., How bad? Worse? Best?).

- Reminisce; tap into their long-term memories.

- Look for a creative solution together (e.g., What did you do when this happened before?). Tap into earlier coping methods that worked.

Nonverbal

- Observe.

- Mirror residents' movements; pick up on their breathing and match movements.

- Link their behavior with an unmet need (e.g., love, need to feel safe, need to be useful).

- Maintain genuine eye contact.

Most elderly people respond well to therapeutic activity programs, especially programs designed around their former leisure interests or those adapted to a cognitive impairment. Leisure interest surveys upon admission can help create an inventory of interests among the entire population so that both small and large group programs can be established to appeal to a broad array of interests. A resident's mental and physical health is largely a function of attitude. Residents who remain active and engaged will be able to maintain a positive outlook, treating themselves to a higher quality of life.

REFERENCES

Carda, L. M. (1989). *Activity ideas.* Phoenix, AZ: Careage Corporation.

Center for Medicare and Medicaid Services. (2002). *The December 2002 revised long term care resident assessment instrument (RAI) user's manual for the minimum data set (MDS), Version 2.0.* Washington, DC: U.S. Government Department of Health and Human Services.

Feil, N., & DeKlerk-Rubin, V. (2002). *The validation breakthrough: Simple techniques for communicating with people with Alzheimer's-type dementia.* New York: Health Professions Press.

ICR Research Group. (1991). *Marriott seniors' attitudes survey.* Washington, DC: Marriott Senior Living Services.

Manning, W. G., & Wells, K. B. (1986). *Use of outpatient mental health care*. Los Angeles: Rand Corporation.

Pearce, B. W. (1998). *Senior living communities*. Baltimore: Johns Hopkins University Press.

Stephens, J. L., Ackerman, K., & Catherwood, F. (1996). *Incidents of travel in Yucatan*. Washington, DC: Smithsonian Books.

U.S. Department of Labor. (1997). *Guidelines to OBRA. § 1819 [42 USC § 1395i-3]. Requirements for, and assuring quality of care in skilled nursing facilities*. Washington, DC: VeriCare.

Wolfe, D. B. (1990). *Serving the ageless market*. Washington, DC: McGraw-Hill.

Part IV

Private Practice

Chapter 10

Individual Treatment of a Borderline Older Woman: The Case of Mrs. Z.[1]

Vicki G. Semel

Psychotherapists and psychoanalysts have moved slowly away from Freud's early admonitions against treating the patient over 50 (Freud, 1953), and toward attempts to treat the aging patient. Interest in treatment of the elderly in private practice has been growing and is expected to continue increasing, especially as the baby boom generation ages. The federal government has acknowledged this emerging trend as well as the counseling needs of many older adults today by enabling those covered by Medicare to be reimbursed for psychological services. Consequently, psychotherapy has become more accessible to the aging population, and virtually every psychologist is faced with requests to provide mental health services to older adults (Qualls, Segal, Norman, Niederehe, & Gallagher-Thompson, 2002).

[1]A modified version of this chapter was presented at the American Psychological Association annual meeting, 1990, in Boston and published in *Modern Psychoanalysis: The Journal of the Center for Modern Psychoanalytic Studies, 15,* 215–224.

In keeping with this developing social need, the American Psychological Association (APA, 2004) has generated "Guidelines for Psychological Practice With Older Adults." These guidelines were designed specifically to help psychologists evaluate their own readiness to counsel older adults and to help them prepare academically and clinically to treat this population.

Although there is an inclination to see the treatment of the older patient as requiring distinct approaches (Qualls, 1998), studies confirm that similarities often outweigh differences between older adults and younger adults in therapy (Knight & McCallum, 1998; Knight, 1999), and there is an expectation that older patients can be treated like patients of any age who come to therapy in an effort to ameliorate symptoms or make major life changes. In fact, an optimistic view of treating the elderly has been an essential part of Robert Knight's work for decades (Knight & McCallum, 1998; Norcross & Knight, 2000). The question for this chapter is how to combine an acceptance of a patient's unique issues with an approach that maintains the psychodynamic treatment modality whatever the age of the patient. Therapists who do not change their treatment modality simply because the patient is of advanced age offer new insights into the treatment of this cohort.

In addition to recognizing that older adults comprise the fastest-growing segment of our nation's population, it is further important to note that the majority of these aging adults are women (Trotman & Brody, 2002). This "feminization" of the aging population raises a variety of issues. Therefore, it is essential that clinicians be both aware of potential gender differences when working with older adults and "well informed about women's development across the lifespan and the implications for women of growing up and growing old in a sexist and ageist society" (Crose, 1999, p. 58).

In this chapter, following a review of recent clinical literature on the aging patient and a brief outline of the Modern Psychoanalytic approach that informs my work, I present the case of Mrs. Z., a seriously narcissistic woman with paranoid features, who began treatment at age 60. The difficulties encountered in this ongoing, seven-year therapeutic relationship are representative of the challenges such patients offer almost any practitioner. As noted earlier, whereas a traditional bias prompts therapists to believe they need to apply different treatment methods when working with older adults, it can be argued, as demonstrated in this chapter and as the literature supports, that both older and younger adults can benefit from the same treatment methods and approaches. Patients like Mrs. Z., who often appear to be hopeless in terms of analytically oriented psychotherapy, have required therapists to rework their strategies and theories. However, working with patients like this aging woman with preoedipal disorders helps expand the therapist's commitment for psychotherapy with elderly patients in private practice.

RECENT CLINICAL LITERATURE ON AGING

The increasing interest in treating the aging patient does not exist in a vacuum. Freud is castigated for his early warnings against analyzing people of advanced age, but he later revised his position after developing his structural theory. He then presented a more open and questioning view of developmental issues occurring later in life (Freud, 1958). Abraham (1927) considered the successful treatment of patients of advanced years more related to the length of their neuroses than to the length of their life.

Literature on treatment of the elderly patient remained quite sparse until a sprinkling of authors began to write about their dynamically oriented approaches in the 1940s and 1950s. Atkin (1941), commenting on a paper by Kaufman (1940), described the personality rigidity of an unmarried aging woman. He argued that her inelasticity of mental functioning appeared to be a defensive response to unexpressed anxiety rather than an automatic part of the aging process. Grotjahn (1940, 1951) described the dynamics of a senile patient. It was not until 1958 that Segal presented an 18-month analysis of a man in his seventies.

Various dynamically oriented clinicians have described their work with the geriatric patient. Although this review will concentrate on the clinical and case literature, it is worth noting that in the 1960s, the Boston Society for Gerontologic Psychiatry presented several books on their work (for example, Berezin & Cath, 1965; Levin & Kahana, 1967; Zinberg & Kaufman, 1963), and the society has been publishing the *Journal of Geriatric Psychiatry* since 1968.

King (1974, 1980), who employed a developmental perspective in her work, argued that the aging process leads to a resurgence of the issues evoked by adolescence, as the patient regresses to that earlier stage in order to resolve the issues of aging. Sandler (1978, 1982), in two detailed presentations, also provides a developmental perspective. One case was of a two-year analysis of a 69-year-old woman who had used a defense of pseudo-independence throughout her life to avoid difficult and unbearable feelings of sadness and anger. Sandler conceptualized this woman's illness as a result of the derailment, in her old age, of her ability to adapt to the tasks of maturation. Describing in detail her interactions and the experience of working with this woman, Sandler also cited several countertrans-ference reactions that catalyzed her understanding of the patient.

Sandler offered another study of an eight-year analysis of a man who completed therapy in his sixty-sixth year. His complex problems, which Sandler viewed as related to his self-esteem and his narcissistic fear of humiliation, were described with much process material. The patient wanted to please the analyst and satisfy her. The therapist saw the patient as finally dealing with material not completed during his adolescence. Sandler described this patient as neurotic "within a narcissistic matrix" (1978, p. 34).

Myers (1984) reviewed the treatment of six elderly patients through psychoanalysis and psychoanalytic psychotherapy. He found that several of these patients seemed especially eager to embrace therapy because their age made them aware of the need to deal with symptoms such as alcoholism or impotence before time ran out. The general theme of loss, and its particular qualities in response to the death of loved ones or the effects of retirement, was explored throughout this fine collection.

Myers found that when patients could dream, had good object relations, and could use the transference relationship, they were indeed able to benefit from psychoanalytically oriented therapy, no matter what their age. Myers was concerned, however, that patients lacking these qualities would be ineligible for such treatment.

Miller (1987) understood a 70-year-old woman's experience in psychoanalysis as the wish for immortality. Mrs. T. displayed a relatively strong ego and was a well-functioning woman who had several crises with her adopted children. Miller enjoyed his work with this patient and found her psychologically minded and witty. He had thought the patient's age might be a barrier to her experienc-ing, as younger patients do, oedipal feelings for him. Miller was therefore surprised by the oedipal nature of the patient's transference responses to him. Mrs. T. was a basically healthy patient who was able to cooperate with the therapist and explore her feelings about rejuvenation.

In 1985, Simburg described the psychoanalytic treatment of a 62-year-old woman. Like Miller's patient, she was a neurotic woman who was able to cooperate with the therapist and to use insight effectively in a traditional analysis. This woman had never been able to mourn and experience anger at her mother's early death. In the transference, the patient experienced the love she had felt from her mother and then was able to experience anger at the mother for dying. Simburg felt that age was no determinant of the patient's ability to make use of analysis. He did note the complexity of the transference communications, as he seemed to be dealing with five generations through the patient's associations.

Freed (1987) emphasizes the distinctions in women's life cycle compared with men's. Women's issues relate more to the importance of relationships, she argues, and thus loss, and loss of roles, can have an especially devastating effect on the female. Freed describes three case vignettes of women dealing with loss in relationships and the way in which therapy was used to enable them to strengthen themselves by developing new roles. The cases are of women who seemed well-functioning and were dealing with widowhood, loss of the mothering role, and divorce.

Solis and Brink (1989) employed an Adlerian approach to treating a widow in her mid-sixties. She had experienced the loss of many important people in her life and felt that no one needed her help any longer. No longer serving someone, she fell into a depression. The therapist encouraged her involvement in activities in which she could serve and feel needed. This solution helped her resolve reactions to her life circumstances.

Depression and drug abuse fueled the therapy of a 62-year-old woman whose early developmental problems never permitted her to deal with lifelong conflicts. Liptzin (1985) employed the conceptualizations of Erik Erikson (1959) to discover this woman's lack of basic trust and focused on this developmental need. This approach helped the patient to give up the drugs and improve her relationship with her husband, on whom she had depended completely.

Kivnick and Kavka (2002) cite the example of Mrs. Y., "a spunky Chinese woman in her late 80s" who was constantly so worried that something awful was going to happen to her children and grandchildren that her quality of life was being severely affected. As she learned about Mrs. Y.'s childhood and the abuse she suffered at her mother's hand, even as Mrs. Y. "discharge(d) adult duties while only a child," the therapist was able to establish a therapeutic alliance and sense of trust in their relationship by actively engaging Mrs. Y. on the continuity between her past and present. It became clear that although Mrs. Y. had been a model adult, as she found herself increasingly dependent on her children she had re-experienced the terror and rage that characterized her youth with her own mother. She was afraid of being mistreated and frightened of the destructiveness of her own rageful responses to being mistreated. Through the therapeutic alliance, Mrs. Y. was able to face deep-seated fears and rebalance her earliest sense of trust and mistrust, ultimately relieving her symptoms and enabling her to once again be able to handle the demands of everyday life. Kivnick and Kavka (2002) also used Erik Erikson's developmental perspective to understand and treat this woman.

Nemiroff and Colarusso (1985) also present a developmental perspective in understanding and treating the older patient through psychodynamic psychotherapy and psychoanalysis. They explore whether a developmental arrest can be resolved in adulthood, permitting the personality to unfold and thus enabling the patient to deal with adult life tasks. In Nemiroff and Colarusso's edited collection, therapists working from various theoretical perspectives describe patients from the age of 40 through their 80s, many of whom were able to benefit from therapy by successfully employing insight. The patients discussed tended to be more along the neurotic side of the psychopathological continuum. A common thread in the cases presented by many of these authors is the fact that the patients were comfortable and cooperative with the psychotherapeutic process. Colarusso (1998) continues to examine his interest in the developmental issues that rebound in the aging patients as he studies their continued maturation. In another work, he examines the separation-individuation crises of later life that encompass a growing awareness of the multiple losses that will begin to occur (Colarusso, 1997).

Another approach to the developmental issues for older women is examined by Crose (1999), who studied "the complexities of body image, sexuality, and intimacy in the lives of older women" (Crose,

1999, p. 74). Therapists traditionally believed older women were very different from their younger cohorts and treated them differently. However, a growing interest in the sexuality of older women reveals that aging women are being treated in the same ways as their younger counterparts. Certainly, there may be other issues impacting the older woman and her sexuality (e.g., health, menopause, depression, loss), just as there are issues that affect younger women. But Crose (1999) maintains that aging itself is not a disability that needs direct attention; instead, in developing an approach to therapy, the therapist must discuss issues of concern with the patient and be willing to hear what the patient needs to say.

Altschuler and Katz (1996) bring to therapists' attention sexual, countertransference, and treatment issues associated with older female clients. Unless the therapist understands his or her own ageism, sexism, or countertransference prejudices that might be conveyed unconsciously to older women with sexual concerns, the therapist's ability to work with these clients is limited.

In a study of treating older patients, Levine (1996) emphasizes the issues of countertransference when a therapist is a younger woman and the patient an older woman. Concentrating on the feminist issues that relate to these attitudes about loss, death, and illness is offered as a foundation for shaping the therapeutic relationship.

Valenstein (2000) warns that the age and gender of the therapist are significant in determining the direction the transference relationship takes. He cites the case of a 68-year-old musician who returned to graduate school after retiring from her teaching position. Her analysis enabled her to complete a creative doctoral thesis by the age of 79, growing in insight and awareness. Valenstein thought that the transference of the older patient, especially the old-old patient, tended to regress to a preoedipal type of transference. He described the therapy with this patient as productive, even though she was of advanced age. Similarly productive was the treatment described by Settlage (1996) in which a centenarian, a creative poet, was enabled to work productively in analysis and experience changes in her psychic structure.

In a vignette cited by Plotkin (2000), the therapist overidealized an older, narcissistic patient, thereby preventing productive analytic work. The therapist's boredom with the relationship led to the interruption of the treatment when the patient proposed that she was too old for therapy and the therapist agreed. The more seriously disordered patient is a challenge, whatever the age. And as more elderly are seeking treatment, it is critical that the more seriously ill older patient receive the same attention as the more disturbed younger patient.

One of the questions this chapter addresses is what do we do with the patient who is not comfortable or cooperative with the process, such as a patient with serious lifelong pathology? I believe we can engage in treatment that takes into account the fragility of the ego, the intolerance for insight, and an inability to form a treatment alliance. We can create therapeutic options, even for patients with serious lifelong pathology such as Mrs. Z., whose case is discussed later in this chapter.

THE MODERN PSYCHOANALYTICAL APPROACH

The therapeutic approach I use to help create options for seriously disturbed patients derives from the theoretical perspective of Modern Psychoanalysis, developed by Hyman Spotnitz (Meadow, 2003; Spotnitz, 1987, 2004; Spotnitz & Meadow, 1976). To describe Modern Psychoanalytic techniques quite briefly, I should note that the goal is to permit successful work with the narcissistic or preoedipal patient by means of ego-strengthening approaches. In the early stages of treatment the fragile patient sets the tone for the sessions and a non-stimulating environment is created. The therapist offers no more talking than the patient seeks. This effort to follow the patient's verbal and nonverbal signals is called "following the contact functioning," and the patient's contact with the therapist is studied and respected (Spotnitz, 2004). Interventions during this period help the patient experience the therapist as similar to the self and agreeable, on either a conscious or unconscious level (Margolis, 1986; Meadow, 2003).

At this early stage, the patient does not clearly differentiate him- or herself from the therapist. With the development of this state, a narcissistic transference takes hold and the patient's characterological patterns become amenable to influence within the day-to-day working of the therapeutic relationship (Spotnitz, 2004). As this stage develops fully, the patient is helped to see the therapist as a separate object. Frequently, as the patient begins to experience the therapist as separate, there is an expression of aggression directed against the therapist. Once the patient is able to distinguish between self and other in the therapy relationship, the patient is well on the road to healthier functioning in which he or she can have relationships with people who think and feel differently.

In this approach, the therapist's reactions, too, provide useful information about the unexpressed feelings and thoughts of the patient. These reactions, that is, all the therapist's thoughts and feelings about the patient, are studied under the rubric of counter-transference. A therapist's feelings of hopelessness, then, would be studied not merely as an objective statement about the impossibility of meaningful treatment for a patient, but as offering potentially useful information about the patient. This orientation shapes my work with patients and is especially applicable to therapy with the aging patient, where feelings of helplessness and futility often enter the therapeutic relationship.

To illustrate how this approach works in practice, I will discuss a two-year period, beginning five years after Mrs. Z. began treatment. At this time, Mrs. Z. was coming to therapy weekly and her husband joined her twice a month. Individual treatment combined with couple therapy is frequently used in Modern Psychoanalysis when the patient's main emotional involvement is to a spouse. The individual is treated in the presence of the spouse.

This period highlighted issues especially relevant for the older population: retirement, illness, and selling one's family home and moving to a retirement community. As these life-marking events unfolded, I became more hopeless about the possibility of helping this angry, paranoid woman to have a satisfying life and a cooperative marriage.

Before tracing the treatment in relation to these life events, let me review the background of treatment up to this point. For a review of the earlier period of treatment, see Semel (1986).

CASE: MRS. Z.

A high school graduate, Mrs. Z. had devoted her adult years to raising four children in a New York suburb and, to a lesser extent, to being a wife. She began treatment two years after the shock of learning that her husband, a successful lawyer in a New York firm, had been having a six-year affair with a colleague, whom he wanted to marry. This crisis in their life was resolved by Mr. Z.'s serious depression in attempting to leave his wife and his subsequent decision to remain with her and give up the "other woman."

Mrs. Z. came into treatment feeling she had never recovered from, and was unable to cope with, this situation. She selected a female therapist to "understand her" and also to help "explain men" to her. Mrs. Z. wanted a therapist who was like her. Her husband's psychiatrist had referred her to me with the request that I also consider marital counseling for the couple. The early stage of treatment saw this woman totally unable to talk about herself. She had no skill in observing her own behavior and would speak in an out-of-contact fashion about the weaknesses and failures of her husband. I was aware that, along with a paranoid character structure, she exhibited some degree of thought disorder. She could not hear what was said and often "heard" what she assumed were another's motives. She was easily distracted and frequently scrambled others' messages.

When she entered treatment, Mrs. Z.'s total world-view was bound up with her husband. Every aspect of his behavior enraged *her,* while her paranoid projections led her to describe *him* as in a rage at all times. She also saw him as vindictively attempting to get back at her for not going along with his authoritarian whims. She had no sense of herself as contributing to their conflicts or to the unsatisfying status of their 30-year marriage. Mrs. Z., who was completely out of touch with her own rage, lacked an observing ego. I wondered, at this early stage, if she were not psychotic.

Initially I tried following her contact functioning to help her develop a relationship in which she saw me as similar to herself. When I might slip and offer unsolicited "useful information," such as how raging at her husband might not help her achieve her goals, she simply was unable to make use of this input. I would then, according to Mrs. Z., not understand how truly awful he was. I saw that my silence, in combination with a few questions that might eventually lead her to have an interest in me or an understanding of herself, was the best approach during these early years of work.

Mrs. Z. reported a loving and satisfying family of origin. Seven years younger than two siblings, she had been the much-loved baby.

Her mother may have been a bit overprotective, but she felt loved by her parents and she loved them. She saw her father as "having a temper," but it flared quite rarely and quickly dissipated. She reported an idyllic childhood, no frustrations, no anger. One of her older sisters was given a college education; Mrs. Z. was later refused one, so did not attend college. She experienced no feelings about this inequity.

Mrs. Z. stated that she felt supported by her mother. She once described her mother as passively dominated by her older sisters (Mrs. Z.'s aunts). The mother would submit to these relatives and then cyclically break off ties to free herself from their power. Mrs. Z. described a slight feeling of revulsion toward her mother for allowing them to treat her in this fashion.

Issues of domination constantly shaped her verbalizations. Of course, in the present, these were tied to her husband. A continual battle of wills existed between them. It was he who had ruined her life. Nothing had ever been wrong until she married him. In righteous indignation she explained: "I let him go to grad school . . . I let him advance his career and work late." Her interest remained in the projected image she had of her husband. In keeping with that interest, we explored the idea of bringing him to sessions so I could help her improve her marriage.

As I spent time with her, I realized that she used rage as a defense against any of the "softer feelings," such as hurt, abandonment, longing and, of course, hopelessness. Five years of treatment progressed slowly, but with some evidence that Mrs. Z. could control her rages. And she was just starting to talk about herself, occasionally beginning sentences with the word "I" rather than "He." Thus we arrived at the period of her husband's retirement, illness, and the couple's decision to move to a retirement community in Florida.

At this time, Mrs. Z. continued to think of her husband as the only problem in her life. I had helped her and was therefore idealized. Her rationale seemed to be that if I could not help the marriage it was due to the serious deficiencies of her husband.

To celebrate Mr. Z.'s retirement, parties were held and some of these took place at the site of his betrayal with the "other woman." Mrs. Z. spent much time deciding whether to go to a dinner honoring her husband. She said she would be nauseated by the adulation Mr. Z. would receive. She was sure she could not stand the people who would be there and that her husband would not help make her comfortable. I agreed that Mr. Z. would not try to make her comfortable, but took a stand in favor of her actively solving the problems that her husband allegedly produced. I introduced the idea that she could feel one way and act another, behaving appropriately no matter how she felt. I also encouraged her to seek what she wanted rather than blame her husband.

She did, indeed, want to behave appropriately and attended the retirement dinner in style. Her decision, although showing some of her ability to change and to benefit from the ego-strengthening strategies of therapy, did not relieve my feelings of frustration about this case.

Her true feelings about her husband surfaced in a slip she made when he became ill during the first year of his retirement. Treatment for Mr. Z.'s condition required that a tube be inserted into his ear and then removed. While describing this procedure, Mrs. Z. told me the doctors removed the "tomb," instead of "tube." She, of course, did not hear the slip, so I asked whether she was moving her husband to the tomb. She responded with irritation at Mr. Z.'s incapacity and with annoyance that he could not follow the doctor's orders and sit still when necessary. She did, however, seem genuinely concerned about her husband's health, but expressed even this concern in a hostile and critical fashion. No empathy or fear for his well-being was articulated, only anger—the pervasive emotion she relied on as a defense against other more painful affects.

Retirement, and the close contact it brings some couples, is not all bliss, especially for a couple whose every interaction inflames one spouse. Mr. and Mrs. Z. were now together much more frequently than before. Behaviors that had always irritated each about the other became exacerbated. A pattern that played itself out continually involved Mr. Z.'s obsessive orderliness and neatness, contrasted with his wife's sloppiness and inability to discard or put away anything. Mr. Z. would have breakfast and clean up after himself immediately. Mrs. Z. would have a leisurely breakfast and not clean up. This led to frequent arguments and dissatisfaction.

Feeling irritated and frustrated about ever seeing this couple behave considerately toward each other, I used my feelings in a countertransference intervention and proposed that Mr. Z. truly was hopeless and could not possibly change. After much discussion of his hopeless state, Mrs. Z. replied that she would now have to accept that while her husband did have a problem with overneatness, *she* might just have to stop fighting his obsessive–compulsive behaviors.

From our initial sessions five years earlier, Mrs. Z. had maintained that Mr. Z. was hopeless. I had taken the useless stand of trying to convince her that he might be redeemable if she treated him differently. Because she could not be convinced of another point of view, this strategy had not helped. Now, as the couple was planning to sell their house and move to Florida, I continued the countertransference intervention and suggested to Mrs. Z. that they made each other miserable. I asked why Mrs. Z. would want to stay with her husband in retirement, since he made her so unhappy. I was no longer taking the position of trying to preserve their relationship and was leaving to her the responsibility of convincing me that the marriage could improve. My agreeing with her about his hopelessness allowed her to relax her drive to have him change, and she began reporting that she and her husband treated each other a bit more circumspectly at home. Mrs. Z. also enumerated pleasures she and her husband did share; for example, traveling together, time with their grandchildren, and the fact that they enjoyed having companionship. In truth, I was hardly convinced and pointed out that she could have those pleasures without living with Mr. Z.

Responding to this treatment strategy, Mrs. Z. began to work more cooperatively with her husband on the selection of a place to retire. They even agreed on the model of a house and decided that Mrs. Z. would be responsible for the interior. Mr. Z. was to have a workshop that was exclusively his. They could not actually share responsibilities, but were at least able to delineate areas in which each spouse would dominate.

This effort to get along better did not last long, and a major conflict developed over preparing their present home for sale. In keeping with her habitual pattern, Mrs. Z. claimed to be eager to move, but was unable to mobilize herself to fix up and clean the house in order to put it on the market. As usual, Mr. Z. pressured his wife to undertake these tasks and to discard many of their belongings.

In an effort to resolve this conflict, the couple came to a joint session. However, even there, each spouse tried to dominate the other. Mr. Z. complained that Mrs. Z. wanted him to be her slave, and Mrs. Z. was just as convinced that he wanted her to be *his* slave. "What equally impossible people!" I thought.

I told them this was the scenario repeated throughout their years together and "ordered" them to let themselves be a "slave" to their partner. When Mrs. Z. wanted to save items and go slowly, Mr. Z. should help her do so. If Mr. Z. needed to be active and do cleaning tasks, Mrs. Z. was to encourage and help him. This particular strategy led to significant changes in Mrs. Z.'s therapy.

Shortly after this, Mrs. Z. was able to express annoyance with me. She began a session by stating that she wished she could take me home with her so I could witness firsthand the problems she encountered. But her tone was light and full of humor, something I had not heard her express before. She also noted feeling pressured by me. She felt that when I had told her to submit to her husband, I was asking her to give up her sense of herself, her identity, and that she would then be "stepped on." She even admitted that Mr. Z.'s attempts to influence her or convince her he was right on any issue made her become more obstinate in an effort to protect her "real self." For the first time in our work together, Mrs. Z. was actually talking with self-awareness about herself, her feelings, and her behavior patterns.

In her new insights I recognized that her reaction to her husband's pressure was similar to that which she had felt at her mother's submission to relatives. Knowing that Mrs. Z. could not make use of this connection between two periods of her life and that she would feel misunderstood if presented with this observation, I did not express my thoughts to her at this time. Even so, this session was radically different in content and emotion from previous ones. Humor, involvement and annoyance with me, and self-awareness were new factors that characterized this encounter.

Some change continued to be evident. Later that month, also for the first time in our work together, Mrs. Z. took on blame for the couple's difficulties in selling their house and the need for a costly bridge loan. Her guilt hinged on her slowness in preparing the house for sale. For this woman to believe and verbalize that she was responsible for any problem in her life was progress. Her normal automatic projection of blame did not occur. Of course, a goal of therapy is to enable the patient to function without needing to place blame on the self or others, and Mrs. Z. had not come that far. However, she had shifted her response to life events from blatant overt attacks on her husband to acknowledging her own responsibility; this was an important change.

Thus, some movement was now evident in treatment, but I was still aware of my own pervasive feelings of hopelessness about this patient and could not believe Mrs. Z. was truly improving. Of course, I had seen that her fear of being vulnerable to Mr. Z.'s, or any person's influence, and her continued need to place blame and be angry, reflected her fragile ego and uncertainly of her own value and role in life. I recognized, too, that she needed to be able to work through her preoedipal rage in an environment in which she felt protected. Was I providing such an environment? On reviewing the case carefully, I became aware of how afraid of Mrs. Z's rage I had been throughout our work together. I questioned whether I had used my feelings of frustration about the case to spare myself the burden of having her anger turned on me. This realization freed me from feelings of futility about this treatment and I began to think of ways to talk with this patient about her anger.

In the next session, I described her as a "good attacker," and asked why I was ignored in her attacks. She thought it was because I was not nasty and unfair like her husband. I offered to operate as he did, if this would help her include me in her well-developed attacks and criticisms. Was she ready to direct her rage at me? Apparently, she was ready, and I was also prepared to deal directly with her venomous attacking quality. I began to take stronger stands that frustrated her and I felt freer to confront her. We began to disagree more openly and more regularly. At last we were on our way to having a more open interactive relationship.

The outcome of this case was interrupted by the move. Mrs. Z., however, had made definite progress, and the couple had the opportunity to try out more harmonious coping strategies, even if these behaviors were not fully adopted as a way of life. Mrs. Z. was able to bring some varying degree of insight and self-awareness to her interactions with her husband and to problem solving, and sometimes was able to modify her behavior to achieve her goals. Although anger and rage still were primary emotions, she had begun to look at this mode in therapy and occasionally express other emotions. Her affect lightened somewhat, and although her world-view had been totally centered on her husband, she was acknowledging her own needs and desires and found ways to articulate them, if not always to achieve them. Most importantly, she allowed one other significant relationship to influence her life—the therapeutic relationship with me.

Certainly, age-related issues permeated the content of therapy with Mrs. Z. Her husband's mid-life affair, and later his retirement, serious illness, and the couple's decisions around selling the family home and moving to a retirement community all were relevant aspects of the treatment. However, the part these issues played was primarily to exacerbate the already existing problems and the patterns the couple, and especially Mrs. Z. individually, used for coping. In Mrs. Z.'s case the stress of these late-life events and markers highlighted the inadequacies of her preoedipal survival skills and the serious nature of her psychopathology, causing her enough suffering to motivate her to seek out and persist in treatment.

This case demonstrates the Modern Psychoanalytic approach in patients of whatever age or with seriously entrenched disorders. The barriers to Mrs. Z.'s case, after the basic transference had been established, were my countertransference difficulties with her rageful qualities and my feelings of futility about the case. Clearly, the feelings of hopelessness in working with this woman were more a result of the countertransference issues than a statement about Mrs. Z.'s treatability. These are difficulties I might have had with patients of any age—they were specifically related to her personality patterns and to her resistance to treatment. My use of countertransference interventions allowed the treatment to finally focus on her rage and to create an environment in which she could express it and discuss it. Our accepting relationship helped lessen her need to repeatedly project rage onto her husband and opened the possibility for other change.

I believe that the more seriously disturbed the patient, the less age appears to be the primary factor in treatment. In these cases, the essential factor is the orientation of the therapist to working toward personality maturation, which will help these patients in their later years.

REFERENCES

Abraham, K. (1927). The applicability of psycho-analytic treatment to patients at an advanced age. In *Selected papers on psycho-analysis* (pp. 312–317). London: Hogarth. [Original work published 1919.]

Altschuler, J., & Katz, A. D. (1996). Sexual secrets of older women: Countertransference in clinical practice. *Clinical Gerontologist, 17,* 51–67.

American Psychological Association. (2004). Guidelines for psychological practice with older adults. *American Psychologist, 59,* 236–260.

Atkin, S. (1941). Discussion of Kaufman's paper. *American Journal of Orthopsychiatry, 10,* 79–84.

Berezin, M. A., & Cath, S. H. (Eds.). (1965). *Geriatric psychiatry: Grief, loss and emotional disorders in the aging process.* New York: International Universities Press.

Colarusso, C. A. (1997). Separation-individuation processes in middle adulthood. In S. Akhtar & S. Kramer (Eds.). *The seasons of life: Separation-individuation perspectives* (pp. 73–94). Northvale, NJ: Jason Aronson.

Colarusso, C. A. (1998). Development and treatment in late adulthood. In G. H. Pollack & S. Greenspan (Eds.). *The course of life,* Vol. 7: *Completing the journey* (pp. 285–317). Madison, CT: International Universities Press.

Crose, R. G. (1999). Addressing late life developmental issues for women: Body image, sexuality, and intimacy. In M. Duffy (Ed.). *Handbook of counseling and psychotherapy with older adults* (pp. 57–76). New York: Wiley.

Erikson, E. (1959). Identity and the life cycle. *Psychological Issues.* [Monograph No. 1]. New York: International Universities Press.

Freed, A. O. (1987). Psychotherapy with older women. *Smith College Studies in Social Work, 57,* 171–183.

Freud, S. (1953). On psychotherapy. In J. Strachey (Ed. and Trans.), *The standard edition of the complete psychological works of Sigmund Freud* (Vol. 7, pp. 257–268). London: Hogarth, 1905.

Freud, S. (1958). Remembering, repeating and working-through. In J. Strachey (Ed. and Trans.), *The standard edition of the complete, psychological works of Sigmund Freud* (Vol.12, pp. 145–156). London: Hogarth, 1914.

Grotjahn, M. (1940). Psychoanalytic investigations of a seventy-one-year-old man with senile dementia. *Psychoanalytic Quarterly, 9,* 80–97.

Grotjahn, M. (1951). Some analytic observations about the process of growing old. *Psychoanalysis and the Social Sciences, 3,* 301–312.

Journal of Geriatric Psychiatry. (1968–1992). Vols. 1–25.

Kaufman, M. R. (1940). Old age and aging: The psychoanalytic point of view. *American Journal of Orthopsychiatry, 10,* 73–79.

King, P. H. M. (1974). Notes on the psychoanalysis of older patients: Reappraisal of the potentialities for change during the second half of life. *Journal of Analytical Psychology, 19,* 22–37.

King, P. H. M. (1980). The life cycle as indicated by the nature of the transference in the psychoanalysis of the middle-aged and elderly. *International Journal of Psycho-Analysis, 61,* 153–160.

Kivnick, H. Q., & Kavka, A. B. (2002). Psychodynamic psychotherapy: Psychosocial themes in the Eriksonian alliance. In F. K. Trotman & C. M. Brody (Eds.). *Psychotherapy and counseling with older women* (pp. 125–143). New York: Springer.

Knight, B. G. (1999). The scientific basis for psychotherapeutic intervention with older adults: An overview. *Journal of Clinical Psychology, 55,* 927–934.

Knight, B. G., & McCallum, T. J. (1998). Adapting psychotherapeutic practice for older clients: Implications of the contextual, cohort-based, maturity, specific challenge model. *Professional Psychology: Research and Practice, 29,* 15–22.

Levin, S., & Kahana, R. J. (Eds.). (1967). *Psychodynamic studies on aging: Creativity, reminiscing, and dying*. New York: International Universities Press.

Levine, L. (1996). "Things were different then": Countertransference issues for younger female therapists working with older female clients. *Social Work in Health Care, 22*, 73–88.

Liptzin, B. (1985). Psychotherapy with the elderly: An Eriksonian perspective. *Journal of Geriatric Psychiatry, 18*, 183–202.

Margolis, B. (1986). Joining, mirroring, psychological reflection: Terminology, definitions, theoretical considerations. *Modern Psychoanalysis, 11*, 19–35.

Meadow, P. W. (2003). *The New psychoanalysis*. In C. Lemert (Series Ed.), *Legacies of social thought*. New York: Rowman & Littlefield.

Miller, E. (1987). The oedipus complex and rejuvenation fantasies in the analysis of a seventy-year-old woman. *Journal of Geriatric Psychiatry, 20*, 29–51.

Myers, W. A. (1984). *Dynamic therapy of the older patient*. New York: Jason Aronson.

Nemiroff, R. A., & Colarusso, C. A. (1985). *The race against time: Psychotherapy and psycho-analysis in the second half of life*. New York: Plenum.

Plotkin, F. (2000). Treatment of the older adult: The impact on the psychoanalyst. *Journal of the American Psychoanalytic Association, 48*, 1591–1616.

Qualls, S. H. (1998). Training in geropsychology: Preparing to meet the demand. *Profession Psychology, Research and Practice, 29*, 23–28.

Qualls, S. H., Segal, D. L., Norman, S., Niederehe, G., & Gallagher-Thompson, D. (2002). Psychologists in practice with older adults: Current patterns, sources of training, and need for continuing education. *Professional Psychology: Research & Practice, 33*, 435–442.

Sandler, A. (1978). Psychoanalysis in later life: Problems in the psychoanalysis of an aging narcissistic patient. *Journal of Geriatric Psychiatry, 11*, 5–36.

Sandler, A. (1982). Psychoanalysis and psychoanalytic psychotherapy of the older patient: A developmental crisis in an aging patient: Comments on development and adaptation. *Journal of Geriatric Psychiatry, 15*, 11–32.

Segal, H. (1958). Fear of death: Notes on the analysis of an old man. *International Journal of Psycho-Analysis, 39*, 178–181.

Semel, V. G. (1986). The aging woman: Confrontations with hopelessness. In T. Bernay & D. W. Cantor (Eds.). *The psychology of today's woman: New psychoanalytic visions* (pp. 253–269). Hillsdale, NJ: Analytic Press.

Settlage, C. F. (1996). Transcending old age: Creativity, development, and psychoanalysis in the life of a centenarian. *International Journal of Psycho-Analysis, 77*, 549–564.

Simburg, E. J. (1985). Psychoanalysis of the older patient. *Journal of the American Psychoanalytic Association, 33*, 117–132.

Solis, J., & Brink, T. L. (1989). Adlerian approaches in geriatric psychotherapy: Case of an American widow. *Individual Psychology, 45*, 178–185.

Spotnitz, H. (1987). *Psychotherapy of preoedipal conditions: Schizophrenia and severe character disorders*. Northvale, NJ: Jason Aronson.

Spotnitz, H. (2004). *Modern psychoanalysis of the schizophrenic patient* (2nd ed.). New York: YBK.

Spotnitz, H., & Meadow, P. W. (1976). *Treatment of the narcissistic neuroses.* New York: Manhattan Center for Advanced Psychoanalytic Studies.

Trotman, F. K., & Brody, C. M. (2002). *Psychotherapy and counseling with older women: Cross-cultural, family, and end-of-life issues.* New York: Springer.

Valenstein, A. F. (2000). The older patient in psychoanalysis. *Journal of the American Psychoanalytic Association, 48,* 1563–1589.

Zinberg, N. E., & Kaufman, I. (1963). Cultural and personality factors associated with aging: An introduction. In N. E. Zinberg & I. Kaufman (Eds.). *Normal psychology of the aging process* (pp. 17–71). New York: International Universities Press.

Chapter 11

Modern Psychoanalytic Therapy With an Aging Man: The Failure to Attain Occupational Success

Vicki G. Semel

One belief about aging is that as one moves into old age, one is far less likely to change. Personality traits become more rigid with age, states Freud (1964). Because men are less likely than women to enter the therapist's office, we might assume that such a pattern would hold with older men as well. Sprenkel (1999) notes the difficulty men have in talking about themselves and express-ing affect.

Yet a contradictory theory supports the reverse theoretical position about older people. Colarusso (2000) looks to the continua-tion of separation-individuation periods in adulthood and later life—for example, as men, and now women, upon retiring from work, find themselves needing to redefine their identities separate from their jobs. Kahana and Morgan (1998) similarly review the continuing state of development. There is some literature that compares older men with younger ones. Gutmann (1979) notes the growing comfort that men have with their feelings as they age and as they come to terms with their lives. The pressure from aggressive/competitive values diminishes and men can become accepting of the softer values. Kernberg (1980) also suggests that narcissistic patients, in general, are easier to treat as they age. Thus it may be useful to review the reports that have started to appear in the literature of psychoanalytically oriented private practice treatment of men, as many researchers expect continuing change and development in older adults.

This chapter reviews those reports and examines the therapy of one aging man, Mr. P., with special attention to issues of work success and retirement.

ANALYTIC PRACTICE WITH OLDER MEN: LITERATURE REVIEW

Much of the literature reviewed in chapter 10 of this book is also relevant to this discussion and the reader is referred to that chapter. More detailed consideration of additional reports illuminates some themes specific to practice with older men. Segal (1958) presented an early work on the subject of male treatment. She psychoanalyzed a 73-year-old man who had an acute paranoid psychotic breakdown when he was confronted by the fear that a business venture that had involved some illegality would lead to his being "caught."

Segal believed that the unconscious fear of death led to this man's psychotic episode and that this fear may underlie other patients' acute psychotic breaks. The patient had used denial and idealization, but these defenses had failed to protect him. The analytic work not only helped him to regain his sanity, but also led to a diminution of his persecutory fantasies and idealizations, and an increase in his acceptance of ambivalence in his psychic reality. Segal, a Kleinian psychoanalyst, understood this man's avoidance of the depressive position as necessary until he was able to work through these issues in the transference and become, for the most part, largely cured.

In another detailed case study, Sandler (1978) described her work with a 58-year-old man who remained in therapy until he was 66 years old. Sandler takes a developmental perspective about the resurgence, in older age, of the adolescent issues that have not been totally resolved. Overwhelming and terrifying somatic symptoms brought this patient to treatment. An architect, he was ashamed about a minor problem with a new building project. He also was inhibited by long-standing marital, sexual, and interpersonal difficulties.

She described how he seemed to form an immediate attachment to the therapist and eventually changed fields to be closer to his idea of what might please her. He also left his wife for another woman and was able to be sexually potent with his new choice. In therapy the patient analyzed both his humiliation and easy narcissistic wounding as well as the flip side—his grandiosity. The analyst believed that he was able to deal with issues from his adolescence that were revived by his aging.

Wasylenki (1982) helped his male patient with a more active kind of therapy. A 78-year-old man was suffering in retirement. Others around him were feeling his intense displeasure. Work had been especially essential for his self-esteem. His professional activities were the source of feeling competent. This man displaced his frustration about his retirement onto his wife and family, criticizing and blaming them unmercifully. In a brief six-month treatment experience, the patient was helped to develop different interests. He was guided to find activities that would redistribute his energies from attacks on his family to behavior that was more satisfying and productive.

Myers (1984) described the detailed treatment of three male patients (among other female patients) in a book that emphasized psychoanalytic principles as valid for such an age group. One patient, a man who was 59 years old at the start of therapy, resolved a lifelong potency problem. Not only did he move forward in his career but he felt positively mobilized by his work with the therapist. A positive transference led to these major gains involving both psychological and physiological potency.

In another of Myers' cases, a 62-year-old depressed man, who had been without work since a coronary attack, passively withdrew in all areas of his life. His wife had left him, and the company for which he had worked went bankrupt. Although the patient was described as leaving therapy prematurely, he had made major gains, marrying again and beginning consulting work.

Myers describes the third man he presented as a treatment failure. A narcissistic college professor, aged 60, with little awareness of his unconscious and little interest in introspection, left treatment when he resolved a potency problem by acting out with a mistress. This patient seemed to fear the aging process but defended against exploring its deeper determinants.

Myers, who worked in a traditional mode using interpretative methods, found his classical psychoanalytic and psychoanalytically oriented psychotherapy approach acceptable to those patients who were able to make use of insight and who were comfortable in exploring their unconscious processes, especially through dream analysis. Character and personality dynamics, rather than age, related to treatment success or failure in these cases.

A fine collection of articles by Nemiroff and Colarusso (1985) offers the idea of successful therapy in old age *because* of old age. It is the "race against time" (the title of their book) that frees many patients to make use of therapy. In one article, a serious heart attack brought a 62-year-old man into treatment (Crusey, 1985). Crusey notes, in this article, the timelessness of the unconscious and the powerful sexualized transference that the patient developed toward his younger female therapist and that he acted out with a nurse. The patient was willing and able to make use of short-term psychodynamic therapy, as he had the impression that there was not much to lose by engaging in therapy. Thus the aging process and illness made this man quite receptive to psychotherapy.

In another article in this collection, Cath and Cath (1985) treated a husband and wife. The wife was dying and the therapy helped the two of them deal with this fact through individual work. Couple counseling also improved their relationship and helped them both handle her serious illness.

Grotjahn's contribution in this collection (1985) was unique and personal. In moving fashion, he described the effects on himself, a therapist, of being sick, facing 80, and possible death. One senses the accepting quality in this aging ill man as he confronts his own decline.

Kahana (1985) examines the treatment of two depressed older men and their disparate approaches to work. One had never been able to work, yet had some ability for fun and pleasure, whereas the other, more a workaholic, had never been able to have enjoyment because he was so self-attacking about his own failures. Kahana believed that these men were both helped by ongoing therapy. He offered descriptions of how each man achieved greater self-esteem.

The more isolated, depressed, nonachieving man moved into the world and began to participate with other people in a senior center, and the overworker made changes more assertively in his work style and developed some capacity for pleasure. Each patient met with the therapist either every other week or once a month and made significant changes in functioning.

In 1991, Coltart described her nine-year, five-day-a-week analysis of a 58-year-old man in a suicidal depression, demonstrating her belief that one must settle for limited gains in the case of older patients. This man's depression was resolved; yet he remained alone in his life, unable to establish intimate relations with anyone except his analyst. The therapist believed that elderly patients confront two tasks: one, their need to consider their own prospective death, and two, the necessity to mourn opportunities that are lost forever.

This patient was especially eager for treatment because his pain was so great that he could not imagine continuing to live. Although an outwardly successful man in his occupation, he felt empty and suicidally depressed. Therapy led him to deal with the depression and resolve it; yet it did not permit him to reach out to others and establish meaningful ties with people

Plotkin (2000) describes her treatment of a successful 60-year-old man whose issues of "self-contempt and self-reproach" (p. 1592) did not prevent him from experiencing national renown. When the patient returned to work after an illness, he was unceremoniously replaced. Faced with this patient's issues of depression plus humiliation at his being rejected professionally, the therapist initially colluded with the patient's dependency issues. When she was able to operate as an analyst, and ceased to be distracted by the patient's age and illness, the patient became more able to focus and to "fall back in love with the world" (p. 1595).

There is an interest in treating the narcissistic patient in later life. Jacobowitz and Newton (1999) describe the treatment of an older salesman who previous to an illness and loss of a job was an independent, narcissistic man. The therapist acted as a grandiose and powerful object, enabling the patient to idealize him and begin to work on his previously unsuccessful return to income production on his own. The therapist worked to strengthen the patient's defenses and self-concepts to deal with issues around aging.

With an Eriksonian view of old age, Kivnick (1998) applies this developmental theory to older life. She studied the life cycle of a

76-year-old doctor who was still professionally active. He chose research in medicine and remained detached from his family and his inner self. His rigid commitment to his professional life did not permit him a way to deal with old age and accept his limitations or his losses. The idea of learning to mourn his past losses and reach out to his family to accept and give caring in a generative context, as a way to "learn to accept the care that he himself required, led to movement in the therapy" (Kivnick, 1998, p. 128). Kivnick proposes that resolution of unresolved early issues are resolvable in later life, as they were for this doctor.

Limentani (1995) notes the issues of creativity in old age. In his examination of the "third age" and creativity, he describes the successful treatment of a 65-year-old man whose recurrent depression blocked his ability to work in his office, let alone offer any "constructive creative thinking" (Limentani, 1995, p. 830). Therapy not only helped him return to running his business but also resolved a longstanding problem with impotence. Limentani believes that work with the older patient can help resolve issues that block creativity due to depressive reactions caused by aging, as much of that creativity is bound up in work-related processes.

It is evident in this brief review of articles on the late-life treatment of aging men that work issues were a major factor in the vast majority of these cases.

The effects of socialization on men who were raised in the first third of the twentieth century would most likely make the issues of work especially salient. Men had the jobs outside the home, whereas women were primarily homemakers, caring for the children and the household needs of the family. Just as a woman in her sixties might experience the role of wife and mother as especially central to her self-concept and self-esteem, so, too, for men would the importance of work evoke both intrapsychic and sociological reactions. Changing roles in society might shift this pattern, but we are examining the patient more than 60 years of age, born in the 1940s or earlier.

A further issue in the literature on men, as well as women, is the seriousness of the patient's disturbance. Patients capable of insight and self-awareness, no matter what age, are considered by many of these authors to be candidates for depth psychotherapy. Yet, if a patient has a disorder such as schizophrenia or one of the other serious character disorders, several clinicians (e.g., Myers,

1984; Pollock, 1987) suggest that such a patient may be inappropriate for psychoanalytically oriented psychotherapy. One approach that is recommended for the treatment of schizophrenia in late life is proffered by Bartels, Levine, and Munster (1999). They emphasize a biopsychosocial approach, rather than psychotherapy. Ivey (1999) notes that destructive narcissism made the treatment of a middle-aged male impossible, as he participated in the destructive enactments that destroyed the treatment.

My position is that techniques have been developed to make the psychoanalytic method applicable to patients no matter what the diagnosis. Modern psychoanalytic methods are those used in the following case. The patient to be described would fall along a continuum of psychopathology in the more narcissistic domain (Spotnitz, 2004; Spotnitz & Meadow, 1976); yet he was treated and benefited from the work, slow though it was.

CASE: MR. P.

This case explores the relationship between unsuccessful vocational choices, retirement, and the aging process for one male patient, with the hope of detecting a pattern that may be relevant to other patients. I suggest that the use of psychoanalytically oriented psychotherapy can be seriously considered as a treatment of choice with patients of any diagnosis, at any age.

With this orientation in mind, we can ask what might the effects be on a man who reaches old age and confronts the reality of a life without success in an essential arena for most men—that is, the workplace. With the more disturbed patient we can frequently expect a powerful defense of denial to operate around issues of aging. In these instances issues of success or failure in the workplace may be unavailable to the therapist. In the case to be discussed, however, certain reality intrusions made the issues of work and retirement quite central to the day-to-day talk in the therapy sessions with Mr. P., which occurred on a weekly basis for five years.

Mr. P., a 65-year-old man, began treatment in the 1950s with a seriously debilitating mental disorder. Unable to function, he had been living at home with his mother, in a Long Island suburb, and he was diagnosed as a paranoid schizophrenic at that time. He was raised the oldest of five children—three brothers and two sisters—in an Italian Catholic family. His father, for whom he expressed much love, was perceived as a harsh and even a violent man who would beat him when Mr. P. misbehaved. The children were all afraid of this man, who worked in another city and came home late at night.

The father was seen as successful in his area of work and made a good living as a manager in a midsize corporation, rising to the level of vice president. He demanded quiet, well-mannered children and enforced this goal with a vengeance.

Mr. P.'s parents separated and then divorced when he was a teenager. Mr. P. never knew why and never asked. He thought there might have been some drinking or gambling problems that the father had at that time. After this separation, Mr. P. would have enjoyable visits with his father, who would pick him up at the New York suburb where he lived and take him to the city. His father became less harsh and more fun.

His mother was perceived as afraid of everything. She would retire to her bedroom if upset. He saw her as quite changeable in her moods and this disturbed Mr. P. enormously. He came back to this description of his mother in many different situations. It was her changeable nature and unpredictability that upset him. It seemed that he was describing a labile woman.

During an initial early therapy experience, Mr. P. had experienced physical symptoms, blackout spells, inordinate fear reactions, ideas of reference, delusions, confused thoughts, and autistic-like thought patterns with another therapist. This was a report of successful treatment, with a male psychoanalyst, Dr. D., who had since died, long after this treatment ended. By the time that therapy concluded, 20 years earlier, Mr. P. had married and fathered two daughters, whom he adored.

He had stopped his analysis because he felt contented, had no ambition, was totally enthralled with his children, and wished to be around to help raise them. He had learned to be both a devoted father and a supportive husband to his wife. He had no wish to further himself in any vocational pursuit and also had no wish to attend college. He had obtained work as a clerk in a family-run business and was a loyal employee at that firm for 15 years. Ten years after the conclusion of his first period of treatment the firm went bankrupt, but he was able to find another job.

Then several shocking events eventually led him to return to therapy: the death of his mother; the serious injury, incapacitation, and then death of a younger brother through that sibling's alcoholism; the failure of yet another business that he had joined as a clerk; and his frustration with an authoritarian female boss for whom he had worked in a third firm. He had first liked her considerably and believed she also liked him. Then she suddenly and publicly humiliated him. This combination of events left him with incapacitating migraine headaches that seemed to "rage inside like an inferno," as Mr. P. described his sensations.

He had little energy, but reported that he went to work in the factory every day as a clerk. He had begun to wonder why he was not more successful and thought he would like to be more competent.

He was referred to me when he attempted to reach Dr. D., and found he had died two years before. In his second entry into therapy he was suffering with painful symptoms. He was somatizing, but seemed to be functioning relatively well. He was eager to be relieved of his terrible headaches. Neurological examination did not identify any medical basis for his symptom picture. He believed that his problems were psychological, although what motivated them was unclear to him.

Mr. P. talked about his first therapy frequently. There he had learned that his inability to express anger and aggression was his basic problem. He thought he needed to express these feelings now, but felt out of touch with the power of them.

He would often, however, describe images of wild animals, especially lions, tearing people apart. I soon became one of these people as a fantasized victim of his rage. He also began to relate the story of the events mentioned above that had caused him to return to treatment. Although his mother's and brother's deaths were mentioned as important, it was the rejection by his female boss, almost as a lost lover, that he related to the onset of the powerful migraine headaches.

His talk was immediately comfortable, as if we had been together a long time. In fact, he described the conclusion of his therapy with Dr. D. during which he began to see him with a certain perceptual distortion that he also projected onto me as his new therapist in the first session. He thought I sounded like and reminded him of Dr. D. Yet what struck me was that this man was beginning therapy almost as if it were the next session that followed by one day his last with Dr. D. 20 years before—a tribute both to the timelessness of the unconscious and perhaps a diagnostic tool for evaluating his object-relatedness.

The personality of the individual therapist did not seem to matter—he had little sense of people as real objects in the world. There were no unique individuals, so he fit me into his continuing need for a therapist. Also, I believed if he thought I was interchangeable with Dr. D., a vastly important person in his unconscious life, he would not have to mourn his loss.

His ability to handle his aggressive impulses was definitely deficient. Though he could "talk about talking about" anger, there was little genuine feeling in the sessions. He might tell of wanting to tear my head off and stab me with a knife, but all these reports were rather boringly enunciated, as if he were behaving like a good boy who knew he should be talking out his angry feelings as Dr. D. told him to do.

Mr. P. would often seem afraid of his impulses, but he behaved appropriately during the sessions. He would arrive on time, use the couch, talk cooperatively, and never engage in threatening action. He convinced me he could stay on the couch and talk, no matter what he felt. Yet he did not seem so convinced. During this period he worked as a clerk in a factory and had the afternoon shift. He hated the hours, but was frozen into accepting whatever his boss decided to give him on the schedule.

This shift was probably unconsciously ideal for him. He would have lunch with his wife, then go to work, where he would have few contacts with people, especially any bosses, who were less in evidence during these off-hours. Then he would return home, sleep, and have the house to himself (his wife worked part-time and the children were in college). He needed this non-stimulating environment; it was important to someone trying to control his impulses.

He would frequently talk about wanting to be more successful, but he could not imagine any field to which he could turn. He had ruled out almost every endeavor. He would note that he could not be a salesman. For this he blamed Dr. D., bringing in his name whenever there was some behavior he did not want to pursue. His recollection was that Dr. D. had thought all salesmen were crooks. I wondered aloud to him whether he could find a product in which he could believe and be an honest salesman. He did not think he could, although he recalled selling a product door-to-door one summer during his early adulthood and doing an exceptional job at it.

He was knowledgeable about cars, but thought the hard sell of most car salesmen would make that a terrible field for him. Car salesmen seemed more like criminals because they pushed you to purchase the car with more and more options, he remarked. The pattern behind Mr. P.'s descriptions of jobs seemed related to the idea of criminality, misbehavior, being "bad." All avenues were closed to him. His children were grown, his wife was working, and he seemed to have little purpose in life.

And this, indeed, was his history. Because he behaved as if I were a continuation of Dr. D., his history came out as if he had already related it to me. His parents gave him the message he should be a "good boy" and only that.

Hence, being "good" made him dependent on the views of others, and their changing moods left him susceptible to their shifts in reaction. This aspect of changeability was a recurrent theme for Mr. P. In fact, this was the perceptual distortion he described in his first meeting with me that he had recalled from his last meeting with Dr. D.

When Dr. D. had greeted him at the door at his final session, Mr. P. thought his face looked different, almost like a witch, melting. He noted in the first session with me that I had that same look, like a witch from *The Wizard of Oz*. The patient did not have a unified view of the objects or people in his life—they became alien when their moods changed.

He began to realize that in therapy he could be like these wild animals. He was interested in them, as he might be like them. His impulses were alien forces inside him, not to be used and directed for his benefit but to be controlled and beaten into submission lest they become freed and destroy. He would describe himself as a monster at times. No wonder he had so little inclination to advance in a profession. His energies must be bound up in controlling himself.

During the early years of our therapy, while verbalizing the wish to become successful, he mainly sought relief from the suffering he felt from his headaches. He had great faith in the psychoanalytic process because it had previously helped him so definitively in many ways.

As he talked and became more aware of the monster in himself, the headaches diminished. He could relate their passing to talking more directly in the sessions. Unexpressed anger did, indeed, seem to produce them. When he could put the frustrations into words, the headaches would diminish, until we both realized he was hardly mentioning them any longer. They were plaguing him far less and when they appeared, would diminish quickly if he could focus on what was bothering him.

He was cooperative in working with the transference in the sessions. He tried to see if I annoyed him when the headaches occurred in the sessions. He might be aware of some anxiety in coming to see me, and then get a headache. Soon he was able to relate it to something I might have done that angered him. He stopped talking about wild animals, and our relationship was more the focus of our interactions. He began to notice variations in my mood: Was I bored with him, annoyed, tired? He appeared calm as he noted some possible shift in my moods. I had the impression of a more intact ego, capable of object consistency.

He mentioned that friends and family commented that he was a "nicer person," not as irritable. He was pleased with these changes in his personality, yet worried that this meant he might never be successful, since one cannot be too nice and move ahead assertively.

He then was let go from his clerical job. At first hurt by this layoff, he then admitted to a delight in not working at a job he hated, in avoiding bosses telling him what to do, and in having decent hours, like other people, for sleeping and spending time with his wife. Mr. P. spoke of an eagerness to find work, although he settled comfortably into his retirement. I first found myself an advocate of his alleged interest in finding an occupation (see chapter 13 for discussion of an important countertransference issue in this case).

When I realized he had little interest in finding work, I concentrated on the meaning of retirement for him. It meant having no authority figure to order him around. It meant being lazy like a baby. He had bought a puppy during this retirement period and spent many hours training it lovingly but firmly—his new baby, it seemed. In fact, once I had resolved my countertransference block to having Mr. P. retire, I was able to see that his idea of retirement was a return to the womb or the early nurturing period of his life. And though he felt guilty about his retirement, and lonely, no work appealed to him.

He began to talk about babies, even took a course on infancy in a continuing education program and, in general, settled into his own retirement infancy. He was trying to rework that early period from which he had never completely removed himself. I recalled how much pleasure he would report in raising his children during their infancy, describing them as playful puppies.

This preoedipal longing to remain a baby could be understood in several ways. A baby does not have to be in control of impulses that threaten to break through. Others will care for him even if he is squalling, dirty, or angry. He cannot be held accountable and he will still be loved. He also can do little damage to his loved ones. Being a baby certainly has much appeal. On a more advanced object level, it would also protect him from identifying with his brutal father.

The emotional message of retirement for this patient is a return to the pleasures of infancy. Yet Mr. P. is in conflict between the pleasures of babyhood and the guilt about such pleasures. Thus, retirement arouses the early and unresolved conflicts of the preoedipal period for the more disturbed patient. Mr. P. had resisted occupational success his whole adult life. The freedom from authority, the need to be taken care of totally, and finally, the need for limited stimulation, all led him to a work inhibition and lack of success. Retirement for such a patient may simply support the underlying resistances to maturation. At the same time, the conflicts around such early longings are more visible and amenable to psychotherapeutic interventions, the goal of therapy with all patients.

REFERENCES

Bartels, S. J., Levine K. J., & Munster, K. T. (1999). A biopsychosocial approach to treatment of schizophrenia in late life. In M. Duffy (Ed.). *Handbook of counseling and psychotherapy with older adults* (pp. 436–452). New York: Wiley.

Cath, S. J., & Cath, C. (1985). When a wife dies. In R. A. Nemiroff & C. A. Colarusso (Eds.). *The race against time: Psychotherapy and psychoanalysis in the second half of life* (pp. 241–262). New York: Plenum.

Colarusso, C. A. (2000). Separation-individuation phenomena in adulthood. *Journal of the American Psychoanalytic Association, 48,* 1467–1489.

Coltart, N. E. (1991). The analysis of an elderly patient. *International Journal of Psycho-Analysis, 72,* 209–219.

Crusey, J. (1985). Short-term psychodynamic psychotherapy with a sixty-two year old man. In R. A. Nemiroff & C. A. Colarusso (Eds.). *The race against time: Psychotherapy and psychoanalysis in the second half of life* (pp. 147–166). New York: Plenum.

Freud, S. (1964). New introductory lectures on psychoanalysis. In J. Strachey (Ed. and Trans.), *The standard edition of the complete psychological works of Sigmund Freud* (Vol. 22, pp. 7–128). London: Hogarth. [Original work published in 1932.]

Grotjahn, M. (1985). Being sick and facing eighty: Observations of an aging therapist. In R. A. Nemiroff & C. A. Colarusso (Eds.). *The race against time: Psychotherapy and psychoanalysis in the second half of life* (pp. 293–302). New York: Plenum.

Gutmann, D. (1979, May). *The clinical psychology of later life: Developmental paradigms.* Presented at the West Virginia Gerontology Conference on the Transitions of Aging, West Virginia University, Morgantown, WV.

Ivey, G. (1999). Transference-counter-transference constellations and enactments in the psychotherapy of destructive narcissism. *British Journal of Medical Psychology, 72,* 63–74.

Jacobowitz, J., & Newton, N. A. (1999). Dynamics and treatment of narcissism in later life. In M. Duffy (Ed.). *Handbook of counseling and psychotherapy with older adults* (pp. 453–469). New York: Wiley.

Kahana, R. J. (1985). The ant and the grasshopper in later life: Aging in relation to work and gratification. In R. A. Nemiroff & C. A. Colarusso (Eds.). *The race against time: Psychotherapy and psychoanalysis in the second half of life* (pp. 263–329). New York: Plenum.

Kahana, R. J., & Morgan, A. C. (1998). Psychoanalytic contributions to geriatric psychiatry. In G. H. Pollock & S. I. Greenspan (Eds.). *The course of life:* Vol. VIII: *Completing the journey* (pp. 161–196). Madison, CT: International Universities Press. Revised and expanded version of S. I. Greenspan & G. H. Pollock (Eds.). (1980). *The course of life: Psychoanalytic contributions toward understanding personality development.* Washington, DC: U.S. Government Printing Office.

Kernberg, O. (1980). *Internal world and external reality.* New York: Jason Aronson.

Kivnick, H. Q. (1998). Through the life cycle: Psychosocial thoughts on old age. In G. H. Pollock & S. I. Greenspan (Eds.). *The course of life:* Vol. VII. *Completing the journey* (pp. 119–134). Madison, CT: International Universities Press.

Limentani, A. (1995). Creativity and the third age. *International Journal of Psycho-Analysis, 76,* 825–832.

Myers, W. A. (1984). *Dynamic therapy of the older patient.* New York: Jason Aronson.

Nemiroff, R. A., & Colarusso, C. A. (1985). *The race against time: Psychotherapy and psychoanalysis in the second half of life.* New York: Plenum.

Plotkin, F. (2000). Treatment of the older adult: The impact on the psychoanalyst. *Journal of the American Psychoanalytic Association, 48,* 1591–1616.

Pollock, G. H. (1987). The mourning-liberation process: Ideas on the inner life of the older adult. In J. Sadovoy & M. Leszcz (Eds.). *Treating the elderly with psychotherapy: The scope for change in later life* (pp. 3–29). Madison, CT: International Universities Press.

Sandler, A. (1978). Psychoanalysis in later life: Problems in the psychoanalysis of an aging narcissistic patient. *Journal of Geriatric Psychiatry, 11,* 5–36.

Segal, H. (1958). Fear of death: Notes on the analysis of an old man. *International Journal of Psycho-Analysis, 39,* 178–181.

Spotnitz, H. (2004). *Modern psychoanalysis of the schizophrenic patient: Theory of the technique* (2nd ed.). New York: YBK.

Spotnitz, H., & Meadow, P. W. (1976). *Treatment of the narcissistic neuroses.* New York: Manhattan Center for Advanced Psychoanalytic Studies.

Sprenkel, D. G. (1999). Therapeutic issues and strategies in group therapy with older men. In M. Duffy (Ed.). *Handbook of counseling and psychotherapy with older adults* (pp. 214–227). New York: Wiley.

Wasylenki, D. A. (1982). Psychodynamics and aging. *Canadian Journal of Psychiatry, 27,* 11–17.

Chapter 12

Private Practice With the Aging Couple: Two Unusual Cases

Vicki G. Semel

A joke that has been around for years describes a couple in their nineties who go to a divorce lawyer to engage his services. He wonders what has brought them to this state after such a long marriage. They respond that they had to wait for their parents and their children to die in order to do what they wanted. At last they are free to do as they choose! This black humor succinctly portrays some of our culture's expectations, stereotypes, and beliefs about aging couples, and these factors pervade the (until recently) sparse clinical literature on treating the elderly couple. This chapter presents literature in the field and two case examples of aging couples who either directly or indirectly sought to deal with serious marital disharmony in their later years. Treatment may not be different whether the couple is old or young, but the content of the issues that brings the elderly couple to treatment may be distinctly related to the aging process, whether, for instance, retirement or an age-related physical impairment or medical condition.

CLINICAL LITERATURE ON THE AGING COUPLE

There is a growing clinical literature to note on the marital treatment of the elderly. Apfel, Fox, Isberg, and Levine (1984) note several complications for younger therapists in working with older couples. These complications are linked to the role of the child in relation to the parents' sexuality and the taboos in those areas. The authors describe the countertransference difficulties that two younger female therapists experienced in working with parental figures. Both treatments dealt with sexual dysfunction and its resolution in the marriage. In one case the patients' responses to the therapist were a source for the resurgence of the analyst's oedipal conflict. In the other case the therapist was blocked because parental figures (that is, the patients) expected her to resolve the hostility they hurled at each other. When that therapist, feeling like the child called upon to help her parents' relationship, recognized and resolved this countertransference bind, she could relate as an adult professional to the couple.

Maintaining a professional relationship is not always easy. Salamon (1997) provides case examples of couples in conjoint therapy that demonstrate how difficult counseling can become when the issue of erotic countertransference is approached.

Gafner (1987, 1989) has written on marital therapy with aging couples. In an attempt to involve the older couple in treatment, he described the "exaggerated engagement" of a couple in their sixties who were fighting after the wife's retirement and their move to a small apartment (1987). Rather than concentrate on the marital conflicts initially, Gafner explored what each member of the couple had experienced in the last few years. He found that helping them resolve real-life medical and physical difficulties, which may have led to tension in the marriage, strengthened their commitment to treatment and appeared to ease their conflicts.

In 1989, Gafner presented a brief note on treatment of an "old-old couple," ages 93 and 87, who had been referred for therapy when the husband was in psychological distress regarding a medical problem. The main upsetting force in this couple's relationship was the failure of the husband's health. The need to readjust to growing physical disability is often a primary impetus for older couples to seek therapy. The therapist was swept into a long-standing conflict with a couple who had been married for 66 years, but who had had "no affection since Pearl Harbor" and "no sexual intercourse since the late 1920s" (1989, p. 51). In retrospect, Gafner became aware that the couple had managed to get the therapist to align with the wife. When the therapist made a home visit, the husband became psychotic, accusing his wife of having an affair with the therapist. Gafner thought the therapist should have either aligned with the husband early on, as he was the more resistant patient, or else should have used male and female cotherapists.

In a third, brief clinical comment, Gafner and Uetz (1990) cite work with an aging couple whose marriage was destroyed by compulsive gambling. The pair enjoyed their time together, although the wife was enraged at the husband's squandering tens of thousands of dollars on gambling. This couple separated over this compulsive gambling but sought to continue their social lives together. The irony was that much of the time that they felt excitement was when they were gambling. The couple was satisfied with the outcome of therapy because they were communicating better and, indeed, although involved in divorce proceedings, seemed to want a continuing relationship. Their gambling, however, in no way abated. Gafner and Uetz note that this couple dealt with many of the issues in marital therapy in a way similar to that used by other elderly couples. They note "embarrassment, grief, and coping with the exacerbation of medical problems in the wake of radical loss and change" as important themes (1990, p. 45).

Savitsky (1983) describes the individual and marital work with an anxious, depressed, and highly critical man. These qualities had a negative effect on both him and his marriage. When these were addressed, the marital conflict abated. Carstensen, Gottman, and Levenson (1995) present an empirical study of 156 couples divided into four groups on the basis of age and marital satisfaction: middle-aged, who were married for at least 15 years, and were either satisfied or dissatisfied, and old, married for 35 years or more, who were either satisfied or dissatisfied. The couples were observed, and then "rated" as they discussed and attempted to resolve a problem in their relationship. Overall, the middle-aged couples displayed more emotions in their interactions than did the older couples—more disgust, belligerence, whining, interest, and humor. On the other hand, the older couples displayed more affection. Across the two age groups, the wives were more emotionally expressive (both positively and negatively), whereas the husbands were more likely to respond defensively, but were more neutral listeners. The gender differences in expressing negative emotion were particularly strong in unhappy marriages.

Retirement can be a major life-affecting event for older couples, especially if it is unexpected or comes sooner than planned or desired (Qualls, 1995). A paradoxical approach to treating a resistant couple, married for more than 40 years, was presented by Gilewski, Kuppinger, and Zarit (1985). The husband was inactive in his retirement, whereas the wife was energized and critical of the husband's inertia. The couple's fighting had worsened after the wife's retirement. She was the one who initiated treatment, although it was with a request for an evaluation of her husband, who she believed was becoming senile. Although being with each other was a goal of treatment, the therapist, using a paradoxical approach, urged the couple to spend *less* time together. This reduced the fighting and the therapist was able to influence the marriage. The couple was then able to see one another as different, not as one partner conducting retirement correctly while the other was a problem partner.

Retirement was the impetus for a case study of a couple treated individually, with the marital conflict as the focus of the work. In that paper, Wolinsky (1986) combined a theoretical model of treating the "mature-stage marriage" with a case study of a 72-year-old retired schoolteacher who had expected her husband, who had always needed much time alone, to provide passion and excitement in her life. Therapy helped her realize that her husband was unable to give her the degree of involvement she expected and that she needed to plan her own retirement goals. She then found another teaching job and became less depressed as she realized she still held a central role in her extended family, especially with her grown grandchildren.

ILLNESS AND DISABILITY IN AGING COUPLES

Besides the aging process, illness and the limitations caused by illness can impact a couple's relationship. The role of physical impairment leading to crises in the marital situation seems to underlie much of the available clinical literature. As couples age, conflicts may surface due to shifts in roles. Greenbaum and Rader (1989) explore the effects of illness on couples. As one of the pair becomes a caregiver, chronic underlying marital conflicts can arise.

Beckham and Giordano (1986) present a theoretical approach to the possible effects on different types of marriage, using the example of one spouse becoming increasingly impaired and the effects of the other becoming a caregiver.

In another case, the husband's physical impairment led the caregiving wife to move from a dependent and passive position to a more independent and assertive role in the marriage (Crose & Duffy, 1988). As the husband's health declined, the formerly subordinate wife initiated a "limited marital separation" (p. 71) while still taking care of him, cooking for him, and visiting him daily. The rigidly structured marriage could not sustain the effects of the role shift, and the wife's own health worsened and led her to remove herself from her difficult partner.

A different issue arose in the marriage of a couple dealing with a terminal illness. Rosowsky (1999) describes the case of a couple that first came to couple therapy for support during the early phases of the 69-year-old husband's terminal illness. The couple subsequently returned to therapy for "a meaningful closure to their marriage" (p. 263). The husband, though seriously ill, was expending much of his limited energy on finishing a community service project he had been working on. The wife wanted her husband's time to be spent with her and to focus on their relationship and life together. But instead of coming together, they were being pulled apart, and her anger and his guilt were only adding to their already heavy emotional burden. Their therapy enabled the couple to explore the dynamics of the situation and better understand each other's feelings, somewhat easing her anger and his guilt. Nevertheless, when the husband died, the wife still felt some resentment, as this was not the ending to the relationship that she wanted, but she was comforted somewhat for having been supportive of her husband.

In Knight's description of case histories (1992), both of his studies of couples in conflict were presented with issues that are more likely to be specific to the older patient: retirement and serious illness. These life-impacting events shaped the therapy in these cases. From the initial contacts with the therapists, "Elaine and Warren," a couple in their seventies, were dealing with the husband's lung disease. The challenge for the therapists was to help the couple deal with their denial of Warren's serious illness and inevitable death. The psychological issues around their interaction were overshadowed by the husband's and, to a lesser extent, the wife's physical problems. The therapists worked with the couple in both individual and conjoint sessions to help Elaine and Warren confront the reality that faced them.

In Knight's case of "Jerry and Bea," a younger-old couple in their sixties, couple therapy was required because Bea felt the need to see herself as a better counselor than the therapists, though it was Bea's serious illness that needed to be addressed. The couple's difficulty communicating was apparent; they rarely discussed Bea's illness. Further, the couple found it difficult cooperating and establishing rapport with the therapist. Although the therapists concluded that their relationship with this couple was unsuccessful, it seems that the patients were comfortable being negative about everything in their lives, including their therapists. So the therapy continued and ultimately seemed to help the couple deal with their situation in a way that was comfortable for them.

Rolland (1994) discusses illness and disability as skewing the couple relationship along several "fault lines" addressed in therapy. These include ownership of the problem/illness, the space the illness takes up in the marriage, the amount of "spouse time" the role of patient and caregiver consumes, and the amount of togetherness and separateness required of the couple.

Frey, Swanson, and Hyer (1989) studied the marital system among aging chronic psychiatric outpatients. The authors warn that therapists frequently become enmeshed in a couple's conflict and they recommend strategic brief therapy with such patients. A case is described in which the therapist, a long-term ally of the male chronic patient, began to accept the fact that the couple's interactions would not change. He accepted a "one-downmanship" (p. 30) position and reframed his view of the patient's failure to progress, praising the patient's tenacity in pursuing solutions to his problems.

The same authors describe a case in which the therapist tried to "shake up the system" by encouraging a couple to continue their negative interactions. The therapist thus removed the onus of solving the couple's difficulties from himself, suggesting that nothing was likely to change and that there might even be some advantages to keeping the situation as it was. This approach led the couple to more appropriate interactions.

In addition to such "routine" issues of aging as retirement, physical ailments and disabilities, and loss, chronic issues that have long affected a relationship, but were given minimal, if any attention because of other more pressing issues (e.g., children, parents) now emerge, often as crises, driving couples to counseling. Croake and Kelly (2002) conducted structured group therapy with seriously ill patients and their wives and found that the couples experienced improved marital satisfaction through this process. With more leisure hours in their later years, couples find they have both the time and opportunity to address serious personal problems that they had ignored for decades and that now, untreated, could seriously impact their "empty nest" relationship.

SEXUAL ISSUES AND THE AGING COUPLE

Along with retirement and loss as aging-related issues, there is growing recognition that the elderly are as interested in sexual functioning as younger couples, and citations of the elderly in treatment more and more seem to echo issues expressed by younger patients. Additionally, literature on sexual dysfunction and treating the elderly are far more prevalent today than even ten years ago (Morrisette, Zeiss, & Zeiss, 1996). The importance of recognizing sexuality in older patients and treating their sexual conflicts are addressed by Gussaroff (1998).

Whitlatch and Zarit (1988) note that literature on treating sexual dysfunctions in the elderly was based on clinical findings using younger clients. Although there are similarities between sexually dysfunctional younger and older adults, there are also aging and cohort differences that may affect treatment. As such, the authors present a case study in which an older married couple received successful behavioral therapeutic intervention for their sexual dysfunction.

In her studies, Kaplan (1990) observed more than 400 patients over the age of 50 who had sexual complaints. She found that many of the underlying factors contributing to their complaints—cultural attitudes, neuroses, and general marital dissatisfaction, among them—could be addressed with physiological and psychodynamic therapy.

Guttman (1982) adds to an understanding of work with aging couples by noting the types of sexualized and nonsexualized transference and countertransference that abound. She also proposes techniques for dealing with such natural occurrences in couple therapy.

Although the literature indicates there are not many elderly couples in therapy with private practitioners, there is much potential for such patients. There are signs that the aging of the population may produce more elderly individuals and couples who will be more comfortable with psychotherapy and who will use this approach to handle life's crises. Aging individuals who have either experienced therapy in their younger years, or know family and friends who have done so, are likely to feel less resistant to consulting a therapist to deal with a developmental crisis. Therapists must be attuned to and comfortable with the aging patient, and equally sensitive to the aging marital couple.

Two cases of elderly couples are presented here. They were encouraged to seek treatment when a family medical crisis led their physicians to insist upon psychological evaluation along with medical care. The therapy was modified to deal with the resistances these couples, or one spouse, had to psychotherapy. In fact, in one case, a spouse did not even come to the sessions, but participated by writing his comments.

CASE: MR. AND MRS. F.

An 82-year-old patient, who had recently had a stroke, was referred for psychological consultation by his internist. The patient was physically debilitated, needed a wheelchair, spoke clearly but with some word-finding deficits, and had become totally dependent upon his wife of 56 years. Following the stroke, Mr. F. could not stop crying and his neurologist said this form of crying was atypical for a stroke victim. During these tearful outbursts, Mr. F. would sob with great pain, stating that his wife was going to die. No reassurance from his wife or physician would comfort him and the tears persisted.

Mr. F. was at first unwilling to seek psychological help, but his wife, perplexed and concerned about him, insisted. Mr. and Mrs. F. came to four sessions, and Mr. F. came alone for two sessions.

Mr. F., who had been raised in a poor Irish home, had become a brilliant and successful entrepreneur—a self-made man. Mrs. F. was also from a poor background and an Irish immigrant. She was devoted to her family, and while Mr. F. developed his business, she stayed home raising their five children and caring for her parents. A natural salesman, Mr. F. became more worldly while Mrs. F. remained a somewhat dowdy wife. His business gave him much freedom as he traveled about selling his product. He became quite a womanizer and totally enjoyed this life. His wife appeared oblivious to his wanderings. However, as Mr. F. aged, moderate vascular problems began to impede his free lifestyle. He became less mobile and less able to hide his extramarital interests.

His increasing ill health and physical frailty made the possibility of moving to a retirement community appealing to both of them. In a joint therapy session, Mr. and Mrs. F. discussed their plans to move. Mr. F.'s second and more serious stroke now limited his mobility even further, and retirement had become a necessity. Indeed, he was in a far more fragile state than his wife; yet he still cried about his wife's imminent demise.

Mrs. F. was perplexed, but also clearly irritated by her husband's fear of her death. Although she continued to reassure him, it did seem she was aware of some hostile note in his concern. She did not think he was worried about her taking care of him, but nonetheless she reassured him she would be there to do so. She also argued with him about her health. He remained inconsolable and almost delusional about the likelihood of her dying.

Her irritation alerted me to his aggression toward her. She noted that his health made his death more likely than hers. They both wanted me to cure him of this painful symptom.

In the two individual sessions we began to explore what would happen if his wife died, shifting the emphasis from reassuring him of her good health. Mr. F. began to talk about how awful it would be for him. "What about it would be awful?" I wondered. "Well," he said, "nobody would be there to take care of me." He might have to find somebody else to take care of him, and I wondered whom he had in mind for the job. It seems he had looked forward to the retirement community as an opportunity to enjoy the attention of the vast numbers of widows. He had hoped to have a wonderful time. His last stroke had taken away that hope. Now, with this more serious stroke, he was not only limited in his mobility, but also totally dependent on his wife and unable to avoid her scrutiny. According to Mr. F., his wife had him just where she wanted him, "right under her thumb." He unconsciously wished her dead in order to regain his freedom in the fertile soil of a retirement community. He was crying in recognition that his choices were limited by old age and infirmity.

While he was addressing the future loss of pleasure, my thoughts were on the loss of hope. He had been comfortable in his marriage as long as he had had the ability to roam. His wife had the ultimate revenge in preventing his marital infidelity. In effect, he had been unconsciously plotting his wife's death in order to give himself an enjoyable old age.

After this session, Mr. F. stopped crying. This crisis intervention, using a psychodynamic approach, helped him make conscious and express what was a partially unconscious wish. In the final session, Mr. and Mrs. F. noted that his symptom had disappeared, and they were satisfied. Neither wanted to go further in therapy. Neither seemed to want to discuss the hidden secret of their marriage: his philandering and her acceptance of it. They stopped treatment because they were not ready to examine their relationship. The decision to solve only one spouse's symptomatic problem might also appear in a resistant younger couple when marital frustrations of which neither partner is aware create physical symptoms.

CASE: MRS. AND MR. R.

There are some elderly couples, however, who *are* more interested in dealing with the marital relationship when they begin to have the impression that it is impinging on their health and producing physical symptoms. Mrs. R. and her husband are an example. The unusual aspect of this case is that Mr. R. never came to a session, but rather sent me notes commenting on his wife and her behavior. It was Mrs. R., a 65-year-old, attractive, energetic woman, looking many years younger than her stated age, who began individual treatment when her internist recommended therapy to help her explore causes of symptoms—shortness of breath, heart palpitations, and headaches—for which no organic basis could be found. She complied willingly, having sought out and benefited from therapy twice in the previous 30 years. In the first instance, having had three children within a four-year period, Mrs. R. was with a colicky infant son when she was overcome by dizziness and a thought that she might kill this child. Mrs. R. had been a loving mother and was shocked and frightened by her reaction. She immediately began therapy and, in a supportive relationship with her therapist, resolved conflicts she had with being an overburdened mother.

Her second period of therapy occurred when her husband's father made a sexual overture to her. She was horrified at this behavior but decided not to tell her husband. In order to handle its effect on her, she began another period of psychotherapy. She started treatment believing that her father-in-law was her problem, but soon realized that she was talking about a long-held secret of incest in her own family. This early incident had involved a paternal uncle, her, and two sisters. Her parents had not been able to protect their children from a hypersexualized environment that broke firmly entrenched societal taboos against incest, and Mrs. R. grew up alienated from her parents for their passivity.

Through treatment she came to terms with the lack of caring and concern she had felt from her parents. As her father had lived into old age beyond her mother, Mrs. R. was able to develop an accommodation that even forgave the passivity her father had believed was necessary in his position.

We come now to the situation that brought the patient into therapy with me; Mrs. R. was experiencing growing physical difficulties for which the physicians could find no source and admitted to being under stress. She began immediately to relate her physical symptoms to the uncaring quality of her husband, whom she loved, but was thinking of divorcing. Mrs. R. described her husband as rejecting and herself as loving. Yet many contradictory messages were obvious in her presentation. She thought her physical symptoms were due to his cold and distant qualities.

Mr. R. was a pharmacist who owned a relatively successful store that supported the family in a moderate fashion. Mrs. R. described his total absorption in his work as difficult to tolerate. She said he dominated their decisions about money, although she was a careful and even cautious spender. When she thought he would disagree about an expenditure, she obtained a part-time job rather than argue with him or speak up. She also experienced him as putting her down and as subject to angry outbursts. Although she thought of him as unsupportive and unduly frugal, he willingly supported her visit to a psychotherapist.

While describing Mr. R. as unaffectionate, Mrs. R. noted that their sexual relationship had always been a good one. However, about three years earlier she realized that any overtures for affection or sex came from her. This awareness upset her considerably and, in her mind, proved that she was not truly loved by this man. After this, Mrs. R. stopped initiating affectionate actions and although they would still have sex, there seemed to be no warmth in their contacts. This led her to the thought that the only solution for her health would be to leave him.

In fact, over the years when Mrs. R. had found her husband's behavior intolerable, she would take off alone or with the children for a few days and come back when she calmed down. These episodes, oddly enough, were never discussed between the two of them. Life went on as usual after Mrs. R. returned. She had dealt with him by avoidance. Her visit to me, in fact, presented the first arena in which she had been assertive about something with which she felt he would disagree.

The patient's descriptions of conversations with her husband most clearly supported my doubts about her claims that he was rejecting. Her reports suggested that she was always thinking of getting rid of her husband and might be perceived as rejecting by him. For example, one day she described how handsome he was and told me she had commented to her husband that his next wife would be quite proud of him. She would continually refer to the future and mention his "next wife." There was an undercurrent of hostility and rejection that seemed to permeate her relationship with him. She noted that he would not talk much to her and certainly would not tell her his reactions to her subtle threats.

Because she seemed to be trying to get rid of him rather than figure out how to make the marriage work for both of them, I asked whether she would like me to help her get what she wanted from the marriage or if I should help her husband. She did not believe that he could change, but thought divorce would be difficult for her and the family. At this point I suggested that she might be trying to drive him away. Now, this was a woman who had had prior experience with therapy, and she was able to consider the intervention and make use of it to become aware of the hostile nature of her comments to her husband.

We could then talk about whether a man who experienced his wife as trying to get rid of him would sound loving and romantic. This discussion, in which she seemed to take her husband's side, had the paradoxical effect of helping her look at herself and her role in his behavior. She became more hopeful about the possibility of improving her marriage and influencing her physical symptoms.

At this point, I asked her about inviting her husband for couples counseling. She was willing, but thought he would not "go for" this suggestion. Therefore, as a way to include him while still respecting his hesitancy, we developed the idea of having him write any comments he would like. His wife encouraged him to write about her and what she was doing that irritated him. Thus, we engaged in marital therapy in which one partner would communicate through notes to me. Mrs. R. at first gave her husband topics such as, "How am I like my mother?" She suggested to her husband that his comments would help her become a better wife. And she was, indeed, interested in her role in contributing to her husband's seeming withdrawal.

As Mr. R. wrote about what he saw as negative in her behavior, she, in turn, began to express direct anger about him in the sessions. This release led her to be more assertive in asking for what she wanted from him outside the sessions. She began to realize that though resentful about his lack of interest in her, she was not attempting to influence his behavior and get what she wanted. In effect, she was behaving in the passive fashion that her parents had modeled for her. It was also clear that her physical symptoms began when she stopped reaching out to her husband to initiate the kind of warmth that was necessary for her.

Mrs. R. underwent a frightening biopsy of the colon during this period. She thought she could not bear her husband's distance. He, too, was especially anxious and frightened about the implications of this procedure and therefore was inclined to withdraw. However, she was able to ask him for affection and he was able to respond supportively and she felt cared about and loved. The biopsy results at first seemed questionable and then turned out to be benign, and she had evoked a reaction from her husband that brought them closer together.

Soon after this, although he began writing critical notes again, she continued to be more assertive. For example, she enjoyed going out for dinner and he did not; yet she would approach him by asking if *he would like* to go out for dinner. If he responded in the negative, stating the preference for which she had asked, Mrs. R. would feel rejected. She would resent his refusal to go out and feel furious with him.

She learned that she was defeating herself and became more direct, stating that *she wanted* to have dinner out with him. One night he agreed to venture out for dinner. She said where she wanted to go; he complained that he did not like that kind of food and would wait in the car for her while she had dinner. Rather than retreating and saying they could stay home, she responded with eagerness to go out with him and to have him support her choice. He did so!

He even became more affectionate when Mrs. R. came up with a proposal that he touch her and act affectionately one day, and she would do so on the next day. If he forgot, she would not pressure him, but rather accept his less demonstrative nature, yet make sure she reached out and initiated affection with him on "her" days. Thus, she stopped withdrawing from him, reversed the pattern, and was asserting herself and improving her marriage. At the same time, she was curing herself of her somatic symptomatology.

With input from both spouses, this case became, in my view, a marital therapy case with a resistant spouse. Because the wife was encouraged to work on the relationship rather than divorcing her husband, true marital improvement occurred as a result of both spouses expressing their opinions and needs, he in notes to the therapist and she directly to Mr. R. Her physical somatizations disappeared and her husband seemed willing to participate with her in activities from which she had once alienated him.

I had the distinct experience with these two cases that age was irrelevant to the therapy, although it was true that the content may have been influenced by the issues around aging. Age-related health issues forced Mr. F.'s retirement and subsequent move to the retirement community, with the attendant marital problems. However, the decision not to upset the marriage, as well as the couple's interactions, can be found in relationships of people at any age.

The same conclusion applies to Mr. and Mrs. R. Their willingness to pursue treatment creatively, using notes as well as the normal input at sessions in order to change their interaction, has an ageless quality. Marriage—of whatever duration, with partners of any age—responds to stresses and role changes based on its own dynamics and partner willingness to communicate and learn.

REFERENCES

Apfel, R. J., Fox, M., Isberg, R. S., & Levine, J. (1984). Countertransference and transference in couple therapy: Treating sexual dysfunction in older couples. *Journal of Geriatric Psychiatry, 17,* 203–214.

Beckham, K., & Giordano, J. A. (1986). Illness and impairment in elderly couples: Implications for marital therapy. *Family Relations Journal of Applied Family and Child Studies, 35,* 257–264.

Carstensen, L. L., Gottman, J. K., & Levenson, R. W. (1995). Emotional behavior in long-term marriage. *Psychology and Aging, 10,* 140–149.

Croake, J. W., & Kelly, F. D. (2002). Structured group couples therapy with schizophrenic and bipolar patients and their wives. *Journal of Individual Psychology, 58,* 76–86.

Crose, R., & Duffy, M. (1988). Separation as a therapeutic strategy in marital therapy with older couples. *Clinical Gerontologist, 8,* 71–73.

Frey, J., Swanson, G. S., & Hyer, L. (1989). Strategic interventions for chronic patients in later life. *American Journal of Family Therapy, 17,* 27–33.

Gafner, G. (1987). Engaging the elderly couple in marital therapy. *American Journal of Family Therapy, 15,* 305–315.

Gafner, G. (1989). Marital therapy with an old-old couple. *Clinical Gerontologist, 8,* 51–53.

Gafner, G., & Uetz, F. (1990). Compulsive gambling and the aging marital system. *Clinical Gerontologist, 18,* 45–47.

Gilewski, M. J., Kuppinger, J., & Zarit, S. (1985). The aging marital system: A case study in life changes and paradoxical intervention. *Clinical Gerontologist, 3,* 3–15.

Greenbaum, J., & Rader, L. (1989). Marital problems of the "old" elderly as they present to a mental health clinic. *Journal of Gerontological Social Work, 14,* 111–126.

Gussaroff, E. (1998). Denial of death and sexuality in the treatment of elderly patients. *Psychoanalysis & Psychotherapy, 15,* 77–91.

Guttman, H. A. (1982). Transference and countertransference in conjoint couple therapy: Therapeutic and theoretical implications. *Canadian Journal of Psychiatry, 27,* 92–97.

Kaplan, H. S. (1990). Sex, intimacy, and the aging process. *Journal of the American Academy of Psychoanalysis, 18,* 185–205.

Knight, B. G. (1992). *Older adults in psychotherapy: Case histories*. Newbury Park, CA: Sage.

Morrisette, D., Zeiss, A. M., & Zeiss, R. A. (1996). Sexual problems. In J. I. Sheikh (Ed.). *Treating the elderly* (pp. 131–162). San Francisco, CA: Jossey-Bass.

Qualls, S. H. (1995). Marital therapy with later life couples. *Journal of Geriatric Psychiatry, 28,* 139–163.

Rolland, J. (1994). In sickness and in health: The impact of illness on couples' relationships. *Journal of Marital & Family Therapy, 20,* 327–347.

Rosowsky, E. (1999). Couple therapy with long-married older adults. In M. Duffy (Ed.). *Handbook of counseling and psychotherapy with older adults* (pp. 242–266). New York: Wiley.

Salamon, M. F. (1997). On love and lust in the countertransference. *Journal of the American Academy of Psychoanalysis & Dynamic Psychiatry, 25,* 71–90.

Savitsky, E. (1983). Psychotherapy of the elderly. *Journal of Geriatric Psychiatry, 16,* 57–61.

Whitlatch, C. J., & Zarit, S. H. (1998). Sexual dysfunction in an aged married couple: A case study of a behavioral intervention. *Clinical Gerontologist, 8,* 43–62.

Wolinsky, M. A. (1986). Marital therapy with older couples. *Social Casework, 67,* 475–483.

Chapter 13

Countertransference and Ageism: Therapist Reactions to the Older Patient

Vicki G. Semel

An older patient calls me for an appointment. As a therapist I make arrangements for the first office contact. I am demonstrating no visible bias if, in that initial session, I proceed as I would usually, asking, "What brings you here?" "What should I help you with?" and reach a contract about frequency, time, fee, and then begin my typical therapy relationship. And yet the literature about working with the older patient in private practice presents many caveats and warnings about the older individual's limited potential for maturation. I believe such an orientation of doubt is created by underlying biases toward the older patient—doubts that take the form of either countertransference and/or ageism.

In a growing literature that reflects a dynamic or psychoanalytic orientation, it is obvious that one's perspective on treating the elderly patient is clearly related to potential countertransference and ageism issues. When the therapist is experiencing the older patient as untreatable or hopeless and then refuses to provide treatment, modifies it, or discharges the patient for age-related reasons, we are talking about countertransference and ageism. This chapter reviews these general concepts in relation to work with the older patient and then presents clinical examples of how countertransference intertwined with ageism operated and was resolved with two aging patients.

DISTINGUISHING AGEISM FROM COUNTERTRANSFERENCE

Countertransference reactions are distinct from the bias of ageism, although they are frequently enmeshed in some fashion. Ageism can influence the mental health practitioner in deciding whether to accept older patients into treatment, and in thinking that they might only be capable of limited gains or should only be offered palliative therapy, regardless of their wishes. These forms of prejudice are examples of ageism.

The conflicts presented in the concept of countertransference relate to the reactions of the therapist, conscious and unconscious, once therapy has begun. They concern a therapist's responses to the behavior, thoughts, and feelings of the patient within the treatment relationship. The patient's ways of responding to the therapist are evoked from past relationships, especially the earliest ones with parental figures—that is, the transference.

The effect of countertransference on psychoanalytically oriented clinical studies has a long history, starting with Freud's earliest admonitions on the subject in 1914 (Freud, 1958). Reviews of clinical thinking and controversies on this subject are available (Epstein & Feiner, 1979; Gorkin, 1987; Searles, 1979; Spotnitz, 2004; Wolstein, 1988). The framework I have found most useful in approaching a clinical understanding of countertransference derives from Spotnitz (2004) and Winnicott (1958).

These clinicians conceptualized countertransference reactions as either objective reactions any analyst would experience toward a particular patient (Spotnitz, 2004; Spotnitz & Meadow, 1976; Winnicott, 1958), or subjective responses to the patient, which are derived more from the unique background of the therapist (Spotnitz, 2004). Neither subjective nor objective countertransference reactions are a problem within the therapy *if* they are understood and consciously accepted by the therapist. They only become problems when the therapist reacts unknowingly in response to the patient. Then they become a resistance or a barrier to forward movement in treatment. In fact, the more regressed the patient, the more the therapist can make use of his or her own countertransference reactions to understand the preverbal messages of the patient (Meadow, 2003).

These constructs are especially useful in any understanding of countertransference as it operates with the older patient, and especially the older patient who is more disturbed. With such a patient the therapist has a potential multiplicity of objective as well as subjective responses to the patient's losses, helplessness, and impending death.

There are some relevant articles and books that attempt to deal with the specific issues that come to bear in the countertransference as it appears in work with the elderly patient. The concern with the death of the patient arouses fears of one's own death or that of family members (Berk, 1989; Fieldsteel, 1989). Fears about patients who may die leave therapists vulnerable to feelings of guilt (Lardaro, 1988). Nemiroff and Colarusso (1985) believe that a major influence on the development of countertransference is the therapist's reaction to his or her own aging, including such experiences as biological deficits, major losses, awareness of one's own limitations, and ability to deal with death. Fears of such difficult feelings as helplessness, loneliness, or dependency also may influence the countertransference of therapists (Cohen, 1982; Jaques, 1965; Knight, 1986; Smith, Tobin, & Gustafson, 1987).

Another concern is the degree to which the therapist has resolved feelings toward his or her parents. Countertransference blocks may occur as one seeks revenge on one's parents (Grotjahn, 1955; King, 1974) or even toward one's psychoanalyst (Myers, 1984).

Myers (1986) illustrates the relevance of past transference issues with one's parents and one's analyst in a description of his awareness of countertransference. He reflected upon his own dreams that alerted him to countertransference resistances with two particular older patients. In one dream, idealization of a male patient and a wish to save him reflected both the therapist's personal history in relation to his dying father (subjective material) as well as an objectively felt countertransference reaction, as the patient, too, was dealing with his own father dying. A second dream was about a female patient with whom he experienced irritation when she rejected suitable males. This alerted him to a revival of his own oedipal feelings toward his mother and his female analyst. Neither of these responses seemed uniquely tied to the age of the patient, but rather to the emotional issues that were alive in the treatment.

Hillman and Stricker (2001) describe the issue of sexualized countertransference with older adults as potential blocks to therapeutic progress. The ideas of sex and incestuous issues may seem especially uncomfortable when working with the older patient. But Hillman and Stricker also think that the management of the countertransference reaction to sexualized dynamics can be helpful in understanding the older patient's issues, as it would be with patients of any age.

Altschuler and Katz (1996) address the countertransference and treatment issues for therapists working with sexual content for older women. In order for therapy to be effective, the researchers urge practitioners to examine their own ageism, sexism, and countertransference limitations, which might be conveyed unconsciously to clients who have sexual concerns. This team (1999) subsequently developed a methodology for uncovering countertransference reactions toward the elderly. Their sentence completion exercise can be used in a variety of treatment settings to teach therapists how to work with older adults.

Hildebrand (1982) notes the effects on the countertransference when the older patient responds as if the therapist were a son or daughter. Besides these inverted transferences, Knight (1986) considers the possibility of grandparent countertransference reactions. Nemiroff and Colarusso (1985) also discuss multiple generational transferences and countertransference reactions.

In fact, it is at this point that the interference of ageism might be used in the service of avoiding a relationship with a patient, refusing to discover that patient's uniqueness. Ageism may intervene and lead to stigmatizing the potential patient under some general rubric of "older patient." Ageism occurs when the therapist has not even met the patient, but has decided a priori that psychoanalytically oriented psychotherapy would be inappropriate due to age. Wasylenki (1982) believes that the inclination to see psychological problems in the elderly as purely organic leads to "therapeutic nihilism," a form of ageism. Genevay and Katz (1990) seem to use the concept of countertransference to describe hesitancies in working with older patients; yet it seems more a prejudice related to ageism.

A further bias toward the aging can emerge when a patient appears to have dementia. Even the Alzheimer's patient who seeks therapy has a right to treatment where ageism and countertransference on the part of the therapist are monitored and held in check. Kane (2002) acknowledges that memory-impaired clients often receive unequal treatment because of bias perceptions.

Wylie and Wylie (1987) offer an example of how the therapist can become distracted from thinking of the patient's resistances by concentrating on the older patient's somatic symptoms, which might be left to the internist or relevant physician rather than the psychiatrist or psychotherapist. One patient in her sixties used urinary tract problems as an unconscious symbol (somatization), acted out, and displayed reaction formation to avoid sexual feelings toward the therapist, who was 15 years her junior. Specifically, the patient experienced urinary incontinence in place of sexual arousal. Wylie and Wylie state, "In the course of this analysis, the analysand brought a number of issues into the hour, all of which wore the exclusive look of age-specific reality concerns. Upon closer inquiry they were seen to mask both transference and countertransference issues" (1987, p. 350). When the analyst in the treatment recognized the problems as symbolic and not age-related, the therapist focused concentration away from the physical symptoms and continued to analyze the patient. The symptoms then disappeared.

Hinze (1987), who examined analytic treatment of the elderly patient in Germany, believes that after the initial stage of treatment, therapists have more problems with the age of the patient than the patient does with the age of the therapist. Transference takes hold and the patient brings all the early, unresolved issues into therapy, no matter what the age differential. In his article, an older woman developed a sexualized transference to a younger therapist and an older male patient developed a competitive transference, which did not seem too different from that of a younger patient.

Muslin and Clarke (1988) believe that the study of the self psychology treatment of the older patient reveals the countertransference of the therapist getting in the way of the work with the elderly patient. Conflicts with parents can interfere with the therapist's being empathic with the patient. The authors describe two cases in which older patients had to deal with the therapist's unconscious replay of some aspect of an original relationship with parents. These issues, however, could occur with a therapist and patient of any age. Where age is presented as an issue, it may reveal bias toward the patient and a block by the therapist. As the literature indicates, there are fruitful areas for both objective and subjective counter-transference difficulties plus ageism, but also for increased amounts of information about the patient as a result of the countertransfer-ence processes.

On a bright note, Settlage (1996) worked with a centenarian during the last ten years of her life. Although historically there might have been some question about the suitability of this client for psychoanalytic treatment, the work utilized creativity, specifically the patient's poetry writing, to reflect the experience of very old age and the confrontation with death. Transference and counter-transference reactions to the elderly patient did not interfere with a successful outcome.

THE AGING THERAPIST

Looking back on the ten years since the first edition of this book, I realize how much my views toward my older clients have evolved as a result of general feelings I have about my own aging (or *maturing,* as I might prefer to call it). Coincidentally, over that same ten-year period, therapists and the mental health system in general have realized that there are new issues related to aging that need to be examined in our relationships with our patients and with ourselves as practitioners when we deal with the older patient. Pollock (1994) has edited a book with a collection of psychiatrists describing their own reactions to aging. The chapters range from those mental health practitioners who always felt old and for whom there seemed to be a continual awareness of this process (Fleck, 1994) to those who did not even begin to see themselves as old or think such a factor would influence their work (Eisenstein, 1994). Many psychiatrists who themselves write about treating older patients describe the meaning of the aging process for themselves (Cath, 1994; Sim-burg, 1994).

Solomon (1997) describes a particular crisis related to aging. She cites an example of aging issues that might lead the therapist to enacting fantasies that idealize a particular patient. Solomon suggests that maintaining satisfactory personal relationships should help limit this type of countertransference. An internal red flag might be raised if a therapist feels either a wish to act out in this way or to withdraw from the patient.

In interviews with 15 psychiatrists between the ages of 69 and 77, Weiner (1990) reports that these therapists most feared a decrease in referrals due to possible ageism bias unless illness prevented them from practicing. Sadly, the study revealed, although the therapists had gained wisdom and expertise over a lifetime of practice and their transference and countertransference difficulties seemed minimal, they were now faced with a societal bias toward the aged that involved professional rejection.

Perhaps the most optimistic work is presented by Strauss (1996), who, at the age of 80, discussed becoming an elder analyst herself and the transference and countertransference changes that come with aging. She urges both patients and therapists to welcome aging and all that comes with it, good and bad.

Once again it appears that conflicts that reverberate in the therapist, whether they are related to unresolved issues about one's early family relationships or about issues of aging and their meaning, require that the psychotherapist monitor any reactions that interfere with the patients saying whatever is necessary to solve the problems that brought them to treatment. It is the block within the therapist to hearing whatever the patient might want to say that is most relevant to countertransference binds that develop in treatment.

In the following section I present two cases in which issues of countertransference become intertwined with the prejudice of ageism.

CASE: REVISITING MR. P.

As described in chapter 11, Mr. P. was a 65-year-old clerical worker who was freed from an unhappy job situation when he was laid off. He claimed that his goal was to find a job that he finally might like. I, too, thought he could find some satisfying profession. But his earnest wish to find satisfying work was balanced by behavior that revealed his pleasure in "having no boss." He would agonize about what kind of work he should do. I found myself encouraging him to become trained as a child care worker or as a teacher, because he seemed to love children so much. I also had the impression that he was excellent at raising small children and truly able to understand their, and perhaps his own, symbiotic needs.

I wanted him to find satisfying work—a profession. I wanted him to attend college. "Never," he would say. My ideas came from the conscious thought that because he was older, he might want to make better use of the time that was left to him. This belief was, in itself, a form of ageism on my part.

With a man as stubborn as this, and as unwilling to find a satisfactory occupation, I had stopped behaving like an analyst and had become more of an advisor—and a rather unsuccessful advisor at that.

My concerns with his life were also related to a countertransference bind. It was as if being older meant he had both the time to pursue a new path and also the pressure to do so. Nemiroff and Colarusso (1985) noted that patients found the pressure to "race against time." In this instance, however, it was an issue for me, the therapist. I was concerned with his "race against time." I was selecting the form of old age for the patient rather than helping him resolve blocks to his selection of his own form of old age. This aspect of the countertransference would be considered the subjective part, the part I brought to my relationship with Mr. P. My personal values about older age led me to a counterproductive situation with this patient.

In a deeper sense I was like his parents, who must have pushed him to behave the way they wanted. This aspect of the countertransference describes an objective part of our relationship. The objective countertransference experience reflects how most therapists would feel with such a patient. He was stubborn and held rigidly onto his own choices, while feeling guilty for not going along with them (and me).

The difficulty with our interactions during this period was not that I had the wish to help him find a career and feel satisfied nor that I was frustrated with his stubborn passivity. The problem was that, somewhat unaware of these two forces, I had acted and verbalized interventions that interfered with his directing his own therapy, which is surely the way patients learn to become their own genuine selves. Recognizing both subjective and objective countertransference led to my more accepting stance in our work.

CASE: MRS. T.

In the case of 67-year-old Mrs. T., a different dynamic shaped treatment. Mrs. T. entered therapy because of a lifelong drive to become cured. She had experienced a psychotic depression at age 20, when she tried to leave home and take a job in another state. She was hospitalized for several months and received shock treatment. From that period on she sought out different therapies to help her with almost incapacitating symptoms of inertia and anhedonia. Yet despite this, she became a college-educated teacher, married another teacher, and raised two children, one of whom seemed to have problems similar to hers.

She began therapy with a most optimistic view of its potential. She reported in the first sessions that she had read about Modern Psychoanalysis and Hyman Spotnitz's work and thought this was the approach for her. She soon developed a positive transference to me in which I was idealized and even worshiped. Such feelings were physically painful to her as well as upsetting. Nevertheless, the therapy seemed to be progressing. The intensity of the patient's feelings, while painful to her, boded well for the treatment. They signaled the beginning of a positive narcissistic transference state (Spotnitz, 2004), which is the beginning of a useful therapeutic relationship, according to Modern Psychoanalytic theory.

After this, Mrs. T. moved with equal levels of passion into the negative aspects of this narcissistic transference phenomenon. After being a worshiped figure, I became a sarcastically denigrated, incompetent therapist. She frequently talked for the entire session of finding another therapist. She attacked Modern Psychoanalysis and me unmercifully.

A therapist may realize the therapy is moving along and that the patient is beginning to perceive a world where people, including the therapist, can become separate figures with their own ideas and values. The therapist may also understand that this separation is frequently accompanied by much aggression directed toward an object seen as separate from the self. Yet the actual onslaught can become quite wearing.

Mrs. T. had a particularly denigrating and off-centered way of delivering barbs and criticisms. She would make frequent assumptions about what I was thinking. Then, dripping sarcasm, she would attack me for these assumptions. Many of her criticisms had the quality of "Have you stopped beating your wife?"

In the sessions I felt both angry and hurt. The patient, however, reported improvements in her external life. She described her relationship with her husband in more pleasant terms. She was getting along with her daughter and her troubled son was actually seeking her out for social contacts.

She and I, however, were not having such a good time in our sessions. I was aware of a strong wish to discharge this patient. Ideas circulated through my mind about how I might not be the right therapist for this woman (a wish even I could recognize). I also began to become increasingly conscious of her age, something that had never concerned me before this point in the therapy. Suddenly it was as if Mrs. T. had become an old patient, perhaps too old to be successfully treated by analysis. Freud's admonitions about the elderly patient with rigid personality traits flitted through my mind.

After a particularly painful session, I reminded myself of the distinction between helping a patient verbally discharge aggressive impulses in the sessions versus the patient gratuitously and sadistically attacking the therapist. I was becoming too passive in the face of this onslaught.

Emboldened, I asked Mrs. T. if she knew that she was making me feel so terrible. She responded with real and direct feeling, rather than her indirect attacks: "Yes, and I hope you feel as bad as I do! Now you'll know how I feel!" Because I did not know how she was feeling, and because criticism is not the same as an expression of feeling, this was a useful turning point in the therapy. I could now better help her to talk more directly in the sessions about what she was feeling. This method of inducing feelings in the therapist as a useful message from the preverbal patient is a rather typical and necessary part of treatment. She also began to explore how her sarcasm was a family trait, one she learned simply by modeling the adults in her life. She despised this trait in them, often felt demeaned by them, and was upset to realize she had assumed the same style of communication.

The purpose of this case description is to show how negative ideas about aging can mask or become melded to countertransference issues. I initially had no concern about analyzing a woman in her sixties. The long-term nature of her psychopathology was also no barrier to my beginning treatment. Patients with early developmental disturbances are usually the most suited for a Modern Psychoanalytic approach. So when did age suddenly become a barrier to treatment? These thoughts about aging arose when I was in the grip of powerful and hostile feelings toward the patient.

When I was able to get some distance from the patient's objectively distressing verbalizations, I noted that thoughts of age once again disappeared and the treatment continued. The objective aspects of this countertransference reaction were the feelings of anger and frustration caused by her behavior. Rather than being fully aware of how angry I was, I began to use the idea of age as a resistance to understanding the objective countertransference I was experiencing with Mrs. T.

The subjective aspect of the countertransference had led me to accept the attacks in a passive fashion rather than dealing with them directly. This fit an aspect of my personality developed during my youth. Sometimes it helped me work with patients who took much patience and I was relatively accepting of serious psychopathology.

In the cases of both Mr. P. and Mrs. T., analysis of both aspects of the countertransference, and sensitivity to the way ageism appeared were helpful in resolving the block. Although these two forces, countertransference and ageism, operated as problems, they also offered useful information about treatment and the unexpressed feelings and thoughts of the patients.

REFERENCES

Altschuler, J., & Katz, A. D. (1996). Sexual secrets of older women: Countertransference in clinical practice. *Clinical Gerontologist, 17*, 51–67.

Altschuler, J., & Katz, A. D. (1999). Methodology for discovering and teaching countertransference toward elderly clients. *Journal of Gerontological Social Work, 32*, 81–93.

Berk, R. J. (1989). Differential aspects of psychoanalysis of the aged: Discussion. *Psychoanalysis and Psychotherapy, 7*, 44–48.

Cath, S. H. (1994). Some autobiographical notes by a psychogeriatrician in "That Time of Year": The role of devalued fathers and adopted great parents. In G. H. Pollock (Ed.). *How psychiatrists look at aging:* Vol. 2. Mental Health Library Series, Monograph 3 (pp. 213–227). Madison, CT: International Universities Press.

Cohen, H. C. (1982). On loneliness and the aging process. *International Journal of Psychoanalysis, 63*, 149–155.

Eisenstein, S. (1994). The aging of therapists. In G. H. Pollock (Ed.). *How psychiatrists look at aging:* Vol 2. Mental Health Library Series, Monograph 3 (pp. 137–152). Madison, CT: International Universities Press.

Epstein, L., & Feiner, A. H. (Eds.). (1979). *Countertransference.* New York: Jason Aronson.

Fieldsteel, N. D. (1989). Analysts' expressed attitudes toward dealing with death and illness. *Contemporary Psychoanalysis, 25,* 427–432.

Fleck, S. (1994). Aging. In G. H. Pollock (Ed.). *How psychiatrists look at aging:* Vol 2. Mental Health Library Series, Monograph 3 (pp. 127–136). Madison, CT: International Universities Press.

Freud, S. (1958). Observations on transference-love: Further recommendations on the technique of psycho-analysis III. In J. Strachey (Ed. and Trans.), *Standard edition of the complete psychological works of Sigmund Freud* (Vol 12, pp. 157–171). London: Hogarth. [Original work published in 1914].

Genevay, B., & Katz, R. S. (1990). *Countertransference and older clients.* Newbury Park, CA: Sage.

Gorkin, M. (1987). *The uses of countertransference.* Northvale, NJ: Jason Aronson.

Grotjahn, M. (1955). Analytic psychotherapy with the elderly. *Psychoanalytic Review, 42,* 419–427.

Hildebrand, H. P. (1982). Psychotherapy with older patients. *British Journal of Medical Psychology, 55,* 19–28.

Hillman, J., & Stricker, G. (2001). The management of sexualized transference and countertransference with older adult patients: Implications for practice. *Professional Psychology: Research & Practice, 32,* 272–277.

Hinze, E. (1987). Transference and countertransference in the psychoanalytic treatment of older patients. *International Review of Psycho-Analysis, 14,* 465–473.

Jaques, E. (1965). Death and the mid-life crisis. *International Journal of Psycho-Analysis, 46,* 502–514.

Kane, M. N. (2002). Awareness of ageism, motivation, and countertransference in the care of elders with Alzheimer's disease. *American Journal of Alzheimer's Disease & Other Dementias, 17,* 101–109.

King, P. H. M. (1974). Notes on the psychoanalysis of older patients: Reappraisal of the potentialities for change during the second half of life. *Journal of Analytic Psychology, 19,* 22–37.

Knight, B. (1986). *Psychotherapy with older adults.* Beverly Hills, CA: Sage.

Lardaro, T. A. (1988). Till death do us part: Reactions of therapists to the deaths of elderly patients in psychotherapy. *Clinical Gerontologist, 7,* 173–176.

Meadow, P. W. (2003). *The New psychoanalysis.* In C. Lemert (Series Ed.), *Legacies of social thought.* New York: Rowman & Littlefield.

Muslin, H., & Clarke, S. (1988). The transference of the therapist of the elderly. *Journal of American Academy of Psychoanalysis, 16,* 295–315.

Myers, W. A. (1984). *Dynamic therapy of the older patient.* New York: Jason Aronson.

Myers, W. A. (1986). Transference and countertransference issues in treatments involving older patients and younger therapists. *Journal of Geriatric Psychiatry, 19,* 221–239.

Nemiroff, R. A., & Colarusso, C. A. (1985). Issues and strategies for psychotherapy and psychoanalysis in the second half of life. In R. A. Nemiroff & C. A. Colarusso (Eds.). *The race against time: Psychotherapy and psychoanalysis in the second half of life* (pp. 303–329). New York: Plenum.

Pollock, G. H. (Ed.). (1994). *How psychiatrists look at aging:* Vol 2. Mental Health Library Series, Monograph 3. Madison, CT: International Universities Press.

Searles, H. F. (1979). *Countertransference and related subjects.* New York: International Universities Press.

Settlage, C. F. (1996). Transcending old age: Creativity, development and psychoanalysis in the life of a centenarian. *International Journal of Psychoanalysis, 77,* 549–564.

Simburg, E. J. (1994). A psychiatrist looks at his own aging. In G. H. Pollock (Ed.). *How psychiatrists look at aging:* Vol 2. Mental Health Library Series, Monograph 3 (pp. 181–201). Madison, CT: International Universities Press.

Smith, G. C., Tobin, S. S., & Gustafson, J. D. (1987). Perceptions of geriatric practice: The role of theoretical orientation, age, and gender. *Clinical Gerontologist, 6*(3), 29–46.

Solomon, M. F. (1997). On love and lust in the countertransference. *Journal of the American Academy of Psychoanalysis & Dynamic Psychiatry, 25,* 71–90.

Spotnitz, H. (2004). *Modern psychoanalysis of the schizophrenic patient: Theory of the technique* (2nd ed.). New York: YBK.

Spotnitz, H., & Meadow, P. W. (1976). *Treatment of the narcissistic neuroses.* New York: Manhattan Center for Advanced Psychoanalytic Studies.

Strauss, H. M. (1996). Working as an elder analyst. In B. Gerson (Ed.). *The therapist as a person: Life crisis, life choices, life experiences, and their effects on treatment* (pp. 277–294). Hillsdale, NJ: Analytic Press.

Wasylenki, D. A. (1982). Psychodynamics and aging. *Canadian Journal of Psychiatry, 27,* 11–17.

Weiner, M. F. (1990). Older psychiatrists and their psychotherapy practice. *American Journal of Psychotherapy, 44,* 44–49.

Winnicott, D. W. (1958). Hate in the countertransference. In D. W. Winnicott, *Through paediatrics to psycho-analysis* (pp. 194–203). New York: Basic Books, 1949.

Wolstein, B. (Ed.). (1988). *Essential papers on countertransference.* New York: New York University Press.

Wylie, H. W., & Wylie, M. L. (1987). The older analysand: Countertransference issues in psychoanalysis. *International Journal of Psycho-Analysis, 68,* 343–352.

Part V

Relevant Issues and Approaches for Therapy

Chapter 14

The Political Reality of Medicare: History and Treatment Issues

Miriam E. Lemerman

Medicare is the national health insurance program established by the Social Security Act of 1965 as the government health program for citizens 65 years of age and over. This program is dedicated to helping fund the medical expenses of seniors, individuals of all ages with permanent disabilities, and persons with end-stage renal disease.

Medicaid and Medicare were established simultaneously. These two programs, however, are distinctly different. Medicaid's focus is on assisting the poor and those individuals at the lower end of the income scale. In 1977, the Health Care Financing Administration (HCFA) was created to coordinate the policies and procedures governing Medicare and Medicaid. In 2001, HCFA was renamed the "Center for Medicare and Medicaid Services," or "CMS" (Centers for Medicare and Medicaid Services, 2004a).

This chapter concentrates on Medicare. There are two major sections to Medicare: "Part A" and "Part B." "Part A" entails coverage for hospital care and subacute care in a qualified nursing home or rehabilitation facility. Workers contribute to this insurance fund through deductions from their monthly paychecks. Everyone eligible for Medicare receives "Part A."

"Part B" is optional, although most people subscribe to it by paying a monthly premium. "Part B" provides coverage of expenses for skilled medical professionals (i.e., doctors, nurse practitioners, physical therapists, speech therapists, and so forth) who care for patients on an inpatient or outpatient basis (*Medicare and you*, 2004).

President Lyndon Johnson signed the Medicare bill in Independence, Missouri, Harry Truman's hometown. This location was selected in recognition of Truman's earlier attempts to create national health coverage (Centers for Medicare and Medicaid Services, 2004b). In the early 1950s, senior citizens were facing a health care crisis. "Two thirds of older Americans had incomes of less than $1,000 annually, and 1 in 8 had health insurance" (Medicare Rights Center, 2004a). Medical care was simply too expensive for the majority of individuals to afford.

A debate as to how to handle this health care crisis ensued for several years. By 1960, it became apparent that private insurers were not capable of providing affordable health care coverage to the growing number of elderly citizens. Studies indicated that between 1960 and 1965, only one out of four senior Americans had adequate hospital insurance (Medicare Rights Center, 2004a).

Medicare's introduction in 1965 represented a social insurance plan intended to provide all senior citizens with comprehensive health care at an affordable cost. If individuals or their spouses work at least 10 years in Medicare-covered employment, they automatically qualify for hospital insurance ("Part A") and do not have to pay a monthly premium (*Medicare and you,* 2004). People enrolled in medical insurance ("Part B"), however, must pay a monthly premium (Medicare Rights Center, 2004b).

Seniors must be properly advised as to the limitations of current Medicare benefits. For example, Medicare does *not* pay for "Long-Term Care" and assistance with the tasks of daily living (e.g., toileting, washing, and dressing) (Centers for Medicare and Medicaid, 2004c).

The intricacies of Medicare have expanded throughout the years. The program consisting of "Part A" and "Part B" comprises the original fee-for-service plan. Medicare has now become more complicated as a result of added options. It can be difficult to distinguish the benefits of one plan versus another. For example, in 1997, as an alternative to the original fee-for-service Medicare program, "Medicare C Plans," or "Medicare Plus Choice Plans," became available. These plans, now known as "Medicare Advantage," provide managed care as well as private fee-for-service Medicare (Centers for Medicare Advocacy, n.d.). People often choose the managed care option because it is less expensive than the original fee-for-service Medicare plan. The primary disadvantage of such managed care plans is that they generally limit the choice of doctors, whereas the original Medicare plan permits the patient to select the physician of his or her choice.

Another added Medicare feature is "Medicare Supplement," or "Medigap." Medigap is sold by private insurance companies and is intended to fill in Medicare's original gaps of coverage. It pays for additional coverage in hospitals, skilled nursing facilities, and services covered by "Plan B." There are ten standardized Medigap Plans, labeled "A" through "J." Consumers select the plan that best fits their needs. Medigap serves as an adjunct to Medicare and pays for expenses not covered by the individual's basic plan (*Medicare and you,* 2004). If a person has insurance that has been carried over by a former employer, this may be used as Medigap, or supplemental, insurance.

Over time, a clamor has taken place to revise the system providing drug benefits to senior citizens. In 1965, there essentially were no expensive prescription drugs. Today, pharmaceutical costs continue to spiral upward (Murtha, 2004). The 2003 "Modern Medicare Act," or "MMA," was intended to enhance medical benefits in the area of prescription drugs. MMA's provisions include a voluntary drug benefit and enhanced health plan choices. The new drug benefit will begin in 2006; in the interim, drug discount cards for seniors are offered by many pharmaceutical companies. A study by Antos and Pinell (2004) writing for the American Enterprise Institute found that low income seniors who are entitled to a $600 government subsidy per year could save between 50 percent and 78 percent in drug costs by purchasing generic prescription drugs with their Medicare discount card at retail pharmacies.

In 2006, all Medicare recipients, regardless of which plan they are enrolled in, will be entitled to prescription drug benefits according to the following guidelines:

1. A person will choose a prescription drug plan and pay a premium of approximately $35 per month;

2. A person will pay the first $250 (called a "deductible");

3. Medicare will pay 75 percent of all drug costs between $250 and $2,250; the beneficiary will pay only 25 percent of these costs;

4. A person will pay 100 percent of drug costs between $2,251 and $3,600;

5. Medicare will pay approximately 95 percent of drug costs after a person has spent $3,600 in a 12-month period.

Extra aid will be available for people with low incomes and limited assets. Nearly 11 million beneficiaries with limited means will participate in this low-income subsidy and receive substantial additional assistance from Medicare (*Medicare & you*, 2005).

The second aspect of the 2006 "Medicare Modernization Act" entails additional health plan choices. There will be an expansion in the availability of coordinated health care programs through Medicare Advantage. Individuals enrolled in Medicare Advantage will obtain significant out-of-pocket savings compared to the costs associated with the traditional fee-for-service Medicare plan. Regional "Preferred Provider Organizations," or "PPOs," will be available to all Medicare Advantage beneficiaries (*Medical News Today*, 2004a).

The Centers for Medicare and Medicaid Services (2004d) summarize the 2005 Medicare premiums and obligations as follows:

Part A: (Hospital Insurance) Premium

1. Most people do not pay a monthly Part A premium because they or a spouse has 40 or more quarters of Medicare-covered employment. Part A premium is $206 for people having 30–39 quarters of Medicare-covered employment.

2. The Part A premium is $375 per month for people who are not otherwise eligible for premium-free hospital insurance and have fewer than 30 quarters of Medicare-covered employment.

Part B: (Medical Insurance) Premium: $78.20 per month

Medicare Deductible and Coinsurance Amounts for 2005

1. Part A: pays for inpatient hospital, skilled nursing facility, and some home health care. For each benefit period Medicare pays all covered costs except the Medicare Part A deductible (2005 – $912) during the first 60 days and coinsurance amounts for hospital stays that last beyond 60 days and no more than 150 days.

2. For each benefit period you pay:
    a. A total of $912 for a hospital stay of 1–60 days;
    b. $228 per day for days 61–90 of a hospital stay;
    c. $456 per day for days 91–150 of a hospital stay (Lifetime Reserve Days);
    d. All costs for each day beyond 150 days.

Skilled Nursing Facility Coinsurance: $114 per day for days 21 through 100 each benefit period

Part B Coverage

1. Medicare-eligible physician services;

2. Outpatient hospital services;

3. Certain home health services;

4. Durable medical equipment;

5. $110 per year (after meeting the $110 deductible, consumer must pay 20 percent of the Medicare-approved amount for services).

Health care products and services cost Americans nearly $1.6 trillion in 2002. See Table 14.1.

While looking forward to enhanced Medicare benefits, one cannot help but be bewildered by the political swirl regarding the procurement of prescription drugs for our growing senior citizenry. Many believe that the individual Medicare Advantage Plan administrators should bargain with the drug companies in order to obtain the best prices for their insured. The American Medical Association

TABLE 14.1   How the Money Was Divided

	Portion of health spending
Hospitals	31%
Physicians	22%
Other professional services	10%
Prescription drugs	10%
Nursing home and home health	9%
Administration and overhead	7%
Research and construction	4%
Medical devices and equipment	3%
Government public health activities	3%

Source: Centers for Medicare & Medicaid Services Office of the Actuary (numbers do not add up to 100% due to rounding).

is urging Medicare officials to replicate the efforts of the Department of Veterans Affairs and the Defense Department by negotiating directly with the drug companies for better prices (Pear, 2004). Senior citizens should not have to resort to traveling across the border to Canada to obtain their medications at a more affordable rate.

Other aspects of the Medicare kaleidoscope include President Bush's advocacy of Health Savings Accounts, or HSAs. The establishment of HSAs would allow consumers to take responsibility for contributing to their own health care coverage. Individuals must place $2,600 into their health care account annually. A consumer who invests in an HSA can have no other health coverage and is not eligible for Medicare (Money Guide, 2004).

Some people who analyze the health care system in this country believe that the traditional Medicare single payer plan would be a good model for our entire health system. It would permit the freedom to choose one's own physicians and would result in lower overhead costs. The implementation of the universal health concept prevails in almost every highly industrialized nation except the United States, at half the costs that Americans expend (Relman & Angell, 2004).

By the end of 2005, Medicare "Part B" premiums will have risen by 17.5 percent, jumping from $66 to $78.20 per month. Why have costs risen so significantly? The Medicare Modernization Act of 2003 established increased payments to medical providers and great monetary incentives to privatize Medicare. In 2006, there will be increasingly greater roles for private plans within Medicare. Such plans will provide prescription drug coverage to those subscribers in the traditional fee-for-service plan as well as to HMO and PPO subscribers.

Doctors and hospitals charge much more in the United States than in other countries, and Americans pay a greater amount for prescription drugs and administration (Madrick, 2004). The Medical Rights Center, the largest independent source of Medicare health care information and assistance in the United States, advocates the support and expansion of traditional Medicare and the elimination of private health plans. "Focus groups reveal that older Americans are very satisfied with original Medicare and view notions of privatizing Medicare—that is, shifting control over payment of insurance benefits to HMO's and other private corporations—very negatively" (Medicare Rights Center, 2004b).

Upon examination of the total health care package in America, Alan Greenspan, Chairman of the Federal Reserve, as cited in *Medical News Today* (2004b), warned that quick action is necessary to lower costs for Medicare. With the baby boomer generation quickly ascending to their senior years, how can the Medicare system continue to adequately function? The birth rate is declining and life expectancy is increasing. Michael Mandelbaum (2004), of Johns Hopkins University, echoes Greenspan's ominous warning and discusses the tremendous financial problems caused by excessive health care costs. Mandelbaum cites Peter Peterson, whose book, *Running on Empty* (2004), details the monumental expense of new technologies used to keep people alive as long as possible.

Joining the ranks of conservative advisors is Dallas L. Salisbury. He anticipates the problems Medicare and Social Security will have in serving the baby boomer generation as it approaches the age of 65. Salisbury (1997) states that current workers need to assiduously save in order to have enough money to subsist on in later years. He asserts that boomers have done a better job saving through employment plans than their parents did, but their Social Security benefits will not cover their future needs. He recommends that people determine from Social Security what their probable benefits are and confer with their employers to save for their retirement years. Salisbury strongly recommends that employees save diligently each year to ensure the employer "provides a defined savings opportunity." He advises that people familiarize themselves with all available savings plans. The idea of preserving lump-sum distribution upon retirement or a change in job is key to achieving the goals of retirement income. Finally, Salisbury urges the baby boomer generation to be mindful of the escalating costs of health care and the increase in longevity and, accordingly, save a substantial amount in order to meet their future needs.

Robert Lebow was a physician of great courage, determination, and social conscience. In his book entitled *Health Care Meltdown* (2004), he advocated the concept of a "one risk pool" of health insurance that is modeled on the original Medicare protocol. Under the "one risk pool" plan, everyone in America would be covered by the same health insurance plan regardless of socioeconomic status or geographic location. In effect, every American would be covered for health care. He believed this to be a satisfactory concept and maintained that the administration of this type of insurance program would save us billions of dollars every year. To those who assert that this type of insurance would limit our choice of doctors, Lebow countered with the idea that it would, in fact, expand our choices because "a person could go to any provider of his/her choice—including an H.M.O" (p. 271).

Rettenmaier and Wang (2002) estimated that health expenditures constituted 5.7 percent of the United States economy in 1965. By the year 2000, that figure increased to 13.2 percent and Medicare costs entailed 17 percent of all health care costs in the nation. They advised that as baby boomers retire, there will be a significant increase in the number of Medicare enrollees and retirement years will increase as a result of longer life expectancy. By the year 2035, Medicare expenses are anticipated to be twice the amount they were in 2002.

Our country may not yet be ready to streamline the Medicare Plan to be incorporated into a universal health plan for all Americans. Yet, the idea is appealing on a number of levels. Our medical problems, both within the Medicare system and in general, need continued examination in order to be dealt with more effectively. Evening out the bumps in Medicare would be a good first step.

What is it like to be old in America, both now and anticipating the future? What is it like to be alone after years of living with family? Who will take care of me if I cannot take care of myself? Where will

I live? Can I afford to live alone? Who will support me if I run out of funds? Who will visit me? Will I be isolated and lonely? These are common concerns of the elderly and those approaching their senior years. Multiply these concerns by thousands, and then millions, and one begins to comprehend the future demographics of our country.

It is instructive and sobering to study the statistics that relate to our expanding aging population. It is important to envision the expansion of services and funding necessary to support this natural evolution. These conditions draw the connection between one individual and the global picture of aging in America.

In 2004, the elderly constituted approximately 13 percent of our population. By the year 2030, however, the elderly will increase to 20 percent of our population. The costs of housing the elderly, particularly if they require nursing care or assistance, will be astronomical by the year 2050. It is recommended by the Administration on Aging (U.S. Department of Health and Human Services, 2004) that home care be encouraged on a larger scale, and that friends and relatives pitch in to ensure the success of this residential arrangement. It is further advocated that intensive health educational programs be targeted to middle-aged males, who statistically succumb at an earlier age than their spouses. The growing awareness of a future elder care crisis has sparked such new and creative approaches.

A Profile of Older Americans: 2003, prepared by the Administration on Aging and the U.S. Department of Health and Human Services, and developed by S. Greenberg (2003) provides the following statistics on the growth of the geriatric population: In 2002, people 65 years or older in the United States numbered approximately 35.6 million, representing 12 percent of the population, or 1 in every 8 Americans. Since 1992, the number of older Americans has increased by 3.3 million compared to an increase of 13.5 percent for ages 65 and younger. However, the number of Americans aged 45–64 who will reach 65 over the next two decades will constitute approximately 38 percent of the general population.

The elder population is clearly increasing significantly. The slowing down of the population of seniors in the 1990s was due to a smaller number of babies born during the Great Depression of the 1930s. Between the years 2010 and 2030, when the baby boom generation reaches 65 years of age, the elder population will greatly expand. By 2030, there will be more than twice as many older persons than in 2000. In the 85-and-over population group, there is projected to be an increase from 4.6 million in 2002 to 9.6 million in 2030.

In 2002, 72 percent of older men (approximately 10.2 million) and 40 percent of older women (approximately 7.8 million) lived with a spouse. Thirty percent (10.5 million) of all non-institutionalized older persons lived alone in 2002. In the year 2000, only 4.5 percent of the 65+ group (1.56 million) lived in nursing homes. Nursing home residents constituted 1.1 percent of all seniors 65–74 years of age, 4.7 percent of seniors age 75–84, and 18.2 percent of seniors age 85 and over. Five percent of seniors lived in senior housing residences.

As people age and become frail and sick, a nursing home is sometimes sought as a caregiving environment. The ability to perform activities of daily living (ADL), including bathing, dressing, eating, and getting around the house, is a primary criterion used by individuals and families to determine whether a nursing home is an appropriate option. "Although nursing homes are being increasingly used for short-stay, post-acute care, about 1.6 million elderly are in nursing homes (about half are age 85 and over). These individuals often have high needs for care with their ADLs and/or have severe cognitive impairment, due to Alzheimer's disease or other dementias" (Greenberg, 2003, p. 14). In 1999, over 27.3 percent of noninstitutionalized Medicare recipients 65 years and over had difficulty performing one or more ADLs. Ninety-three percent of comparably aged seniors in nursing homes had difficulties with one or more ADLs, and 76.3 percent of institutionalized seniors had difficulty with three or more ADLs (Greenberg, 2003).

MEDICARE AND MEDICAID

A large number of nursing home long-term care residents are recipients of Medicaid. This is a program that accommodates the health care needs of individuals with very little money and assures that these seniors will be provided long-term care protection. Medicaid recipients are classified as living at or below the poverty level. In order to qualify for Medicaid, many seniors are forced to "spend down" their assets—that is, spend or liquidate their funds or holdings. Doing so is difficult for people who are reluctant to lose their independence and to depend solely upon the government for their care (Stum, 2002).

Seniors who are at the poverty level or below are eligible for both Medicare and Medicaid. Full Medicare and Medicaid coverage includes payment of nursing home services, premium deductibles under Medicare, and prescription medication (Medicare Rights Center & Centers for Medicare and Medicare Services, 2004). Additionally, Medicaid pays for dental expenses, vision care, and, most importantly, long-term care. Eighteen percent of Medicare beneficiaries are dual-eligible. Medicaid pays the Medicare Part B premium, which was approximately $800 per year in 2004 (Kaiser Commission, 2004).

A host of issues pertain specifically to Medicare in nursing homes and community mental health centers. In the year 2000, 1.5 million people aged 65 and over lived in nursing homes. A good portion of the Medicare dollar is slotted to go to these facilities. There are times when Medicare will not pay for physical rehabilitation and simultaneous psychotherapy for a patient in a nursing home unless a physician specifically orders the psychotherapy and asserts that it is medically necessary. For example, if a person leaves the hospital with a broken leg and is sent to a nursing home for rehabilitation, Medicare will pay for physical therapy. If that same person becomes depressed, Medicare will sometimes only pay for psychotherapy after the regimen of physical therapy is completed. To put it differently, Medicare cannot be billed for two services on the same day. Although this has been the experience of some nursing home patients, Medicare officials at the 1-800-MEDICARE telephone number advise that if a doctor orders a particular treatment as necessary, Medicare must provide services simultaneously. Such discrepancies illustrate the fact that Medicare policies are sometimes unclear or are interpreted inconsistently and it is up to the patient and/or the patient's advocates to pursue the Medicare appeals process to obtain services deemed necessary.

Other examples of Medicare usage are services that are sponsored by private community mental health centers. Programs focusing on senior health care issues are prevalent. In a program for caregivers, the mental health center provides counseling both within and outside of the home for those caregivers who need support and perspective as they perform their caregiving roles.

A turning point in Medicare reform was achieved in 1989 when the Congress passed the Omnibus Reconciliation Act. The bill authorized the services of psychologists and other non-medical, licensed mental health professionals to treat patients in nursing homes and to receive reimbursement for these services (Brody & Semel, 1993). This act acknowledged the "creative" capabilities of psychologists and social workers and affirmed their value, along with psychiatrists and nurses, in a nursing home environment. Appropriate treatment fees for these mental health professionals were built into the structure of the act.

It seems foolish and exclusionary that licensed mental health counselors, whose training is comparable to licensed clinical social workers, are still not permitted to participate in the Medicare system. Surely nursing home patients would benefit from expanded mental health coverage. Additionally, the high suicide rates of older Americans mandate greater mental health coverage. Older Americans in rural areas are not always served adequate mental health treatment; these individuals would profit tremendously from the additional support of mental health counselors.

All seniors would benefit from a reduction in the 50 percent copayment presently required by Medicare for outpatient mental health treatments, given the immeasurable importance of mental health treatment for the older generation (American Counseling Association, 2004).

A crucial part of the psychological services in a nursing home entails group work. The following material is a reprint of a portion of Claire Brody's chapter entitled "Medicare" from *Strategies for Therapy With the Elderly* (original edition), written by C. M. Brody and V. G. Semel.

Designing a Pilot Project for Psychological Services in a Nursing Home

In order to encourage support for this projected work, it would be important for the nonmedical therapist to specify the goals for the residents, as well as how the project will be of benefit to the institution (Abramson & Mendis, 1990). It would be desirable for such goals to be outlined in a formal agreement between the professional and the administrator. To accompany this document, the therapist would probably also have to provide evidence of current licensure and liability insurance, even though the institution assumes ultimate responsibility for the services rendered.

Reference is made in the formal agreement to any corollary work that might be done with the residents' families, as well as the in-service training that should be provided for nurses and other staff members. There should also be provision for access to medical records and a commitment to assistance from nursing department personnel, as needed.

Identifying a Target Population for Groups

To the degree that a prospective group member is cognitively impaired, it could affect any individual member or the purpose of a particular group as a whole. Assessment for appropriateness of membership could be on the basis of a diagnosis on record or, what this therapist has found more useful, on the basis of recommendations from staff members who have daily, ongoing, and more intimate information about the behavior, functioning level, and "quirks" of particular residents. Thus, a resident whose record reads "Alzheimer's disease, early onset with memory deficits," might be described by the director of recreation as someone who is personable, occasionally forgetful, and eager to socialize with other residents. Such a person might be a suitable choice for inclusion in a reminiscence group with other residents who have some cognitive deficits, although different diagnostic labels. Certainly the medical history and specific needs of a person must be integrated into the overall treatment plan. Residents in early or middle stages of a developing dementia disorder may be suitable for inclusion in a particular group, after an assessment procedure by relevant nursing home personnel.

Composition and Structural Features of a Group

Finding a suitable place to meet is a persistent problem in nursing home settings. There is rarely an "extra" space large enough, and with privacy features, to spare. Most often the dining room—with or without doors—is the only space available, and then only for circumscribed portions of the day. If a classroom or "board room" is available, the use of it is often subject to cancellation on short notice for "more important" functions. Because it is very important for residents with any level of dementia to have consistency in their activities and environment, this issue must be discussed with the director and worked through with some commitment before a plan for a group is implemented.

In forming a group, a minimum and maximum number of participants should be established. In a nursing home, four to seven members for once-per-week meetings has been found to be appropriate. If all the members have Alzheimer's disease, and are homogeneous for a moderate degree of impairment, the smaller number of participants is recommended. A list of alternate members for any group should be available to allow for dropouts or no-shows.

Groups with a defined number of sessions at the outset (for example, six), as well as open-ended groups, have both been found effective. The shorter time span can allow more residents an opportunity to participate, especially in a large institution; the longer time span, for more intellectually and socially intact residents has the advantage of developing intimacy, support, and a network of peers to relate to between meetings.

As an ongoing resource for the group leader, as well as an integral support for the goals of the group, workshops, seminars, and in-service training for nursing home staff should be included in the planning for a group (Fernie & Fernie, 1990). In this way, issues around group member selection, scheduling, an appropriate space for the group, as well as the planned structure and goals of the group, can be advanced. These staff sessions can also provide a time for periodic program evaluation. Following is an outline for such a series of in-service meetings for the staff of a nursing home.

Model for In-service Group Meetings for Nurses and Staff

The purposes and roles of a staff psychologist/therapist might include:

- Modification of residents' attitudes toward aging, chronic illness, and institutionalization

- Clarification of psychological diagnosis

- Development of strategies for behavioral changes for individual residents through group and individual meetings with staff

- Program development

- Group and individual treatment for residents

- Consultation with families of residents, in groups

- Consultation with staff, individually and in groups

- In-service training

To evaluate a resident's behavior problem and work out a plan for modification of behavior, the following factors need to be reviewed:

- Medical history

- Currently used medications

- Marked changes in physical condition—for example, weight loss, change in eating habits, sleeping patterns, behavior changes

- Changes in cognitive (thinking) patterns—for example, forgetfulness

- Changes in affect

Then, basic behavior therapy principles can be applied. If the staff wants a behavior to increase in frequency, follow it with something positive; if the staff wants it to decrease in frequency, do *not* follow it with something positive. Put much more emphasis on the first procedure. To develop a plan for a particular resident, work out an individualized plan. One way to do this would be to have a regular time for the staff to meet, perhaps in a group, to talk about particular cases. (Brody, 1993)

Vignettes from clinical treatment with elderly individuals follow. The first three patients (Sally, Tony, and Mary) were nursing home residents who were referred by the social worker to Claire M. Brody for consultation. The last two patients (Clara and Claudia) were seen by Miriam E. Lemerman.

SALLY

Sally, age 87, was referred because staff was concerned that she would not leave her room for meals or participate in recreation activities, despite the fact that she had no significant medical or physical reasons not to do so. Her usual excuse was that she was "too tired" or that she had a vague pain in her ribs. (She had broken ribs just prior to admission to the home and these were now mended). She spent a good deal of time in bed, and expressed anger at staff for nagging her, and at her daughter for having placed her in the home, when she thought she could still have taken care of herself in her own apartment.

The sessions with Sally entailed listening to a litany of complaints about her daughter, whose twice-weekly visits were "not enough" and about nursing home staff, who thought she could do more than *she* thought she could, and did not take her complaints seriously. The therapist listened and encouraged her to talk about her life in her own apartment before she came to the nursing home, and about her children and life in earlier years. Sally remembered the therapist from one visit to the next, and although she would not admit to looking forward to the sessions, used the time available to her to vent her feelings about her daughter. However, there was no significant change in her motivation to socialize in the nursing home in this five-week period.

TONY

Tony, age 85, was referred for depression. He had numerous and quite serious physical problems, including a brain tumor, legal blindness, some deafness, and incontinence. Although he also had a problem with locomotion that required him to use a cane, he nevertheless moved around his room and the corridors when he could. The major problem he was presenting, according to the staff, was that he annoyed nurses and aides by pinching and touching them whenever he could, and making lascivious remarks to them.

Tony remembered details of what he talked to the therapist about from one week to the next. He knew exactly what day and time the therapist arrived. He complained bitterly to her about his roommate, whom he accused of invading his privacy and tampering with his belongings. At the same time, he was concerned about alienating the roommate by asking him to leave whenever the therapist arrived. (The resident's room was the consulting space and staff arranged to have roommates of clients involved elsewhere in the home for the period of the therapy session.)

Tony was eager to talk about his life—his old friends, the work he did—but avoided discussion of his unhappy marriage or the fact that two of his three sons had pretty much abandoned him. One day he said to the therapist, "You know what I would like more than anything else in the world? To start another family!"

His need to reach out and touch someone—anyone—was understandable in light of his dismal life prospects. His behavior that annoyed the staff abated somewhat in the period when he was seen regularly.

MARY

Mary, age 86, was referred because of her hostile behavior toward staff and roommate, her unpredictable outbursts of rage, and her intermittent depression and agitation. She had been diagnosed as having Alzheimer's disease, but this diagnosis was questioned.

Mary was suspicious and hostile when the therapist came the first time to talk to her. "Why are you here? Who sent you? Why should I talk to you? Go away," she said. She was restless and found it hard to sit in a chair. The therapist's offer to walk around with her outside was rejected. The first visit—the longest—lasted about 10 minutes; the therapist left when Mary insisted, "I want you to go away."

In the four subsequent weekly visits, the therapist always stopped by Mary's room to say "hello," and to remind Mary who she (the therapist) was if Mary seemed confused. Each time Mary said, "I don't want you to come; I don't need you." Her angry tone diminished slightly, however, over this period, and it is not certain whether she eventually would have "let the therapist in."

CLARA

Clara was referred to me by her internist. She is in her early eighties and resides in her own apartment. She has an interesting history, having survived the Holocaust and immigrated to the United States as a young woman. She raised three children, all of whom are professionals and with whom she is in close contact. She gets along well with her two daughters-in-law and son-in-law. Clara is intelligent and passionate, and she has many friends with whom she shares cultural interests.

One of Clara's sons is married to an Indian woman. Ostensibly, she and this woman get along, but in reality, there is much jealousy and disapproval on Clara's part. She often feels excluded at family get-togethers in her son and daughter-in-law's home and, at times, becomes very agitated about her daughter-in-law's behavior.

After meeting with me for several months, Clara began to display a pattern of presenting a vignette each week, which illustrated some way in which her daughter-in-law mistreated her children (Clara's grandchildren). "Should I tell her that this is wrong?" she would eagerly ask, and I would smile and ask, "What would be the result of that?" Clara would then smile and say, "It's better to say nothing." She would return the next week with a similar story and, again, would ask if she should tell her daughter-in-law what she was doing wrong. Again, I would ask, "How would that be? How would she react?" and she would, again, smile and sigh and say that it was better to be quiet.

Clara displayed a similar inclination to dispense unsolicited advice to her daughter and son-in-law. She frequently asked me for my opinion, and I would generally reply, "If I tell you what to do, will you do it?" She would smile and say, "I'm not sure." Clara appeared to be able to maintain her wisdom and self-control as a result of talking about, rather than acting out, her aggressive impulses. She approached her treatment as if it were an intense coffee klatch between two old friends who shared a common heritage and a transference based on memories of adolescence.

CLAUDIA

Claudia is a local nursing home resident who is suffering from dementia. She is very depressed and feels that life is not worthwhile. Although the subject of her children and grandchildren initially sparked her interest, even they no longer appear to provoke a positive reaction. She remembers, with longing, her husband who died when he was in his fifties. She had previously been flirtatious with male visitors at her facility, but she now remains in bed with the covers pulled up over her head.

Although Claudia is receptive when we meet for sessions, she displays a strong pull toward giving up and being taken care of like a baby. I commiserate with her about how horrible life can be and ask, "Should I be taking better care of you?" "Yes," she replies. I ask, "How could I do that?" She rarely answers. She once asked me to sing to her and I did, feeling like a mother to a child.

Claudia's depression is not unusual for someone living in a nursing home. With a progressive dementia and limited physical mobility, she has limited vision for any happiness in her future. I will continue seeing her and hope that the tie that unites us can help her rediscover some aspects of life to cherish.

In addition to providing individual and group treatment, the clinician, both within a nursing home facility and in general, has the ability and the privilege of contributing to the understanding of Medicare patients. Practitioners can communicate with legislators and policy makers at the local, state, and national levels to bring clarity and focus to the central issues of the elderly. In addition, they can help educate lay people who may not have sufficient knowledge of gerontology or facility design. Clinicians can effect change by sharing their specific brand of expertise (APA Public Relations Policy Office, 1995).

Medicare is increasingly providing access to mental health care for senior citizens. Historically, only medical services were reimbursed by Medicare; however, now mental health professionals and other licensed clinicians are also compensated by Medicare for their work in nursing homes and senior facilities. The value of assisting individuals to adjust to the realities of aging and helping them cope with their feelings is finally being acknowledged by the Medicare system.

It is the job of mental health professionals to enrich the lives of the elderly by trying to satisfy their basic emotional needs. Increased funding and a greater availability of qualified mental health personnel would go a long way in assisting senior citizens who struggle with a host of issues related to aging.

REFERENCES

Abramson, T. A., & Mendis, K. P. (1990). The organizational logistics of running a dementia group in a skilled nursing facility. *Clinical Gerontologist, 9*(3/4), 111–122.

American Counseling Association. (2004). *Medicare coverage of licensed professional counselors.* Retrieved December 14, 2004, from http://www.counseling.org/

Antos, J., & Pinelly, X. (2004). Private discounts, public subsidies: How the Medicare prescription drug card really works. Washington, DC: American Enterprise Institute.

APA Public Relations Policy Office (1995). *A psychologist's guide to participation in the federal advocacy process* (abridged version). Retrieved December 19, 2004, from http://www.apa.org

Brody, C. M. (1993). Medicare. In C. M. Brody & V. G. Semel, *Strategies for therapy with the elderly* (pp. 141–157). New York: Springer.

Brody, C. M., & Semel, V. G. (1993). *Strategies for therapy with the elderly.* New York: Springer.

Centers for Medicare Advocacy. (n.d.). *Aging parents and adult children together.* Retrieved October 15, 2004, from http://www.ftc.gov

Centers for Medicare & Medicaid Services. (CMS) (2004a). *Medicare informa-tion resource.* Retrieved October 19, 2004, from http://www.cms.hhs.gov/medicare

Centers for Medicare & Medicaid Services (CMS). (2004b). *CMS/HCFA history.* Retrieved September 16, 2004, from http//www.cms.hhs.gov

Centers for Medicare & Medicaid Services. (CMS). (2004c). *Long term care.* Retrieved July 10, 2004, from http://www.nytimes.com

Centers for Medicare & Medicaid Services. (CMS). (2004d). *Medicare premiums for 2005.* Retrieved November 15, 2004, from http://www.medicarenhic.com

Fernie, B., & Fernie, G. (1990). Organizing group programs for cognitively im-paired elderly residents of nursing homes. *Clinical Gerontologist, 9*(3/4), 123–134.

Greenberg, S. (2003). *A profile of older Americans: 2003.* Washington, DC: Adminis-tration on Aging, U.S. Department of Health and Human Services. Retrieved December 5, 2004, from http://www.aoa.gov/prof/Statistics/profile/2003/IT.asp.

Kaiser Commission. (2004). *Dual eligible: Medicaid's role for low income Medicare beneficiaries.* Retrieved December 19, 2004, from www.kff.org/medicaid.

Lebow, R. H. (2004). *Health care meltdown.* Chambersburg, PA: Alan C. Hood.

Madrick, J. (2004, July). *Studies look at health care in the U.S.* Retrieved July 10, 2004 from http://www.nytimes.com

Mandelbaum, M. (2004). *Still ducking the entitlement crisis.* Retrieved December 14, 2004, from http:sais-jhu.edu/

Medical News Today. (2004a). *Private insurers object to US government's plan to establish multistate Medicare coverage areas.* Retrieved August 24, 2004, from http://www.medicalnewstoday

Medical News Today. (2004b). *Greenspan warns congress to consider reducing future Medicare, Social Security spending.* Retrieved December 14, 2004, from http://www.medicalnewstoday.com

Medicare & You 2005. (2004, September). Centers for Medicare and Medicaid Services (CMS), Publication No. CMS-10050.

Medicare Rights Center. (2004a). *The history of Medicare and the current debate.* Retrieved August 17, 2004, from http://www.medicarerights.org

Medicare Rights Center. (2004b). *Policy & advocacy priorities privatization of Medicare.* Retrieved November 27, 2004, from http://www.medicarerights.org

Money Guide. (2004). *Health savings accounts.* Mark Kolakowski and Clique Friends, LLC. Retrieved November 27, 2004, from http://www.river2u.com

Murtha, J. (2004). *Jack Murtha's prescription drug fact sheet* (par. 1). Retrieved November 23, 2004, from http://www.house.gov/murtha

Pear, R. (2004). *AMA urges feds to negotiate for best drug prices.* Retrieved October 17, 2004, from http://www.lilacblindfoundation.org

Peterson. P. G. (2004). *Running on empty.* New York: Farrar, Straus & Giroux.

Relman, A., & Angell, M. (October 25, 2004). Single-payer system offers solutions Bush plan doesn't. *Newark Star Ledger,* p. 15.

Rettenmaier, A. J., & Wang, Z. (2002). *Explaining the growth of medicare: Part II.* Retrieved December 13, 2004, from http://www.ncpa.org/pub

Salisbury, D. L. (1997). *Retiring baby boomers: Meeting the challenges.* (Statement before the U.S. Senate Special Committee on Aging, March 6, 1997). Retrieved December 13, 2004 from http://www.asec.org

Stum, M. S. (2002). *What is it like for families of elders to spend down to medical assistance?* Retrieved December 19, 2004, from http://www.financinglong termcare

United States Department of Health and Human Services, Administration on Aging (2004). *Aging into the 21st century.* Retrieved December 15, 2004, from http://www.aoa.gov/prof/statistics

Index

Women in the Middle, Second Edition
Their Parent-Care Years
Elaine M. Brody, MSW, DSc (Hon)

"[Brody's] perspective is timely and highly welcome at this time…She has enriched our field and our lives…"
—From the Foreword by **Barry D. Lebowitz,** PhD
Chief, Adult and Geriatric Treatment
and Preventive Interventions, Research Branch
National Institute of Mental Health

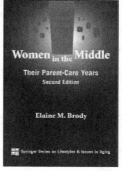

"Women in the Middle" was so-named because daughters, who are the main caregivers to elderly disabled parents, most often in their middle years, are caught in the middle of multiple competing demands on their time and energy. Since the first edition, women's responsibilities and the pressures they have experienced have increased and intensified. Dr. Brody revisits this phenomenon in this new, updated edition of her ground-breaking work.

Partial Contents:

Part I: Background • Effects of Caregiving • Values About Women's Roles and Care of the Aged

Part II: Subjective Experiences • The Caregiving Daughters and Their Siblings

Part III: Diversity Among Caregivers • Diversity in Age and Stages • Diversity in Marital Status • Married Daughters and Their Husbands and Children • Daughters Without Partners • Caregiving Daughters-in-Law • Commentary on Marital Status and Parent Care • Diversity in Work Status • Ethnic and Racial Diversity, *A.R. Saperstein*

Part IV: Services and Living Arrangements for Older People: Effects on Women in the Middle • Nursing Home Placement: A Painful Decision • Community Services and Residential Settings, *A.R. Saperstein*

Part V: Unfinished Business • Unfinished Business on the Parent-Care Agenda • References

Life Styles & Issues in Aging Series
2003   400pp   0-8261-6381-5   hardcover

**11 West 42nd Street, New York, NY 10036-8002 • Fax: 212-941-7842
Order Toll-Free: 877-687-7476 • Order On-line: www.springerpub.com**

Home and Identity in Late Life
International Perspectives

Graham D. Rowles, PhD
Habib Chaudhury, PhD, Editors

To use the words of volume editors Rowles and Chaudhury, "Home is where we belong. It is our experience, recollections, imagination, and aspirations."

Presenting insightful essays and findings from empirical studies, leading contemporary scholars examine the meaning of home to elders and the ways in which this meaning may be sustained, threatened, or modified in association with both normal and pathological changes with growing old. For example, health and well being can be affected by an environmental change, such as a change in an established neighborhood or a forced relocation.

August 2005   416pp   0-8261-2715-0   hardcover

Psychotherapy and Counseling with Older Women

Cross-Cultural, Family, and End-of-Life Issues

Frances K. Trotman, PhD
Claire M. Brody, PhD, with contributors

Psychotherapists Trotman and Brody, along with expert contributors, view older women through a feminist lens and examine social constructs concerning older women, aspects of aging, caregiving, elders' relationships with family, health, body image, and sexuality concerns. The authors define issues that are important to older women and their emotional health and bring into sharp relief some of the painful issues professionals must confront in counseling older women.

A must for all professionals who work with older women in the fields of psychology, gerontology, social work, and nursing, and for students.

Partial Contents:

Part I: Gender Issues Across Cultures • Introduction: Gender Issues of Aging Women, *F.K. Trotman, C.M. Brody* • A Woman's Aging Body: Friend or Foe?, *R.G. Crose* • Cross-Cultural Perspectives: Grandmothers, *F.K. Trotman, C.M. Brody* • Older Women Working: Life Goals, Achievements, and Retirement Issues, *C.M. Brody* • Being Female, Old, and African American: Political, Economic and Historical Contexts for Older Women, *F.K. Trotman* • Women in the Middle: Caretaking Issues, *S.H. Qualls*

Part II: Therapy Issues • Mental Health and Older Women, *C.M. Brody, M. Denninger, F.K. Trotman* • The Therapeutic Alliance with Older Women, *H.Q. Kivnick, A. Kavka* • Feminist Psychotherapy with Older African American Women, *F.K. Trotman* • Older Lesbians Concerns and Psychotherapy: Beyond a Footnote to the Footnote, *B. Greene* • Strategies for Working with Women with Dementia, *M. Duffy* • Working with Women with Severe Communication Disorders: Three Cases, *C.M. Brody* • Commentary: *V. Molinari*

Part III: End-Of- Life Issues • Dying and Death: Decision About Care at the End of Life, *K.M. Coppola, F.K. Trotman* • An Existential Therapeutic Approach to End-of-life Issues for Women, *C.M. Brody*

Focus on Women Series
2002   272pp   0-8261-1468-7   hardcover

11 West 42nd Street, New York, NY 10036-8002 • Fax: 212-941-7842
Order Toll-Free: 877-687-7476 • Order On-line: www.springerpub.com

Custodial Grandparenting
Individual, Cultural, and Ethnic Diversity

Bert Hayslip, Jr., PhD
Julie Hicks Patrick, PhD, Editors

No other book exists that centers on the variability among custodial grandparent caregivers. With a focus on diversity among grandparent-headed families in domestic and international settings, over 35 contributors explore the many parameters of diversity among custodial grandparents. It also provides a wealth of information and a basis for which national and state-run services can evaluate their current policies and devise funds, services, and programs which can help this growing population successfully raise their grandchildren and our nation's future leaders.

Special areas of exploration:
- Age
- Ethnicity
- Race
- Rural/Urban location
- Gender
- Culture
- Religion

Partial Contents:

Part I: Diversity Across Individuals • Determinants of Role Satisfaction in Traditional and Custodial Grandparents • Diversity and Caregiving Support Interventions • Diversity Across Grandparent Caregivers Needs for Formal and Informal Social Support

Part II: Diversity Across Age and Gender • Grandmothers' Diaries • Depression and Caregiver Mastery in Grandfathers Caring for their Grandchildren • African-American Grandmothers

Part III: Cross Cultural and Intra-Cultural Variation • Cross-Cultural Differences in Traditional and Custodial Grandparenting • Social Support Among Custodial Grandparents Within a Diversity of Contexts

Part IV: Variation Across Race and Ethnicity • Latina Grandmothers Raising Grandchildren • African American Grandmothers as Health Educators in the Family • Religious Beliefs and Practices Among African American Custodial Grandparents • The Voices of Black Grandmothers Parenting Children with TANF Assistance

August 2005   352pp   0-8261-1998-0   softcover

11 West 42nd Street, New York, NY 10036-8002 • Fax: 212-941-7842
Order Toll-Free: 877-687-7476 • Order On-line: www.springerpub.com

SPRINGER / PUBLISHING COMPANY

Cultural Changes in Attitudes Toward Death, Dying, and Bereavement

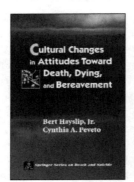

Bert Hayslip, Jr., PhD
Cynthia A. Peveto, PhD

Hayslip and Peveto compare the findings from the landmark 1970s Kalish and Reynolds' "Death and Ethnicity Study" to their own present study and examine the impact of cultural change on death attitudes.

Focusing on African-American, Asian-American, and Hispanic-American subpopulations with Caucasians treated as a comparison group, the authors explore to what extent what we knew 30 years ago holds up to the present. Detailed comparisons are made between the results of the earlier Kalish-Reynolds study and the authors' own recent findings. Several broad findings include: the shift toward more interest in being informed of one's own terminal prognosis, a more personal approach to funerals and mourning observances, and a greater focus on family and relationships.

This book is must reading for researchers, educators, and students interested in death-related studies.

Contents:
- Introduction
- An Overview of the Death-Ethnicity Relationship, *Kalish* and *Reynolds*
- Factors Influencing Death Attitudes, *Kalish* and *Reynolds*
- The Impact of Cultural Change on Death Attitudes
- The Present Study
- Analysis of Findings: Instrastudy Variability
- Analysis of Findings: Interstudy Variability
- Hypothesis Regarding Interstudy and Intrastudy Variability
- Discussion
- Appendix A
- Appendix B
- References

Death and Suicide Series
2005   208pp   0-8261-2796-7   hardcover

11 West 42nd Street, New York, NY 10036-8002 • Fax: 212-941-7842
Order Toll-Free: 877-687-7476 • Order On-line: www.springerpub.com